Islam and Violence in the Modern Era

Islam and Violence in the Modern Era

Beverley Milton-Edwards

palgrave
macmillan

First published in 2006 by
PALGRAVE MACMILLAN
Houndmills, Basingstoke, Hampshire RG21 6XS and
175 Fifth Avenue, New York, N.Y. 10010
Companies and representatives throughout the world.

PALGRAVE MACMILLAN is the global academic imprint of the Palgrave Macmillan division of St. Martin's Press, LLC and of Palgrave Macmillan Ltd. Macmillan® is a registered trademark in the United States, United Kingdom and other countries. Palgrave is a registered trademark in the European Union and other countries.

ISBN-13: 978-1-4039-8618-4
ISBN-10: 1-4039-8618-5

This book is printed on paper suitable for recycling and made from fully managed and sustained forest sources.

A catalogue record for this book is available from the British Library.

Library of Congress Cataloging-in-Publication Data

Milton-Edwards, Beverley.
    Islam and violence in the modern era / Beverley Milton-Edwards.
        p. cm.
    Includes bibliographical references and index.
    ISBN 1-4039-8618-5 (cloth)
        1. Violence – Religious aspects – Islam. 2. Political violence – Religious aspects – Islam. 3. Islamic fundamentalism. I. Title.

BP190.5.V56M55 2005
297.2'7—dc22   2005051502

10 9 8 7 6 5 4 3 2 1
15 14 13 12 11 10 09 08 07 06

Transferred to digital printing in 2006.

For my beloved sisters Lynne and Trudy

Contents

Preface

Although the genesis of this book lay in the research I had undertaken for several years before the events of 11 September 2001, it would not be so much hyperbole to assert that the shadow cast in the wake of the attack has altered the shape and outcome of this project. The attack launched and carried out by Muslim members of the al-Qaeda in assaults on the Pentagon, the World Trade Centre of the United States of America and the US civil aviation network left thousands dead. The attacks moreover demonstrated a vulnerability that affected the majority of citizens of the United States of America and many more elsewhere. The attack has been interpreted as the ultimate evidence of Islam's attachment to terror and blood. It reinforces a stereotype of the faith system and its followers that built up in the West over recent decades. The militant mantle of Islam is today utilised to explain and understand the rise of new movements and parties and the general political mobilisation of Muslim citizens across the globe. This movement includes those who seek to resist the western-led movement towards globalisation with capitalist culture at its centre.

The notion of a fanatic and violent Muslim mass stopping this process of new Enlightenment has fascinated the Western audience and been actively buoyed by a media animated by the portrayal of the armed and bearded fundamentalists betraying their own antipathy towards the West. Indeed, the closing decades of the twentieth century have been dominated by the realisation that although communism was eventually vanquished a new force has risen in its place. It is true that the new force of radical Islam has engaged a militant anti-western element that has perpetrated terrible acts of violence against western tourists and civilians in their own home countries. Yet, unfortunately such truths do not the whole picture make. This perspective underscores the belief that Muslims today promote a counter-culture of violence in an age of global peace. Muslim immigrants in Europe, for example, are seen as representing an outsider–insider threat to the values that lie deep in the heart of contemporary European societies.

Muslims and Islamists are increasingly portrayed as implacable enemies who eschew plurality, diversity, modernity, negotiation, dialogue and conciliation in favour of total victory and domination achieved through force of arms. In respect of this portrayal of a particular Hobbesian state of nature, it is no surprise then that the response to such a representation of Islam is also now predicated on uncompromising force, more popularly understood as the war on terrorism. Such contentions underscore the argument that an intimate link exists between Islam and conflict and thus assert that the dimensions of resolution are repudiated in favour of jihad and global Muslim domination.

My contention in this book is that since 9/11, the meaning of modernity has been altered and is now embedded in the expression of western security interests and the arguments for democratic protectionism. However, this war on terror in defence of modernity and democracy is also increasingly understood within Muslim communities as a declaration of war against them and the values that define them and their faith system.

Today modernity is promoted as a necessary prerequisite to political stability. New conceptions of modernisation or globalisation are employed as the major instruments in the war on terror. But, it is a blunt instrument that is primarily allied to the military response that has dominated the way in which the war on terror is conducted. Political Islam is now portrayed as a critique of modernity focusing antipathy on processes of modernisation, not only in Muslim societies but also in those *modern* Western societies to which Muslims have migrated. Muslims are seen as the enemy of western defined modernity and the political values of secular liberal democracy that are associated with it.

The common factor here is the belief that modernity demands of Muslims a form of cultural, religious, political and economic *submission* in the face of that construct known as secularism. This is the literal antithesis of Islam that also fundamentally requires its adherents to *submit* themselves to Allah. What room then exists for a connection between modernity and Islam?

Muslim resentment at western models of modernisation that have been imposed on their own societies has not only radicalised Islam, but has increasingly divorced it from faith systems such as Christianity. An Islam humiliated and marginalised has provoked widespread anti-Western feeling among its followers. A malign or benign reluctance to perceive the discourses of counter-modernism is a negation of dimensions of politics that are on the margins of western subconsciousness. The veracity of Muslim experience against the western version is constantly questioned because it appears out of kilter with a narrative of modernity that is dynamic and linear.

Because of belief in this narrative it is easy to devise anti-terror measures to protect the citizens of the West from the menace of the *Green Peril*. The consequence of such an approach is that millions of Muslims are increasingly portrayed as potential terrorists. Muslims are represented as engaged in a divine duty to bring Islam to the point of global domination, not only in the political sphere but in economy and other areas too. This divine duty is understood as finding expression in the bloody acts of violence and terrorism that characterise so many modern Muslim communities today.

I wish to signal from the outset that in this book I make no claim to comprehensively cover the modern-day radical phenomenon in its many real or imagined forms. I do, however, try to draw instances widely, in terms of examples, from across the contemporary globe. I do this because the task of this book is to look at the bigger issues rather than the activities of individual groups as part of some empirical study held together by a theoretical framework. This may mean that I have been selective in my choices, but no more than others who tackle such topics. Where I may differ is the way I choose to highlight a particular issue and the thread throughout the book, which draws on my own experience of living in so-called violent societies. Thus, although the purpose of this book is to examine and explore the dimensions of violence that lie within the Islamic realm, and to wrestle with the notion that Islam distinguishes itself from other faiths because of its passionate attachment to violence, I feel it is important to remain cognisant of the same issues in a non-Muslim context. Addressing such issues helps to contribute to a fuller multi-dimensional vision of Islam and its violent episodes that in turn should assist in the task of distinguishing the terrorists from the freedom fighters, the just from the unjust, those with an internationally legitimate claim and those who have not. This does not mean that by engaging in this task I am constructing an apologia for acts of terrorism perpetrated in the name of Islam. I am looking at the Janus-faced messy and morally fluid field of politics and international relations in the modern era and casting an eye to that which has been dangerously generalised and turned into potent myth, on both sides. I will draw out significant distinctions as they relate to the all-important and wider meta-narratives of global politics in the twentieth and twenty-first centuries. In this respect the reader should be forewarned that what appears on these pages may not conform to the hitherto-held stereotypes held on either side of the divide. In respect of this task, I am merely engaging in a more in-depth explanation of an important phenomenon that at present most of us have a superficial understanding of. In abhorring the violence carried out by Muslims I look for specifics and that which may be taken as a theme more common to other faiths and modern-day political phenomena. In this respect I often address discourse and debates, for I believe they provide us with the clues to seek and encourage alternative routes out of relationships of conflict and violence. Thus, I also believe that the time for the blame game is long gone, and that routes out of the impasse that beset so many relationships in the political sphere between the Muslim domain and other worlds should be sought.

Scholarship of political Islam has become a *hot business* since 11 September 2001 and the changing global tempo around this issue weighs on the shoulders of anyone tackling this topic. Such scholarship, however, although undertaken as an individual task depends on a whole series of interactions taking place across time and space. In this respect, I owe a great debt of gratitude to the award made by the Arts and Humanities Research Board for my research into Islam and violence because it allowed me the opportunity to begin my odyssey at a time when there was very little interest in the topic. At the Centre for Islamic Studies at Oxford University where I was awarded a Visiting Fellowship, I encountered materials and individuals from a variety of disciplines engaged in the study of Islam who alerted me to the immense depth and breadth of the topic I was working on. This immersion whether by thinking about Islam through arts, poetry, anthropology, geography or political science kept me alert to the changing features of Islam and I am grateful to the fellows and staff at the centre who pushed me to pursue the study of Islam and violence. This debt of gratitude stems from supporting a project that was conceived to challenge important assumptions about contemporary Muslim politics. Additionally, the Centre for Muslim–Christian Understanding at Georgetown University offered me an opportunity to research my ideas whilst there. These awards allowed me to begin my early exploration of this topic. A number of colleagues and friends have offered their wisdom and time during the formulation of the ideas and discourse presented in the following pages. In this respect I would like to thank Tony Pfaff, Jorgen Neilsen, Danny Casson, Rema Hammami, Larbi Sadiki, Mohammed Hafez, James Piscatori, John Barry, Touraj K. and John Esposito, who between them have encouraged me in this task and read the manuscript. Tony in particular helped me to try and break my *straw man* habit and opened up alternative perspectives to old debates. Mari Palmer generously provided research assistance relating to the gender in this book. There are also many people who have assisted me in the fieldwork for this book and who deserve special mention; they include Randa Hinnawi, Mohammed Debs, Haj Faysal al-Sater, Amal Saad and Haj Saad, Azmi Keshawi, and Khaled Hroub. I would also like to thank Alison Howson at Palgrave Macmillan for picking up this project and supporting me in the quest for publication. My appreciation is also extended to Vidhya Jayaprakash for the copyedit process. In the increasingly risk-based research environment that constitutes contemporary Islamism in the twenty-first century, I wish to acknowledge with thanks the help of many who have taken risks to secure research access for me and for those who have been generous with their time and attention in engaging with me on the issues that this book addresses.

Finally, I want to extend my thanks to my children, Cara and Joshua, who have often travelled with me during periods of research and who now know more than they really ought to about political Islam! It should go without saying that furthermore, none of this would have been possible without the support of Graham.

Beverley Milton-Edwards

Introduction

A plane drives into the twin towers of the World Trade Centre in New York, another into the Pentagon in Washington and thousands perish in the flames and debris that engulf them. The perpetrators are young Muslim men and their leader has declared a jihad against the West. In balmy Bali as thousands of tourists enjoy a relaxing vacation, a bomb is detonated by a Muslim militant, killing and maiming people in an attack hailed by its perpetrators as a jihad. In Kabul, Afghanistan thousands of women are banned from working and confined to their homes; a form of house arrest designed to deny them their rights. They are discriminated against in the name of Islam by a ruling regime known as the Taliban. In the Russian city of Beslan, Islamic terrorists waging jihad in the name of Chechen freedom massacre hundreds of school children. News stations across the globe broadcast reports that Muslim militants in Iraq have murdered Western hostages such as the British–Irish aid worker, Margaret Hassan. In London home-grown suicide bombing attacks lead to national soul searching and major legislative changes affecting all aspects of life in the United Kingdom. Is it any wonder then that in the opening decade of the twenty-first century, Islam is defined and understood as a phenomenon of monotheistic faith associated with fear, violence and terrorism? Such a view was summed up in an editorial that appeared in the wake of the Beslan massacre. It opined, 'It is certainly true that not all Muslims are terrorists, however, sadly we say that the majority of terrorists in the world are Muslims.'[1]

Identity dynamic

This study does not deny that Muslims commit violence and acts of terrorism. Such Muslims who claim and legitimate their actions according to a myth that Islam must either in reasserting itself or in defending itself inflict deliberate terror on vulnerable civilians must have their purposes examined for its veracity and held to account. Islam is the faith system of some billion men and women as well as their children, across many regions of the globe

1

including Asia, Africa and the Middle East. Muslim-ness or being understood as Muslim is part of the explanatory identity of people of the multi-ethnic communities of Europe, the United States of America, Australia and the former Soviet Union, as well as the southern fringes of the Eastern Europe bloc states, including the former Yugoslavia. Muslims come from many diverse ethnic backgrounds including African, Arab, Asian, Berber, Chinese and the Kurd. Muslims speak many different languages and enjoy cultures that distinguish them from each other. They live in social, political and economic units and nation states that are representative of many aspects of the modern ideological spectrum. Yet, there exists an argument that disregarding all these differences – the ethnic, linguistic, geographic, cultural, economic, political, social and technological – Islam 'unites' them. Being Muslim alone, and not the kind of Muslim one is, establishes a powerful monolith. Jonathan Raban explains this monolithic unity of identity in relation to a Muslim prayer, 'So, as the world turns, the entire *Umma* [Muslim community of one billion] goes down on its knees in a never-ending wave of synchronised prayer, and the believers can be seen as the moving parts of a universal Islamic chronometer. In prayer, the self and its appetites are surrendered to God, in imitation of the prophet Mohammed, the "slave of Allah" '.[2] In this respect, being Muslim or acting Muslim is understood and constructed as unique from other religions and identities, such as those associated with gender, class or ethnicity.

Islam is a label attached to good and bad Muslims, fanatical Muslims, religious Muslims, secular Muslims, nationalist Muslims, socialist Muslims, Muslim resistance fighters, Muslim statesmen and women, Muslim conservatives, Muslim reformers, Muslim fundamentalists, Muslim moderates, Muslim terrorists, Muslim women, Muslim men, Muslim rebels, Muslim states, Muslim welfare workers, Muslim immigrants, Muslim asylum seekers and Muslim radicals.

Islam or 'Muslim-ness' is also, of course, self-defining and often denotes a conscious and active attachment to a particular interpretation and understanding of the faith. Increasingly though the label, particularly as it relates to certain co-joined nouns, is attached to Muslims by others. In this process Islam takes on a particularly important but negative connotation. Islam becomes pejorative. Islam is signified as damaging to values as well as to human and other kinds of security in the modern era. Thus, while it may be true that Islam contributes to a sense of unity that has the potential to transcend other 'borders' to identity, such as linguistic or ethnic differences, in the modern age there have truly been very few, if any, occasions when this transcendence was successfully achieved.

More often than not, despite the desire for unity, the house of Islam has been much divided in itself. Division and schism is understood as a historical phenomenon. The validity of a concept of Muslim diversity and division – even a plurality within the ranks – however, simply runs against the grain of much western perception and understanding of the faith in the western arena. A contemporary illustration of such division and conflict, including its most violent dimensions, is apparent in even the most cursory glance of life in a country like the formerly conflict-ridden Lebanon.

In contemporary Lebanon, not only have Muslims been pitched against Muslims during a bitter 15 years of civil conflict, but also Christians have fought Christians and Muslims have waged war (and vice versa) on Christians too. In this respect no one religious group enjoys a monopoly on violence or terror tactics. Christians have been as guilty of terror and atrocity as Muslims. Here too, in Lebanon, the label of Muslim has meanings not meaning. To be a Muslim in Lebanon can mean to be *Shi'a*, *Sunni*, or *Druze*, secular or religious, even religious and secular at one and the same time.[3] To be a Muslim can mean to be anti-western or pro-western, pro-Iranian or pro-Syrian, anti-Palestinian or pro-Palestinian, to be for the empowerment of women as a religious duty or against it, to support the Lebanese political system or protest against its culture of corruption and nepotism. For some, such as for the Lebanese *Shi'a* spiritual leader, Ayatollah Mohammed Hussein Fadlallah, being Muslim is defined by a preoccupation with 'justice and not aggression ... as a matter of principle'.[4] To be a Muslim in Lebanon can mean to walk downtown on a Friday night and stop at a bar for a drink and a meal, or it can mean to sit in the salon of a home in Hrat Hreik in the southern suburbs and share quiet moments with one's family. It can even mean both of these things in the space of not only a single lifetime or generation, but also in the space of a day.

For this is the form of Muslim-ness that applied to Ziad Jarrah, the 26-year-old Lebanese *Sunni* Muslim who played his part in perpetrating the attack on United Airline's Flight 93 on 11 September 2001. He was a Muslim and became a terrorist even though he had been brought up in a secular household and educated at a Christian school. In this case being Muslim was signified by a dynamic transition in identity from a life-loving party-goer to a Muslim nihilist. What is Muslim identity then? In this respect, it is better to recognise the diversity and difference within Islam than attempt the same fixed branding to all. The alternative unitary approach traditionally attaches to Islam a form of power that is cosmic and, therefore, a meta-force that can define or shape life, culture and politics almost to the exclusion of other forces.[5] As Kedourie remarked in relation to the Middle East, 'Muslims, but equally non-Muslims dwelling in the Muslim domain, are strongly marked by the Muslim tradition, and what may be called the Muslim civilization.'[6] Yet, it can be contended that the modern-day reality rests on Islam, divided and unable to transform itself through unity to mount and re-establish such an empire of faith. Islam as a resurrected empire of faith remains a dream and ideal held by the elements of political Islam. To wrestle with what makes something Muslim – even for the non-Muslims living in Muslim societies – creates dangerous and unsettling distinctions that could even be said to ethnicise Muslim identity in the same way that Jewish identity has been ethnicised through the establishment of the state of Israel in 1948.

For a faith in common can also do as much to rent hearts apart and create disunity as to unify them in harmony. Examples of this are not exclusive to Islam. In Northern Ireland the common faith of Christianity contributes (along with other factors) to the notion of divisiveness of society rather than its unity.[7] Faith does as much to label people as apart as a part of each other.[8] Faith is used as a political label. As a label, it is applied by outsiders as well as insiders. It is a means of creating or sustaining a form of difference that in turn increasingly centres on conflict not peaceful coexistence. In this context, as with many Muslim domains, the epithet of religion – 'he's Muslim, she's Catholic, he's Jewish, she's Protestant' – is still employed by a variety of actors, including political actors, as a means of explaining conflict at a time when the relevancy of religion as a political or major social force in western European societies had appeared to diminish but not entirely disappear from the public landscape. The media also plays its role in sustaining a stark difference between religions. Hence, headlines and articles consistently reflected by the international media speak of 'British Protestants', 'Irish Catholics' and 'Protestant Battalions'. The label is a misnomer. Catholic violence and Muslim violence are terms applied to describe and explain violence in a city like Belfast or Beirut. Such violence is ascribed as political, and therefore religious, by outsiders such as the international media, even if it is not experienced as such or even understood as such on the ground by those who are engaged or affected by it. In this respect the Muslims, especially those in poor migrant communities, are like their Irish/Ulster counterparts in being made responsible, often by others, for creating a sense of political dynamism that has inserted religion as violence back into modern secular contexts. Thus, they give the modern contest for power a new meaning through attaching a religious dimension to it. The specificity of context and meaning attached to the struggle for power becomes irrelevant to the broad picture mounted to explain the nature of politics in the twenty-first century as adversarial on a grand scale. Islam is universalised and labelled, then, through specific values that are attached to it.

The divine peacemakers and damned bomb-makers

There is, however, an argument to be made against the universalisation of Islam as a unitary modern nonpareil that can subsequently be read, understood, interpreted and represented to others as some overwhelming whole. For in this way Islam is represented as a superpower in its own right. In this case the challenge is to generate an account of the diversity of Muslim definitions, experiences, connection, debate, discourse and acts of violence in the modern age. The natural corollary to this is a work that also reflects processes of Muslim discourse, debate, experience and acts of peace and peacemaking in the modern age, and it is my aspiration that this account reflects that to some extent. At present, Islam as a mainstream phenomenon is not labelled or understood in this way. 'Muslim peace-maker' is not part of the modern lexicon of Islam. The 'blessed peace-maker' while part of the lexicon of Judeo-Christian culture is absent from western popular understandings of Islam. Muslims are perceived and represented as neither 'blessed' nor as 'peace-makers'. Such a perspective enshrined in many non-Muslim popular cultures associates Muslim leaders – political and religious – to be at the far end of the spectrum between peace and violence. This then establishes a certain blindness to those Muslim leaders and to all that, which signifies a unity within the Islamic experience to peace rather than to war. For example, one of the tiny phrases that does symbolise the delicate attempt at harmony (rather than unity) and peace within the faith that exists within the realm of the Muslim experience is the invocation: '*assalamu alaykum*' (Peace be upon you [all]). The invocation is made upon Muslims meeting, greeting, entering anew and welcoming others. As a salutation it is symbolic of a desire for peace. The common return greeting: '*Wa alaykum assalam*' (And peace be upon you) gives verbal affirmation of a faith aspiring to peace. Yet in the modern era the salutation to peace is lost to the stronger images of conflict and more specifically jihad. Jihad not *salam* is the byword for Islam; the Western imposed brand image of the faith in the twenty-first century.

A number of questions begin to emerge from this point: Is Islam a faith founded, predicated and motivated by bloodlust and violence that marks out its adherents from all others? Why does it appear that Muslims embrace violence and terrorism over peace and harmony in the modern age? What motivates Muslims into acts of violence and terrorism? Is Islam an existential threat to the West? To answer these questions, and others that come up on the path of inquiry, it is useful to explore a series of themes and associated debates. This in turn generates a discourse that should move one forward from a one-dimensional conceptualisation of Islam in the modern age, revealing the variable intertwining motivations at work in Muslim polities, communities, states, movements and organisations across the globe. In this respect there is little to either generalise or universalise out of the modern Muslim experience as it relates to the phenomenon of violence and terrorism. This approach creates a space to allow for an examination of the acts of terrorism perpetrated by Muslims in the name of Islam. This draws a distinction between Muslim terrorism in the name of other ideologies and draws attention to the factors that motivate such terrorism as Muslim or Islamist. Terrorism is not explained away or denied in terms of being perpetrated by Muslims. Thus the phenomenon of terrorism carried out by radical Islamist movements, their motives, ideological impulses and world view, including dimensions of their anti-western rhetoric are outlined and explored. The point here is to also highlight the context in which such terrorism and other kinds of violence occur and to question whether it is faith alone or other factors in combination that may account for it. For, if it is faith alone that compels Muslims to violence and terror, then there are important lessons to be learned for those who seek to promote global projects founded on liberal democratic values with their inherently secular biases.

Framing the debate

Since 11 September 2001 a significant amount of new literature that explores, analyses, reveals and examines the myriad manifestation of violence across the globe has catalogued – often in gory detail – the expression of political violence or terrorism that is then labelled as Muslim or Islamic. Countless journalists have related their journeys into the training camps, hideouts and urban haunts of Muslim terrorists in the western press. Each account portrays the dangerous domain of Islam and the acolytes and leaders of extremist movements and organisations that populate it.[9] Such accounts have contributed to the rising fear and tension associated with the expression of Muslim protest, its politics and the activities of Muslim communities and organisations globally. Although many journalistic accounts of Muslim terrorism detail the extent of the violence perpetrated and the motives behind such attacks, they rarely question the terms of reference that they themselves employ in describing the violence they label as Muslim terrorism or the context in which such events are occurring. There are never enough column inches to question the prevailing orthodoxies or critique the contexts in which Muslim violence is manifest.

There are, however, more extensive studies and accounts that have emerged as a contribution to the debate about Muslim violence since 11 September 2001 that have been published by numerous academics within various disciplines and fields. Political scientists, historians, anthropologists, psychologists, sociologists, specialists in war studies, security studies, media studies, conflict studies, Islamic studies, Middle Eastern studies and terrorism studies have scrutinised Muslim violence since 11 September 2001 from every angle. The normative content of these accounts reinforces a doctrine that contemporary terrorism has lost many of its previous characteristics and become an increasingly (or even exclusively) Muslim preserve.[10] There are some disagreements among scholars regarding the extent to which Muslim terrorism now dominates discourse on international affairs, security doctrines and the wider global tempo, but the frequency of their accounts since 11 September 2001 confirms to the wider scholastic community that Muslim violence matters. Hence contemporary Islamist organisations and groups are studied as if guilty (of violent beliefs) until proven innocent. Disagreements arise largely on the extent to which contemporary Islamist movements are engaged in the promotion of extremist politics that encourages violence and terrorism against western targets. The violent antagonism with the West is a pertinent theme that is addressed in many current academic works leading to a sense of mutual exclusion of political, social and cultural values that are commonly associated with wider discourses of modernity.[11] The global proportions of Islam when mobilised as a global threat becomes a recurring motif of many works. In this way Islam is increasingly represented as the antithesis of the world order that so many westerners have struggled to shape through the principles of secularism and modernity as the progression of rational scientific thought. These themes have led some scholars to pontificate on the diametric clash that exists between Islam and the West, reasoning that the irrational dimension of modern Islam is exhibited in the limitless capacity for violence that Muslims seem prepared to inflict on the rest of the modern world. The message of violence 'preached' by Muslims is construed as using means of political action that 'might be far outside the norms of political activity as we usually understand it'.[12] Scholars believe this is because Islamist movements operate according to a particular world view shaped by a religious lexicon.[13] The religious lexicon also emphasises an ethnic or 'neo-ethnic' dimension to modern Muslim identity and identity politics that is open to a variety of interpretations. Moreover, it is clear that ascribing this ethnic character to Islam (whether primordial or instrumental in construction) illustrates the extent to which post-Cold War conflicts and the place of Muslims within them have been employed instrumentally to promote the clash of civilizations thesis.[14]

Other scholars have argued for a different starting point of analysis for Muslim politics, more generally as a tool by which violence committed in the name of Islam can be rigorously examined for its true portent. They represent Islam less as a unique and violent response to modernity as spearheaded by the West and contend that the demands of many Islamist movements are part of a wider response to globalisation. Moreover, such scholars argue that there is much about Islam that is simply misunderstood or reductive so as to render the faith system of over a billion people as alien to other people who adhere to alternative faith systems or civilisations.[15] In these accounts Islamism and the West share commonalities in terms of faith systems, history and culture but – its authors point out – are generally not known or understood in this respect. Common sources of multi-layered identity are introduced into such works in an attempt to pull down the rigid monolith that increasingly labels Islam as violent and fanatic.[16] Islam and violence carried out by Muslims in a political context is also unpacked and subject to more specific scrutiny in attempts to move Islam 'beyond violence' and view such acts within alternative frameworks such as discourse on nationalism, national movements, breakdown of the state, globalisation and resistance.[17] This literature demonstrates that violence currently associated with Islam can be explained in other ways and thus de-couples it from core spiritual values identified with the faith system. Such accounts, however, only hint at what I believe to be the necessary theoretical exploration of theories of force and violence in the modern age. Muslim violence is characteristically represented through actions and not thought. Because such actions are experienced as irrational, limitless and 'more lethal' than other forms of violence, the strategic motive and calculations based on particular theories of modern politics that the leading figures of contemporary Islamism espouse are overlooked. While it is true that studies that examine particular Islamist movements or leaders who are commonly associated with advocating violence provide the reader with a fuller account of why Muslim violence occurs in particular contexts – be they Chechnya, Iraq, Algeria or Afghanistan – there are few accounts that explore Muslim violence in terms of a theoretical debate of major themes such as force and violence, theology and modernity.

Given this gap in the literature, this study seeks to address such thinking. It begins with a few necessary points of methodological clarification. This is because we need to be clear about who and what we are discussing. As the opening pages of this book have already demonstrated, there is more than one type of Muslim and more than one type of Islam. The terms of reference that will be commonly employed throughout this book, however, will be explained as I go along. The types of Muslims represented in this book span history and geographic location and where possible I have employed data and sources that allow particular Muslims, more commonly labelled as Islamists, to convey their perspective themselves. This has often made the collection of data for this book a haphazard occupation that has lasted over many years and dependent, more often than not, on the real-time political contexts in which so many Islamists groups, organisations and leaders operate under. While the execution of research has been haphazard due to volatile political contexts this, by and large, has been the only obstacle to research in this account of Islam and violence in the modern era. I approached the research remaining ever conscious of my own identity as a potential obstacle to the ideas and issues that have been articulated to me whether first hand or through primary and secondary sources. No one can remain distant and immune from the theme of violence whether experienced by first or second hand. What the task before me has allowed me to do, however, is to use my skills as a political scientist to marshal my individual feelings through the framework of the theoretical debate. In this way I believe that the constituent elements of my identity: woman, mother, westerner and so on, has not impinged directly on the research that has been employed in this book. My experiences of working and living in violent environments both in the West and the Muslim world moreover, while desensitising me to aspects of violence that others recoil in horror to, also alerted me to the empirical fact that no one organisation or group or faith system has a monopoly on violence in the modern era. The cross-cultural and geographic scope of this book, therefore, is obviously related to the 'lived experience' of this researcher in Northern Ireland and the Middle East.

Conflict-ridden domains

In the modern era there have been many locales that are defined and shaped by violence of the politically motivated kind.[18] Political violence or terrorism is increasingly understood at an individual level in an ever-increasing number of domains. Many of these territories have Muslim majority populations, and conflict in the absence of democracy appears to define such societies.[19] In these territories a masculine dominated environment presents itself. It is dominated by men who act out roles as 'hardened' bombers, killers, soldiers, politicians and religious leaders on a variety of sides in a variety of conflicts.[20] This territory also reveals an extraordinary gendered dimension to such a study; for with respect to this kind of terrorism and violence, women are often the victims and rarely the perpetrators. In the modern era, war and violent conflict has a direct impact on women, killing them, turning them into refugees, making them the victims of sexual violence, for as Cockburn reminds us, 'war has the most serious effect on the reproduction of everyday life and therefore the greatest impact on women who are most responsible for those duties in society.'[21] In this sense, the gendered dimension matters in labelling the domain particularly in politically motivated ways. Conflict can then be recognised as manifest at a number of levels as political actions that have implications in both the public and private sphere.

The phenomenon of Islamist inspired violence is important, in terms of the actions as well as consequences, for relations between and within states, values, cultures and people in the twenty-first century. This is important because in order to strike out terrorism, and for a particular form of terrorism to be eradicated, the ideological impulse at the root of such a manifestation of modern life needs not only to be identified but examined as well. This requires more than a military or intelligence-based solution coupled to the propaganda offensive. This requires a sustained engagement and critical counter-offensive in the realm of the powerful discourse that motivates and propels others to acts of political violence or terrorism. Such work, therefore, demands that the concept of justice enter the equation when examining the ethics of violence and terrorism in the modern world. Yet notions of justice must also be tempered by the reality that shapes the experiences of communities (rather than one community) across the globe. The relativism of justice and its relation to political violence must be addressed. Any examination of violence and its Islamic and Islamist dimensions, therefore, should be about the dynamic interface between the religious realm and its associated symbols and values, interpreted norms and values and the current global reality. This modern global reality is one that has been forged, in a number of dimensions, by conflict and war. Hence conflicts and disputes of power (including their violent dimensions) should be recognised as part of the order of political life.

Back to basics – Islam and its fundamentals

The main argument here then is that there needs to be an understanding of how Islam and violence, and political violence in particular, have come to dominate much analysis of the religion across the boundaries of state, community and ethnic group. Indeed in the contemporary world transnational Islam is regularly portrayed in the West as nothing more than a movement for international terrorism and violence. This perception has apparently been reinforced by the trail of terror perpetrated by al-Qaeda's martyr-seekers and Iraq's insurgents. With much recent research on Islam concentrating on this aspect of political violence, it has come to dominate the lexicon of the religion as a whole. Terrorism is promoted as a primary signifier in the way Islam influences policy-makers, media and the cultural norms of others particularly (though not exclusively) in the West. It creates a sense of fear in any encounter with Islam. The second issue here is to reflect a discussion point that is posited on the argument that the construction of this view of Islam is diametrically at odds with the other relationships between faith and struggle that continue to be important to Muslims. This in turn is reflected on, as different to the debate about jihad, as a form of modern terrorism that blights the global landscape in the early twenty-first century. This discussion brings one to a third and related task, which is to critically debate the approach of authors in other fields of research such as terrorology who, it has been contended, routinely demonise Islam. Ironically, it has been argued that the merits of such an approach are obscured by the political motives behind such an enquiry. As such value-free studies of political Islam and Islam as terrorism cannot be easily discerned. They reflect the time and sense of history that animates those that interact with the topic for any length of time. Finally, this is not just an empirical catalogue of violence in the name of Islam but it also introduces a new dimension to the debates about violence in the name of religion and its relationship to tradition theories of war, force and power in the personal as well as public domain. In this way, even if one believes that Islam is the enemy, such a perspective will be augmented by a different approach to the debate in the contemporary context.

Route map

The historical dimension to religion and violence as made relevant to the contemporary context is never far from current accounts of Muslim terrorism and this is addressed in Chapter 1. In this way, there is an acknowledgment that for others it has been useful to cast back to historic episodes constructed and associated with Islam as a way of making sense of the feelings of insecurity that are experienced in modern society. Some sense of historic dimension is understood as beneficial in trying to understand acts of violence and terrorism that appear to be senseless. Additionally, a historic dimension promotes national unity, and communal solidarity emerges in the face of a common enemy. Historic touchstones and myths can be generated to promote a nation-wide sense of unity and togetherness in stepping up to and meeting the challenges posed by such threats; for historical reflection creates a sense of perspective and evidence that by coming together as a nation – especially a people united by democratic values and love of freedom – the challenge of violence and terror could be met. Such historic episodes in the medium-term, however, can also be deployed to support earlier national policy agendas aimed at servicing old needs to conduct a war against other nations as well as on terrorists themselves. There are some that suggest that there is a degree of selectivity in the employment of such historical motifs and that this may be problematic in the long-term.[22] Such myths and motifs are employed by a variety of actors in modern contexts and they in turn can facilitate dissemination and assistance through mastery or control of modern technologies and media. Such historic touchstones and myths can, thus, contribute to a deepening chasm of hostility and disconnection between people and governments across the globe. This dissonance has been highlighted within a framework that Edward Said refers to as a form of 'cultural antipathy' within the West, with Islam today 'defined negatively as that with which the West is radically at odds'.[23] Yet in the context of historic myths and present relations, I would contend that the cultural antipathy is mutual in terms of political and other actors at odds with each other in both a variety of so-called Western and Muslim domains. Many Islamist actors have knowingly constructed historic narratives of Muslim experiences of the West as dominant and define the West as negative. The Hamas covenant, authored in the late 1980s as a treatise of Islamist-nationalism plays on these antipathies.[24] As I try to indicate in this chapter, it may be more worthwhile to explore the link and resonance for Islamists to the past with the present and western understanding of Islamist violence, if a broader historical survey is on offer. One way to do this is to examine the history of the state on its own, or alongside the current studies which centre on a fascination with the extremes of Islam as illustrated in the stories of the 'Assassins', the 'Old Man of the Mountain' or the Mahdi's revolt against General Gordon of Khartoum. A state-centric historical focus permits a more significant context to emerge in which violent phenomena such as a challenge to power are understood; for if we accept one without the other we cannot fully make sense of the past and its impact on the present. To portray, as has been done, the manifestation of the tiny Nizari Ismai'li sect of the Assassins as historically representative or symbolic of Islam is problematic.[25] The reality, after all, is that it is problematic to portray Bin Laden's agenda and tactics as 'representative' of modern Islam or Islamism. Instead al-Qaeda and its leadership represent what others refer to as killer cults. Such cults are small in number, yet made big in significance through their murderous acts and not according to the scale of support they engender in any one society. Here then a useful linkage may be drawn to Usama Bin Laden as a means of explaining the phenomenon of cults and killing. The next step in the dynamic is to assess the 'representative' nature of such strategies of violence in terms of a mainstream monotheistic faith in the modern era. Indeed, the problem is not the parallel with the past but the generalising of such parallels to the extent that they are emptied of their real meaning. Thus a broader vision is outlined in this chapter. There is an acknowledgment of the role of violence within the faith at not just one but a variety of levels. It establishes the link between the state and coercion and the necessary boundaries between force and violence within such realms. It introduces the discourse about plurality and opposition with historical depth and clarity.

The existence of a perception of an historic tension between Islam and the West and its impact on the modern context is explored in Chapter 2. Indeed the tension is recognised as unresolved and transformed into a threat that Islam is believed to pose to those in the West. The examination of issues covers a number of dimensions including the address of the new sense of fear, heightened since the al-Qaeda attacks on 11 September 2001, associated with Islam in its modern form. This gives rise to the production and growth of images and feelings that a notion of Muslim-ness as associated with violence has been created and established in the modern era. As such political acts, struggles and protests that may engage Muslims are re-assessed. This issue proves challenging when the place and role of Muslims in the West is reflected upon. The dimensions to this issue, particularly in relation to negative or conflicted relations were strengthened in the wake of 11 September 2001. There emerged a discourse that centred on a hypothesis that the presence of such communities in the West creates a threat from within which in turn demand new forms of legislative controls. Such legislative controls have deep implications for the liberal concept and aspirations associated with freedom and democracy in Western societies. In the new war on terrorism, it is difficult to ascertain when such a conflict will be considered at an end and by whom. A sense of threat in democratic polities centres on how democracy can survive when emergency measures may undermine the principle of liberty that underpins democracy in the first place. This is especially true when the political leaders of such societies deploy such concepts as weapons in their war of values against those who engage in terrorism. Counter-terrorism efforts have inevitably been stepped up in the wake of 11 September and as a response to the prevailing belief that al-Qaeda and other Islamist elements can wreck havoc against Western targets, which has been strengthened by their recent acts again. The ethical implications of such efforts, particularly as they relate to minorities or other vulnerable groups such as asylum seekers, should at least be acknowledged and debated. In this respect, the contribution of liberal theorists and political scientists to the earlier debate about Islam as a threat to the West – whether cultural, military, political or otherwise – demands serious evaluation and assessment, as such approaches are embraced and employed by political elites as a form of armour to their foreign and domestic policy agendas.

Chapter 2 ends by trying to assess the logical consequences of an acceptance in political and other quarters that Muslims (even in their radical form) pose a serious threat to the internal order of Western democracies. In this respect, there is a reflection on the wider debate about liberal democratic norms and values in the twenty-first century and dimensions of consolidated international power that have emerged in the wake of the ending of the Cold War. In Chapter 3 the theme of violence and its manifestation as a challenge to power in Muslim domains are examined. In examining the Muslim domains, however, it is important to remember other arenas where that which is increasingly recognised or understood as religious violence take place. This means that modern-day phenomena of 'terrorism' or political violence in Gujarat in India or the Tamil resistance in Sri Lanka also fall into the picture in order for us to broaden our horizons on this issue. Violence is a part of modern life, present in a variety of contexts, and in this respect violence is also a part of Islam – or at least it is recognised as a force either to be regulated or abhorred as a threat to peaceful order. In this sense the relationships outlined in terms of power and authority in Islam remains pertinent to understanding the function of violence and force. This places theological as well as historical restraints on the issue as it is addressed in the contemporary form. This approach also recognises a diversity of positions on violence in tandem with political objectives.

One dimension of violence that is also tackled in this chapter is violence that takes place in the private realm. This includes an examination of violence perpetrated by Muslim men against women and others. In this context, a case may be made that violence is 'sacrilized' by patriarchy in extension of their monopoly on power in Muslim locales. This is especially true if the state has played a part in legislating to allow the use of such force without criminal sanction or punishment. Such an argument may be hotly contested, but it is one way of examining the maintenance of a tradition of male interpretation of a sanctioned force/violence perpetrated against women. Much feminist theory and debate has extensively addressed the issue of the sanction of force/violence in a variety of domains or locales – they expose dimensions of the phenomenon that are male not Muslim. In this chapter the issue is also placed in an alternative context as part of the wider focus on the function of force and violence in this multi-layered arena.

One particular aspect of the wider debate about religion and violence, sacrificial violence or the suicide/martyr phenomenon is addressed in Chapter 4. Here the task is to explore and pull-out that which is currently explained or understood as the unique function of Islam in encouraging people to sacrifice themselves in pursuit of the murder of others. This may or may not necessarily be unique, and it is challenging to seek an answer to the explicit assumption that Muslim leaders are actively encouraging this type of undertaking as an act of faith or spiritual attachment to the faith system of Islam. Does it also emerge as part of other explanations of the disruption of terror and terrorism?; for here there is a problem with definition, and definition matters in determining a response or reaction to something that is perceived and presented as a threat. There is a recognition that much modern political violence is often born in the vortex of complex civilian-embracing contemporary conflicts that span across the entire globe. Such conflicts often reflect an ethno-national root of which religion is but one dimension or marker that is important to recognise. Mary Kaldor refers to these conflicts or wars as ones involving 'identity politics' by which she means 'movements which mobilise around ethnic, racial or religious identity for the purpose of claiming state power'.[26] Identity as Muslim-ness must, therefore, be examined and analysed in the context of such conflicts and the violence associated with them.

While it may not be à la mode to identify other political and social forces, economic, security and environmental factors in the accounts of Muslim violence, there is a value to such a task. It helps draw important distinctions between such acts and, therefore, generates appropriate policies for the amelioration of such phenomena; for in this respect Muslim violence and acts of terrorism committed by Muslims in the name of Islamist causes are multi-explanatory. One can then reflect whether a response to violence and terrorism that has a focus on tackling the root causes of political tensions and conflicts has a better chance of achieving the objectives of counter-terrorism than retaliation and revenge. In this respect, to employ a medical analogy, the diagnosis is as important as the treatment if one's ultimate goal is the eradication of a disease. If the goal is to treat the effects of the disease when they are immediately manifested, then any old antibiotic will do. In the long term, however, such abundant recourse to a broad-spectrum medication may have created as many problems as it had solved. This kind of fear was expressed by the Egyptian President Hosni Mubarak during the Allied War on Iraq in March 2003 when he declared that the war would promote rather than undermine Islamist militancy and anti-Westernism. He remarked, 'If there is one (Usama) bin Laden now, there will be 100 bin Ladens afterwards'.[27] Acts of terrorism perpetrated in Chechnya, Saudi Arabia, Morocco and Israel, and in the West Bank and Gaza Strip in the immediate aftermath of the war in Iraq and the fall of Saddam Hussein's regime were then cited as evidence of Mubarak's sense of prescience.

There is also a need to acknowledge that the notion of 'sacrifice' has been employed at a variety of levels in the Muslim realm to motivate and mobilise nations, communities and individuals in defence of national or Muslim causes. In this respect the example of the Iran–Iraq War of 1980–88 speaks volumes. Here too, the discriminate acts of violence perpetrated by Palestinians in the Palestinian–Israeli arena as well as the 11 September 2001 bombers will be examined in detail. There are many difficult issues that such an examination raises, including the ambiguity of opinion-formers towards that which is sanctioned as 'sacrifice' in the name of others and those acts which debase such notions as we understand them in the modern era. I would contend that here the ethical boundaries are breached as civilians are increasingly caught up in conflicts or become targets of those with political grievances intent on bringing a sense of disorder and instability to modern societies. Here the notion of a tradition of violence becomes harder to sustain and the logic of political manipulation deserves to be exposed.

The scholarly recognition of a phenomenon of 'Holy Terror' is examined in Chapter 5. The manifestation of 'Holy Terror', argue its proponents, is situated in the post-Cold War context. This new dimension to the study of Islam and Islamism, I argue, should be understood as part of an effort by those in such fields as terrorism studies to make sense of the emergence of new wars and conflicts over ethno-national issues. This inevitably alters the ways in which the dimensions of Islam are understood. The authors of 'Holy Terror' approach, for example, maintain that Islam as a faith system encourages or sanctions particular kinds of terrorism to a greater or deeper extent than other religions or cults. The approach raises many questions about the understanding of Islam, the development of terrorism studies and the interface between the academic community, policy-makers and media. It is thus contended that the construction of the Holy Terror thesis with its central fascination with Islam as the primary locus of such violence was deliberate, and reflected a political as well as a cultural antipathy towards Islam.

In undertaking the task of writing about Islam and an interface with dimensions of violence, there is an inevitable generalisation of a threat and, therefore, a failure to draw out the specifics or context that appears to motivate believers of a faith system to acts defined as terrorism. Of course commonalities exist, particularly in our transnational and electronic age, but the question here is whether the commonalities exist at the level of discourse or practice. This in turn highlights the dissonance of interpretation and understanding between cultures and even within cultures despite the transglobal dimensions of modern technologies and media.

One dimension of this is the obvious asymmetry that emerges over the so-called universal concepts and values considered central and important in the modern age. In one respect, this reflects a new division that centres on understandings and constructions of homogenous versus heterogeneous values and mores; for as others have recognised, that which is considered as universal is shaped by a dominant Westernised discourse, which, it could be argued, has distilled ideas from a limited pool. Within this discourse I will explore whether Islamism remains in imposed or self-imposed exile on the margins of the debate about universal values and modernity in the present age. Here the spotlight must fall on the tasks that Muslims themselves must continue to address in relation to violence. The nature of the internal debate must be further scrutinised, for in large measure it is found wanting and merely replicates orthodox rather than innovative thinking in tackling such issues. There is much to be said for recognising that a state of denial with respect to violence and terrorism within Islam exists among its myriad leadership. There is, ultimately, an onus on national and political leaders of Islamist movements who encourage others to embrace violence to reflect on the consequences of such activities in terms of balancing against the short, medium and long-term. There are but few voices within the radical Islamist spectrum that have engaged in such debates providing the much-needed intellectual stimulation from the Islamist perspective that this discourse demands. At present the perception of siege, conflict and tension – in relation to external foes – contributes to a sense of intellectual inwardness that fosters increasing intransigence rather than an openness and flexibility. It is worth remembering that only where Islamists perceive themselves as having successfully reconstructed an evolving polity is there a confidence that in turn contributes to a willingness to engage with counter/other-cultures. This is also true of Muslim migrant populations where individuals have emerged to generate a debate from within the confines of the mosque rather than demanding a response to the critical voices external to the mosque. Even in these contexts, however, an unwillingness to countenance the consequences of faith and violence as part of a wider matrix of modernity perpetrated by Muslims is the norm. The factors involved in these issues deserve to be brought out – for where there has been accommodation there is success. Accommodation, in this respect, should be understood in its political context of power and power-sharing and not as something similar to assimilation or integration.

There is an immediate need to question the perspective of Islam that is underscored by a belief predicated on political, theological and cultural constructs that Muslims are violent and inclined to terrorism in ways which make them unique from other groups of believers or people. Indeed, such an ascription gives primordial dimension and ethno-nationalises the Muslim identity. This study, then, asks if Muslim violence is not something innate or primordial; why do Muslims or to put it more specifically, Islamists, engage in acts of political violence? The contention here is that much of that which is described as Muslim terrorism is occurring in the contexts of complex modern-day civil conflicts and intrastate wars such as those that erupted in the former Yugoslavia, in the Philippines or Chechnya. In other words, I argue that the locale in which most terrorism in a Muslim guise is manifest is in a war-zone, battlefield or urban environment disrupted of stable democratic governance. The absence of democratic governance and the prevalence of either collapsed or contested authoritarian state power is a common feature in relation to this manifestation of terrorism. This locale matters and has an explanatory power in the apparent normalising of violence and particularly terrorism as perpetrated by Muslims. The so-called new wave terrorism of Islam is not so modish after all. Of course this explanation has its limits in that I am referring to most terrorism and not all terrorism. The relevancy of this argument is of course questioned when reflecting on other contexts such as the Madrid bombing attacks of March 2004 and the London attacks of July 2005.

There does appear, though, to be an exception to this. The exception is the al-Qaeda phenomenon under the leadership of Usama Bin Laden. Al-Qaeda is the manifestation of a transnational Islamist force predicated on terrorism. Even here, however, it is not the transnational dimension that is unique but rather the strategy adopted to communicate the message. Dimensions of Islamist revivalism throughout the twentieth century had always been transnational or pan-Islamist. This marked it out from the growing phenomena of locally established national Islamist organisations. Pan-Islamism as a transnational movement of a world Muslim community (*umma*) has remained largely aspirational. Organisations that promote transnational Islamic unity around issues common to Muslim concern – whether that is the Palestinian–Israeli conflict, economy or education – have been consistently undermined by a tendency to faction and cliental behaviours.[28] Fundamentalist *salafi'*ism though had always generated a transnational dimension and those drawn to the flame of *salafi'* thinking, more often than not, turned up as part of the Arab mujahideen forces of Afghanistan or in later years in Bosnia and elsewhere. The manifestation of this form of Islamism with its militaristic foundation, encouraged as part of wider global battles, was missed in terms of its potentiality for violence breaking into or out of the contexts in which it was supposed to operate in terms of achieving the end goals of a variety of parties. The consequences of militarising Muslim domains and leaving largely unfettered the conservative regimes of many states, which in turn worked against liberal and democratic forces agitating for change, are clear to see. Responsibility rather than culpability then lies in every domain in the messy path and in the sidetracks that led al-Qaeda and those influenced by their world view to commit its acts of atrocity.

The concluding chapter of this book takes up these themes by reflecting on the manifestation of Islam and violence in the twenty-first century and the extent to which the phenomenon alone can be eradicated. Here, I argue that in the wake of the Cold War a new norm of Islamic terrorism appears to have been developed and it has generated great fear in international society at a variety of levels. The chapter challenges the dimensions of this fear arguing that new orders of power could do well to find ways of accommodating dimensions of Islamic politics rather than its terrorism in order to undermine and eliminate the violent manifestations that appear to currently colour it.

Finally, this book is based on extensive experience of engagement with Islamist movements and trends, especially in the Middle East. The aim though is not simply to describe a phenomenon that is accounted for in most media of the contemporary globe but to offer a different, albeit evidential perspective that is passionately adhered to by those who eschew the politics of the West for the politics of liberation and faith tied to the expression of an Islamic identity. New wave terrorism and emerging patterns of violence appear to scar the landscape of the international political order in ways that only Islam appears to determine. As such the dynamic of conceptualisation must be re-visited and alternatives examined if violence is to be tempered with the power of peace.

1
Religion and Violence: A History of Entanglement

Today we live in a world that is perceived as increasingly violent. Within the maelstrom of violence in the modern era, religion also has its place. Indeed it is difficult to contradict this image of preponderant violence when it appears that so many societies are now characterised as places where the population is engaged in an atavistic and hateful embrace of the other. This hateful embrace often results in countless deaths.[1] When violence becomes a way of life, or rather a means of maintaining an existence – whether as an individual, a community or as a nation – the process of politics along with the economy, culture and society is altered. Politics as a power struggle becomes infused with negativity and fear. There is trepidation at the prospect that violence can and probably even will disrupt the dialogue that takes place within the political arena and undermine its value. The promise of an end to conflict inherent in the meta-narrative of the New World Order has failed to materialise.

While the major ideological battles of the twentieth century had been fought and won, the prospect of global peace was replaced with what appeared to be an explosion of complex intrastate and transnational tensions and conflicts in which the traditional orthodoxies regarding the rules of war have often been ignored.[2] Collective abhorrence combined with an astounding impotence at the horror of, for example, the genocide in Rwanda and ethnic cleansing in the former Yugoslavia only seemed to reinforce the notion that many societies and polities had in fact entered some kind of 'post-orthodox' age.[3] The major conflicts of the 1990s that dominated the media and grabbed global attention were often presented as more representative of another age or time when the world was smaller and we were less sophisticated creatures. The stars of these new conflicts were represented to us as something more akin to the past than the here and now. The luminaries of modern-day conflict were not clean-cut commanding officers who were career soldiers representing a nation state with internationally agreed borders that were to be defended according to international law and treaties. Nor did such luminaries appear to embrace the kind of technology that reduced the risk of human and particularly civilian casualty. Rather, they appeared to glory in dragging civilians into conflict by turning them into war victims and child soldiers, and deployed weapons guaranteed to reap high human costs. The luminaries or rather the 'villains' of conflict in the 1990s were represented to us as warlords, clan-leaders, mad mullahs, machete-wielding individuals and twisted evil psychopaths who employed the appeal of ancient hatreds and attachments to fuel their battles for power.

Our sense of time and space has been collapsed through exposure to events such as wars and conflicts fuelled by the resurrection and invention of traditions of so-called ancient hatreds that under the old ideological framework had previously been suppressed. Serb leaders urged war against Bosnia's Muslims as part of the rhetoric of revived Serb nationalism founded on old historical grievances re-packaged by political leaders such as Slobodan Milosovic. Yet, as Eickleman and Piscatori remind us, 'all traditions are created, however, through shared practice, and they can be profoundly and consciously modified and manipulated under the guise of a return to a more legitimate earlier practice.'[4] Through invented traditions and myths resurrected and re-cast to meet new religious, ideological and political agendas, new conflicts emerged. Many of these conflicts drew in Muslim populations from across the globe.

Modern conflict now rarely consists of well-matched armies facing each other off on the battlefield. Instead militia-leaders, state forces, warlords, demagogues and terrorists engage in paramilitary and terrorist adventures where often the highest number of casualties is found among civilians rather than uniformed and armed combatants. While it may be true that civilian casualties and deaths are, by definition part of war, conflicts throughout the 1990s have led to increasing civilian casualties. By the 1990s, it was contended that 90 per cent of the casualties of conflict were civilians and most of them were women and children.[5] The rise in civilian casualties of war is concurrent with a decline in military ones. It is this dimension of modern conflict that diminishes the value of comparing such a so-called collateral damage of a civilian dimension in an arena of conflict, such as Afghanistan, Somalia, Bosnia or Iraq with World War I. Additionally there has been evidence of a deliberate targeting of civilians in such conflicts.[6] Finally, the targeting of civilians by parties to conflict, including state actors, introduces a degree of fuzziness as it relates to definitions of terrorism, and who may legitimately be accused of acts of terrorism and brought to justice according to the rules of the international order.[7] It is my contention that these wars and conflicts, in which ethnicity, religion, clan and tribe stand at the foundation of ancient hatreds, symbolise our inability to 'sell' the modern, secular global age to certain constituencies. The politics of ancient blood and nation, religion and ethnicity; and the re-emergence of Serbs and Bosnians, Hutus and Tutsi's, *mollota* Haitians and their ancient animalistic voodoo rites, confound and confuse us. Such conflicts are a challenging and uncomfortable reminder that perhaps all is not well with the modern age. Perhaps the liberalisation or abandonment of old taboos, norms and values, and rites and rituals does not necessarily bring us to a better place where violence is reduced or increasingly absent. In this respect the saliency of realist philosophical arguments rooted in the belief that conflict is part of 'brutish' human nature gains ground. As Clausewitz has remarked, 'We say therefore, war belongs not to the province of arts and sciences, but to the province of social life. It is a conflict of great interests which is settled by bloodshed, and only in that is it different from others ... [and] ... State policy is the womb in which war is developed'.[8]

Yet, we are confounded by the appeal of ancient faiths, tribes and clans in generating brutal conflicts in a modern age. We are, it appears, especially perplexed and even affronted at the audacity of modern militant religious fundamentalists who insist that people embrace, once again, the values centred on faith not secularism. The emergence of Manichean dimensions to modern interstate and inter-cultural or civilisation relations appears to work against the mantra of harmonisation and universalism envisioned within globalisation thinking. In the West, commentators and opinion-formers are shocked that the tactics of some fundamentalists includes an embrace of violence and terror against civilians. We do not understand why Christian fundamentalists bomb abortion clinics, kill doctors and blow up US federal buildings.[9] Nor why Hindu fundamentalists encourage the perpetration of terror against Muslims. We are even more confused by the resort to this tactic in societies where democratic values should have ensured that such opinions and viewpoints can be voiced – and even be influential in the corridors of power. And yet the flourishing of fundamentalism contributes to the landscape of violence under the guise of democracy. Karen Armstrong recognises this as a reactionary force to institutionalised secularism; she states,

> In the US today about 8 per cent of the population can be described as fundamentalists, but they command widespread support from more conservative Christians in many denominations, as became evident during the rise of the Moral Majority in 1979 ... As the primordial, archetypal fundamentalism, the American case reveals important aspects of this religious rebellion. First, it always begins as an assault on co-religionists, and is directed against foreigners and outsiders only at a later stage.[10]

In India, the largest democracy on earth, Hindu fundamentalists have played their part in provoking a breakdown in delicate and precarious communal relations with concurrent recourse to violence against the country's Muslim citizens. This is no more tellingly illustrated than in the communal violence that beset the northern state of Gujarat where Hindu fundamentalists promoted the exclusion of Muslims from mainstream society and motivated violence carried out by Hindu mobs and state forces alike.[11] Writing in 2002 and following the latest bout of violence between Muslims and Hindus in India, the author Salman Rushdie pointed the finger at faith declaring, 'in India, as elsewhere in our darkening world, religion is the poison in the blood. Where religion intervenes, mere innocence is no excuse. Yet we go on skating around this issue, speaking of religion in the fashionable language of "respect" '.[12] This return to faith, for the author Rushdie, contributes to the reactive spiral that engulfs communities and promotes the breakdown of order and democracy. Religious leaders and politicians who espouse religious ideological viewpoints are subsequently blamed for whipping up religiously motivated violence either against minorities, or those that do not value or appear to share their beliefs. The victims of such violence litter the wayside of the contemporary political landscape. These victims include the vulnerable such as the elderly, the young, women and non-combatant civilians. Indeed the battlefield of the modern-day religious fundamentalists is rarely one that finds conventional forces facing-off or engaging in aerial combat. President George Bush may have employed the lexicon of religious symbolism when declaring a US 'Crusade' against terrorism in the wake of 11 September 2001 but it would be entirely disingenuous to suggest that the armed forces of the United States of America bear a resemblance to the Knights Templar of the tenth century. Indeed the traditional image of religiously sanctioned violence – as the army padre blesses the uniformed combatants before they engage with the enemy – is increasingly redundant. This is not to say that the approval of religious leaders are not sought to legitimate such actions. Leaders of faith are still called upon to give blessing to soldiers in battle, and a variety of religious figures, movements and individuals also encourage or sanction violence through the appropriation of divine revelation as relevant to the cause in the modern age. In this way the political machinations and developments of the modern age are subject to a re-interpretation through a primarily theological lens. Paramilitary pastors, militant Mullah's, radical rabbis and politically motivated priests populate a landscape of conflict and violent carnage.[13] They are joined by the padres, priests, imams and rabbi's who bestow their blessings on the soldiers of national state armies despatched into battle.

Irrespective of the particular lens – Muslim, Jewish, Hindu, Buddhist or Muslim – manifestations of modern life and politics are subject to a religious interpretation. Sometimes that interpretation is subtle and lies within a private realm of personal spirituality and piety. Other times that re-interpretation is public, explicit, and linked to a process of making sense of the present political environment by reference to the religious texts and their import. For example, in October 2002, during a mainstream national broadcast of the American CBS programme '60 Minutes', the fundamentalist Christian Minister, Gerry Falwell, branded the Prophet Mohammed a terrorist declaring 'I think Mohammed was a terrorist. He ... was a violent man, a man of war. In my opinion ... I do believe that – Jesus set the example for love, as did Moses. And I think that Mohammed set an opposite example'.[14] His comments, rooted in a wider debate about conservative and neo-conservative Christian fundamentalist support for Israel, deepened the belief that religious motive was a significant element in influencing American popular culture and foreign policy-making that has been consolidated under the administration of George W. Bush.[15] Indeed, Falwell's remarks were linked to the controversy almost a year earlier that was sparked by comments from a close confidante of President George W. Bush and fundamentalist Christian Minister Franklin Graham. Graham had declared that Islam, not Islamists or Muslim terrorists but the faith system itself and in its entirety was 'wicked, violent and not of the same God.' Graham declared, 'I don't believe this is a wonderful, peaceful religion ... when you read the Koran and you read the verses from the Koran, it instructs the killing of the infidel, for those that are non-Muslim ... It wasn't Methodists flying into those buildings, it wasn't Lutherans ... It was an attack on this country by people of the Islamic faith.'[16] Such viewpoints matter in the debate about mainstream public opinion as well as to individual opinion-shapers with the power to influence policy within the political administration. This is not to suggest or give into conspiracy theories that circulate about the ascendancy of the Christian right and its inordinate power over the White House, but to highlight the symbolism attached to Christian faith politics in contemporary US politics and the influences, in competition with other interest groups, that it may have over politicians and administrators. The power or influence of this element was demonstrated in November 2004 when the church-going conservatives of the United State of America cast their vote in support of the re-election of Republican President George W. Bush. As Blumenthal opined in the wake of the 2004 poll, 'Ecclesiastical organisation has become the sinew and muscle of the Republican party, essential in George Bush's re-election. His narrow margins in the key states of Florida, Iowa and Ohio, and elsewhere, were dependent on the direct imposition of the churches.'[17] Faith clearly matters in the politics of the twenty-first century superpower of the United States of America.

Faith and politics: the public–private tension

Such examples of mainstreamed perspectives in the United States of America lead one to question whether the redundancy of the religious text from the public realm is complete in all cases. In some quarters, the religious texts serve as a means of 'making sense' of societal development and are utilised as a vehicle of communication to a broad mass who experience distance from the centre and are excluded from the spoils of the development process.[18] In this respect the modern nation state can be viewed as distant; it is unknown and regarded as weak, failed, tainted and open to abuse. In its place, in many, though not all quarters, the texts and interpretations of the 'old' religions are re-packaged and sold anew as something fresh, relevant and meaningful on a daily basis. With this paradigmatic framework, the world can be broken down into components that are much easier to understand and comprehend. In addition, they can be used to tap into that which is sublimated to the altar of secularised universal rights and norms. Furthermore, in other modern contexts, the attachment of fundamentalist religious elements to the font of power has deepened with the emergence of conservative ideological perspectives. In this sense the boundary in certain secular states or environments between them and the sacred is less rigid. Distinctions between such states and others where the boundary is rigid need to be acknowledged. The French state, for example, is institutionally, politically and mostly ideologically divorced from religious influence. Thus while the inauguration ceremony of the President of the United States of America includes a rite of religious benediction from a fundamentalist Christian minister, this is not the case in a state like France. Hence symbols matter as signs, actions and emblematic behaviours that present a version of present realities where faith has a relevancy. In the 2 November 2001 edition of *The New York Times*, novelist Salman Rushdie addressed the symbols as they related to Islam and the war on terror in the wake of 11 September. He contended that contrary to declaration that the war on terror was not a war on Islam, the symbolism of actions betrayed a certain belief that the war on terror was in fact directly targeting Islam. While acknowledged that 'if the United States is to maintain its coalition against terror it can't afford to suggest that Islam and terrorism are in any way related,' the reality was the opposite. He pointed to symbolic demonstration by Muslims across the world in support of Bin Laden and his cause highlighting that the conflict is about Islam. Yet, as Rushdie bewails, which Islam and what Islam is the current war on terror against? 'After all', he notes,

> most religious belief isn't very theological. Most Muslims are not profound Koranic analysts. For a vast number of 'believing' Muslim men, 'Islam' stands, in a jumbled, half-examined way, not only for the fear of God ... but also for a cluster of customs, opinions and prejudices ... the sermons delivered by their mullahs of choice; a loathing of modern society in general ... and a more particularized loathing of the prospect that their own immediate surroundings could be taken over – 'Westoxicated' – by the liberal Western-style way of life.[19]

Thus from some of these religionised political and ideological perspectives the world can be turned into a dichotomy of good and evil. Individuals are no longer appended with the enveloping adjective of evil, but faith systems and states are also caught in the dichotomy. The complexities and inter-linked diversities of the international system in the modern era is reduced by the bald notion that in global 'wars' and confrontation you are 'either with us or against us'.[20] And from this starting point perspectives can be rigidly fixed and held with little room for compassion about the consequences for creating a world where there are no shades of grey. Inherent in this rigid fixing of positions, however, is a lack of flexibility or compromise if the holders of such positions perceive their system of faith or ideology to be under attack, or under a threat of existence. The 'zero-sum' game becomes the means by which international relations and diplomacy is dominated. Other approaches remain but are marginalised. The 'zero-sum' game becomes a means for mobilising not just armed elements or state forces but entire nations in confrontation with the enemy.

Muslim culprits

In the modern era, chief among the religiously motivated culprits are the Muslims who assault and seek to challenge the modern secular liberal order. Its symbols are motifs for rage, or so those in the West are often encouraged to assume.[21] Indeed, the good versus evil reductive process, it is argued, comes from the Islamic realm and has been visited upon other civilisations and not the other way round. As Bernard Lewis states, 'Islam, like other religions, has also known periods when it inspired in some of its followers a mood of hatred and violence. It is our misfortune that a part, though by no means all or even most, of the Muslim world is now going through such a period, and that much, though again not all, of that hatred is directed against us.'[22] In the secular societies of the West, and beyond, religious revivalism and its militant offshoots are perceived as an attempt to drag people back to ancient times and orders. When secular Jews in Jerusalem engage in discourse with their orthodox co-religionists over the collective keeping of Shabbat, fear and tension dominate the encounter. As Alex Lubotsky decries, 'The association between Shabbat and war is the utter antithesis of the Shabbat, "the Shabbat of peace" '.[23] The secularists are challenged by their co-religionists who appear to embrace a desire to stop time, abandon the demands of the modern commercial age and carve out a bit of sacrosanct religious 'down-time'. Too often, however, the desire for sanctity out of the secular and the desire for an acknowledgement of the divine out of the profane is manifest in some act or form of violence. The haredim Shabbat-keepers of Mea Sharim literally man the barricades armed with rocks to throw at transgressors of the border between the sacred and the secular as the sun sets over the sandstone walls of modern Jerusalem on a Friday evening. In the shopping malls of Saudi Arabia the *mutawwa* (religious police) enforce *Wahabbi*-interpreted Islamic custom, particularly as it relates to their religious codes of prayer, dress and behaviour in public. Enforcement of these local laws includes the sanction of force/violence against alleged transgressors and such punishments may be meted out on the spot. In enforcing strict gender segregation according to *Wahabbi* interpretation of Islamic norms, the *mutawwa* have allegedly arrested women and charged them with prostitution after being found in the company of men who could not be proved as close male relatives. In March 2002, the *mutawwa* hit the headlines after they were reported to have actively hindered Saudi rescue workers at the scene of a fire at a girl's school in Mecca. It was said that the girls were prevented an escape route by the *mutawwa* because they were not appropriately dressed. Rescue workers complained that the religiously motivated *mutawwa* had intervened at the cost of saving lives not Muslim modesty.[24]

Faith in the modern age becomes associated, partly through media portrayal, in a heady mix with ethno-national motives as an incomprehensible force for evil rather than good. The faithful become identified as a major obstacle to the realisation of secular democratic goals. Such religious motives also lie in the wellspring of the kind of Serbian nationalism that encouraged the VRS butchers of Srebrenica to massacre thousands of Bosnian Muslims and deport the rest in July 1995. The profession of faith is raised aloft as a banner by the supporters and members of forces who lead armies into wars and terrorists into acts of mindless atrocity and evil in the present day. A cosmic notion of the 'just cause' and the 'just war' places the acts of violence into the realm of the mundane. And in the face of this banal litany of hate and violence in the name of faith the counter-efforts of those who oppose such forces and their methods can appear to be weak and lacking the focus and direction of their foes.

The notion of foe emanates both from within and outside societies and political systems that would identify themselves as both liberal and democratic. In these plural and often multi-cultural societies, the foe is conversely found in the expression of faith, albeit faith that sometimes sits on the margin and at other times, however, is found in the mainstream as a reflection of the kind of principles that such societies value and strive to adhere to. Indeed, it becomes increasingly apparent that the old twentieth century attempt to 'privatise' religion in the secular liberal project has not always worked as well as its supporters may have wished. In the modern era the secularisation of the political sphere was considered important in the expansion of both old and new political systems for the appropriate development of society and the economy. In this context it didn't matter whether you were a communist or capitalist, there was correlation in the ambition to push religion out of the public realm and onto the margins or removed entirely. This is apparent in the variety of contexts from Titoist Yugoslavia, to Nasser's revolutionary Egypt, to socialist-led France and Sukarno's Indonesia. Indeed, by clinging to religion or making it part of the public forum states such as Saudi Arabia and South Africa, it was considered – and rightly so – less than democratic or liberal. Indeed, in the case of South Africa the generation of a vision of Apartheid with its inbuilt religious ideology and 'chosen people' syndrome could also be identified in other states behaving in less than democratic fashions against subordinate communities such as the Palestinians under Israel's occupation.

The 'chosen people' syndrome is a contemporary exemplar of the way in which religion has been knowingly employed to legitimate state and non-state actors in an economic and political mission, which they believe they have been divinely ordained to fulfil. Here the outcome is a less-than-easy arrangement where religious leaders or religious treaties are employed to legitimate state policies organised and proposed by the dominant elite. Similarly, the religious motif demonstrated through a particular notion of attachment or belief in uniqueness – 'chosen people' – behind the actions of non-state actors in modern nation states can be discovered. Religious markers of this nature become important in the construction of a common cause and history. As a force for social cohesion in beleaguered societies, an attachment or re-attachment to social markers such as religion becomes important. In many respects then, it should come as no surprise that violence is a frequent feature of this uneasy alliance as opposition and subordinate elements rebel against such strictures. The issue is the root of the violence and not necessarily its manifestation. This is nothing new but appears to clash in the contemporary context with the attempt to generate models for life which remove religion from the public sphere because of its very divisive features. This is the challenge in modern multi-cultural and multi-ethnic societies: how to accommodate the religious dimension such pluralism presents, yet maintain the principle of secularism in the public political sphere?

The realm of violence and power

Thus, rather than assuming and accepting that religion and violence – particularly in relation to Islam – is something which confounds us in the secular age, a broader canvas is desirable. Tensions within the realm of religion as well as the divisions (sometimes violent) which have emerged between the secular and the sacred worlds are also worthy of debate; for in many respects one is compelled to question whether it was really such a surprise that with the attempt to disempower the religious establishment of Christianity, Islam and Judaism there would be no attempt to fight back. In some contexts this fight has been successful and significant – and this includes the United States of America where, as I have highlighted earlier in this chapter, the well-documented rise of the Christian right-wing has been significant not only in shaping public discourse on a variety of issues from abortion, the gun law and death penalty but also in influencing the political sphere at both the local and regional and national and international levels. It has been noted, for example, that the shaping of American foreign policy on Israel and the Israeli–Palestinian conflict is today influenced or informed as much by the Christian right as the Jewish lobby in the United States of

America. Indeed, the profile of pro-Israel lobbying which has by tradition always been underpinned by a moral sympathy born out of religious sentiment for Israel's 'chosen people' is in the twenty-first century an up-front and public phenomenon bolstered by America's Christian right. As one commentator pointed out, 'What's the number one item on the agenda of the Christian Right [in the United States of America]? Abortion? School Prayer? No and No. Believe it or not, what's most important to a lot of conservative Christians is the Jewish State. Israel: Its size, its strength, and its survival.'[25] Further evidence of such patterns of identification translating into public and political action is apparent in the battle of the 'flags' that erupted in Northern Ireland in the wake of Israel's re-occupation of the West Bank and the siege of Yasser Arafat's Ramallah headquarters in April 2002. Both sides to the conflict in Northern Ireland engaged in the raising of Israeli and Palestinian flags in loyalist and nationalist/republican neighbourhoods. At interface flashpoints, in various parts of the city, opposing flags symbolised the identification with a cause many thousands of miles distant. For the loyalist community, the identification with Israel appeared to be straight forward. Graffiti in loyalist areas, along with the flags, indicated support for Israel and its Prime Minister Ariel Sharon in meeting the threat posed by Palestinian nationalist elements. Elements of the loyalist community, long motivated by religious fervour and the 'chosen people' syndrome were clearly evident in the representation of the two causes as one. Indeed, the British Zionist Star has been regularly flown by loyalist communities and groups symbolising a minority religious view that the Protestants of Northern Ireland are or are like the Lost Tribe of Israel.[26]

What remains significant of course is the political and religious representation – no matter how crude or incorrect – in politicised and conflict environments. In such an environment the symbolism of religion is pulled out in an often unthinking or haphazard fashion to give meaning or potency to political or economic conflicts. Those who conspire to promote or recognise this process also overplay the importance of faith as an expression of conflict and violence and underplay or fail to enter other factors such as nationalism, economics and geo-strategic location into the equation. Yet, it should be increasingly clear that with the decline of the religious empires of classical civilisation and the processes of historical and contemporary reformation evident in the cultures of Europe, Asia, Africa, Latin America and the Middle East along a timeline of many centuries that such processes would generate resistance, clash and defeats in the realms of religion and politics with its echoes felt in the modern age. Indeed, there are some who would argue that the Middle East is yet to experience a true process of reformation in which the religious establishment is confined to the margins of state power. In too many modern Middle Eastern regimes, the Islamic and other faiths establishment has been co-opted or willingly made part of a state structure that employs faith as a means of regulating an authoritarian social order and concurrently the political and economic order as well.

In this respect, to take Marx at his word, religion is not so much an opiate of the masses but is harnessed by the state elite into the fabric of the state – to varying degrees – as a means of force and order.

> Religion is [the world's] general basis for consolation ... The struggle against religion is ... a struggle against that world whose spiritual aroma is religion. Religious suffering is at the same time an expression of real suffering and a protest against real suffering. Religion is the sigh of the oppressed creature, the sentiment of a heartless world, and the soul of soulless conditions. It is the opium of the people. The abolition of religion as the illusory happiness ... is a demand for their real happiness.[27]

Indeed it has been argued that the Muslim theological preoccupation with and fear of disorder (*fitna*) generates important resonance here; for at the heart of significant theological treatises in Islam has been the focus on how Islam brings order (and peace) to societies that would otherwise be subject to chaos. Fear of chaos lies at the heart of radical, conservative and moderate theological discourse and informs thinking and the formulation of norms and values in Muslim societies across time and the globe. Jurists of Islam like Ibn Taymiyyah or al-Ghazali express the fear of anarchy so much so that tyranny becomes a preferential option. Albert Hourani alerts us to this preoccupation with order noting that al-Ghazali argues that 'the tyranny of the Sultan for a hundred years causes less damage than one year's tyranny exercised by the subjects against one another. Revolt was justified only against a ruler who clearly went against a command of God or His Prophet.'[28] This desire for order and fear of chaos also includes reflection on the means by which order is established and the force-violence paradigm. As will be discussed later in this book, this paradigm throws up some interesting dilemmas, most of which, however, are solved in a not dissimilar fashion to those that focus on the matrix of force-power-violence in Western political and theological philosophy. Political ideas have always informed the theological debates of Islam and a discourse on power, order and leadership is no different in this respect. As Van Ess argues, 'Islamic ideologies of all periods have one thing in common: they are expressed in religious terms. This may look obsolete in our part of the world ... Above all it is efficient; its persuasiveness derives from it being deeply rooted in the past, at least in the Islamic world.'[29] The point here is that the notion that Islamic thought and political ideas reflect a greater concern with violence than peace and order is misleading. Historically, as Islam extended out of Arabia and across Asia, Africa and Europe, the campaign to establish political order and Muslim rule in its many manifestations has as much to do with peace and harmony as defence of belief, political order and homeland.

A historical overview of the great 'religious' battles and tensions will perhaps serve as a means of setting the main debates about Islam and violence into some sort of context. The idea here is to create a sense of continuity along a timeline that reflects on episodes of conflict and violence in their appropriate setting. Of course, this leaves one somewhat at the mercy of the historiographers, but no account of the past is without its difficulties, slants and interpretations, and such preoccupations will not detract from the sense of history which should in reality concern us. The idea of providing historical perspective is to avoid relativism and understand the timelessness of such a discourse.

The state-builders

If the notion of a historical relationship between Islam and violence exists then it can be best illustrated by examining the rise of the Muslim state, rule by Muslim leaders and the consolidation, rebellion, succession and defeat of such powers. Other approaches to the examination of Muslim violence establish the motif as central and explicit to the Muslim project as a means of establishing, consolidating and maintaining the faith and the ideology of expansionism that accompanied it. Such an examination dwells on episodes of violence conducted by such as the Assassin sect, the Mahdi, or the West African Jihad movement as testimony of a seamless history of terror in the name of Islam which explains the murderous tendencies of modern-day actions, such as the kidnapping and execution of western hostages, car bombs or suicide attacks as archetypically Muslim. This approach is evident when Bernard Lewis reflects on the historical relationship between Islam and the West, which he refers to as a struggle (initiated by Islam) that has lasted centuries. This struggle he contends, 'consisted of a long series of attacks and counterattacks, jihads and crusades, conquests and re-conquests', with Islam in a 'defensive' mode for the last 300 years.[30] I chart a different course, one that in respect of mainstream accounts of Muslim history is more conventional in terms of recognising the unit of the state and associated power elites with it as central to explaining the manifestation of violence whether under the Ummayads or Ottomans.[31] In this way historical perspective is engendered that is not predicated on violence as a central symbol or dominator. Instead the function of violence is still acknowledged but within the kinds of frameworks we are used to employing in other contexts.

If the unit of the state is central to any historical overview of violence and religion then one must also be careful to recognise that the notion of the state as a Islamic phenomenon has much in common with the secular nation-state unit of modern times with apparent points of diversity pointed out when appropriate. While it may appear that the state founded and established by the Prophet Mohammed in Medina in the seventh century could have little to do with the modern nation state, there are important resonance's when reflecting the basic functions of this political unit. The development of Muslim state rule – as a manifestation of many types of alliances between the religious and political sphere – is also worthy of reflection in terms of identifying or outlining the sheer variety of state types, opposition and rule that were to emerge under the Muslim header. Additionally, it is important to remember that the Koran does not provide the specific outline for an Islamic state or state type, for government, ruler or institutions of rule. While some may consider the constitution of Medina a form of inspiration, it cannot be considered an optimal and detailed blueprint by which to measure successive Islamic statehood against. Islamic 'state-edness', is a many hued and faceted thing.[32] The notion of a one-dimensional state form is not applicable to historical examination.

Since the establishment of the religion by the Prophet Mohammed, its adherents and thinkers and rulers have devised ways and means of political rule that married the religion into the fabric of the state. Although the religion was initially established as no more than a community of embattled believers whom many in authority feared as a direct challenge to their rule, the emergence of a system of political rule, an Islamic state was always fluid and was not inspired by specific divination from the Koran. As Nazih Ayubi notes, 'Given the limited nature of the political stipulations in the Koran and Hadith Muslims have had from the start to borrow and to improvise in the developing of their political systems.'[33] Muslim leaders were motivated and informed, as state-builders, by more than just the holy texts of Islam or the inherited traditions of the Prophet Mohammed. Additionally, previous traditions of tribal rule in Arabia, as well as experience and knowledge of the administrative systems of the Sassanian and Byzantine traditions have also been cited in informing the early state-builders. Indeed, as Lapidus contentiously reminds us, 'statist ideology was derived from previous empires but its expansion was characteristically Islamic.'[34] Some Muslim state-builders ensured that the state was a unit of administration and power in service of the faith, yet others could clearly be accused of employing faith in service of the state. For some Muslim heads of state, territorial expansionism was a primary motive and hence linked to the military unit of the state, while for others consolidation of existing power and justice remained pre-eminent. These points can be illustrated in the rise of the Seljuk Turks and their Samanid predecessors in the geographic extremities of the Muslim domains. The Samanids predicated their rule on centralisation and strong bureaucratic systems combined with expansionism of the faith in new territories by peaceful means. Their strengths, therefore, lay in their bureaucratic prowess sustained through stringent and heavy systems of taxation. Their Seljuk successors, however, grew and established themselves in the realms of pre-existing power primarily through their military prowess and expertise. Saunders, from the perspective of state-edness, considered the Seljuk capture of Baghdad in 1060 important, because the Seljuk ascendancy 'registered a great triumph for Sunnite orthodoxy: the power of the State could now be employed to put down Shi'ism of all kinds and Isma'ilism in particular'.[35] Additionally schismatic differences as they emerged and related to issues of rule and political leadership contributed to the emergence of clerical-political elements in the highest echelons of the state. Yet, the example of clerics as state leaders is not as significant as one might associate with Islam. For although there is a common belief that Islam and politics are inextricably linked this continuum does not, by necessity, extend to a fundamental principle that the leader of the state is a cleric. The clerical class, like other classes such as the military, have, of course, harboured ambitions of power but not always in an exclusive fashion.

As an ideal, however, it can be argued that the Islamic state has some core elements with other features then subject to historical, geographic, social and other contexts. Islamic theorists writing about the state have spanned a number of centuries and covered wide ideological ground. To begin with the term, the 'state' (*dawla*) in the Islamic sense is actually described as the *umma* (community) or the caliphate. Any discussion by Islamic theorists of the *dawla* – the state – is therefore a relatively recent development linked in large part and in response to the rise of the European nation state and associated political thinking and theorising. The Asian Islamist Mawdudi typifies such theorising. Mawdudi outlined a specific framework of institutions central to his vision of a modern Islamic state to include a president, elected council, independent judiciary and so forth. The path by which this ideal would be achieved was one of jihad. Mawdudi declares,

> Islam wants the whole earth and does not content itself with only a part thereof ... It does not want this in order that one nation dominates the earth and monopolizes its sources of wealth, after having taken them away from one or more other nations ... In order to realise this lofty desire, Islam wants to employ all forces and means that can be employed for bringing about a universal all-embracing revolution ... all possible means are called jihad.[36]

Theories of the state in the Islamic or Muslim domain have emerged in a variety of ways and through a variety of contexts. Such theories or approaches have been retrospectively informed by experience of statehood, rule, expansion and contraction, conflict and peace, internal and external differences and the reflection of such experiences in differing schools of juristic rule or schism. All of this has contributed to the emergence of ideas and provisions for statehood that are as varied as Muslim global and historic experience. It is suggested that some thinkers, such as Ibn Taymiyyah, while not believing that the Prophecy served to establish a political order or state did, however, support or adhere to the notion of the state in the service of Islam. The state is not, in Ibn Taymiyyah's view, a divine function of Islam but a framework in the service of Islamic principles as they relate to the political sphere. This highlights an almost polar opposite position to the way in which Ibn Taymiyyah constructs a critique and attack on *Shi'a* principles of Imamate as it relates to statehood.

In the twentieth century much Islamist discourse on the state was a response or rejoinder to the perception by many Muslim thinkers of European domination of political thinking on this subject. Such discourse then was an attempt to reclaim the Muslim body politic and a result of a particular and specific experience of the nation state through, for example, the experience of globalisation, colonialism and European domination of the Muslim world. In addition, while western theorising of the state and government was largely realised, for contemporary Muslim thinkers the ideal remained the norm and practical examples were few and far between. While many states and their rulers may claim 'Islamic credentials', very few, if any, are accepted within Islam as Islamic. Essentialising or pulling out the common threads of Islamisation of the state as they relate to modern-day Iran, Sudan or Somalia highlight the difficulties associated with the assumption that monolithic frameworks represent and dominate the Islamic political.

The Medinan state

If the truly Islamic credentials of modern Muslim states such as Saudi Arabia, Iran or Pakistan can be questioned, what then of the original sources of inspiration, the model which so many contemporary Muslim theorists and Islamists in particular cite as a goal to which the Muslim community should work to, shoulder-to-shoulder, as liberation from corrupt and un-Islamic rule. It is contended that the Prophet Mohammed was a political as well as religious leader and in order to protect his socially and tribally disparate group of believers he evolved a political-religious community in Medina during the seventh century. In this way it is argued Mohammed was more than just a religious leader for a community of spiritually motivated believers. He is characterised as having developed a leadership role that included deliberation and extension of power as a political, military and legal function. Yet, the balance of such forces is contested by Ibn Taymiyyah with regard to the nature or function of the state and the political in the equation with faith, and other factors such as military prowess. The state cannot be placed over or above the prophecy of Islam as ordained by God through Mohammed. In this respect, Khan argues that Ibn Taymiyyah is not abrogating the need for a state, indeed he is 'proving that the state is essential but that it must be dynamic and progressive in its nature and constitution'.[37]

Through this form of governance not only did the Prophet Mohammed unite the tribes of Arabia and provide new codes of social, economic and political practice but also the adherents of the new faith went on and settled new lands and bolstered their power. It is said that there was a military dimension associated with the function of force attached to this form of political authority. I believe it is debatable that what is described by contemporary writers as 'military' in relation to the establishment of Islam is far removed from the reality of life in seventh century Arabia. The Prophet Mohammed didn't come from a military background. He had not been raised in the bosom of warrior tribes or clans established through prowess in combat. The Kuraysh tribe to which Mohammed was born were traders not warriors. His marriage to Khajida strengthened that connection for she was engaged in trading and business herself. As he sought to prevent any diminishment of his influence among his followers and the prevailing authorities he did encounter conflict and eventually armed confrontation.[38] This was particularly pertinent in the realms of defence. Thus, like other contemporary forms of state/empire power, the founder and supporters of the new religion were compelled to embrace the force-violence matrix as a dimension of establishing power as a unit with authority and legitimacy. As such, rules quickly emerged (although they were not codified till much later) setting the theological or ethical boundaries within the new faith system to such behaviours. In other words, force was regulated and violence and terrorism in particular were prohibited in terms of the symbolism of the faith. When conflict did take place moving to the dimension where physical force became necessary, it became regulated by ethical and theological considerations.[39]

The occupation of Medina was a largely peaceful event and further to the consolidation of the Prophet's power agreements were reached with the leaders of local tribes and other faiths. As Saunders notes about Jews and Christians, 'those who were ... and wished to remain so were taken under Muslim protection (*dhimma*) and guaranteed security of their goods and property and the free exercise of their religion, on condition that they paid the *jizya*, tax'.[40] This is not to deny that Mohammed harboured or expressed territorial ambitions in terms of the reach of the new faith system but to acknowledge that such ambitions would be realised through the disciplined use of armed force rather than wanton violence predicated on little if any respect for human life which is important. Indeed the impulse of discipline and order in the face of disorder and chaos became a defining feature of the new religion and associated forms of governance over its followers. Mohammed had no army or bevy of bureaucrats assembled to devise and administer the rules and raise revenues and remittances for the new community based in Medina. It is hard, given the evidence above, to represent the Prophet Mohammed as a terrorist or leader of a bloodthirsty band of armed Arab hooligans intent of disrupting and wrecking havoc and fear among ordinary civilians.

This state, however, left little literature by which successive generations of Muslims could mould or shape themselves by. Surviving literature – such as the 'Constitution of Medina'(*al-sahifa*) – is general rather than specific, echoing the broad themes and resonance's which can be garnered from the Koran and Hadith on the thorny subject of political rule and government. The *al-sahifa* does, however, address the issue of law enforcement and conduct in times of conflict. In addition, the document outlines a concept of community that is not exclusively tribal or in terms of religion outlining conditions under which certain Jewish tribes enjoy freedom. In this respect the *al-sahifa*, it has been contended, recognises a pluralism and tolerance under the umbrella of Islam that would subsequently be witnessed, for example, in the religiously diverse yet dynamic and exciting community of Cordoba in Spain that characterised Muslim rule in the Middle Ages. Thus, the city-state of Medina can be summed up as a state governed by Allah through his revelations to the Prophet Mohammed. The ultimate source of political authority, therefore, is not the ruler of the state, its courts or judges but Allah and through his revelations in the Koran. The Islamic state is not an ethnic or religious exclusivity, but includes Kurds, Asians, Arabs, Africans, and the People of Book – Jews and Christians – are accorded 'protected status' upon payment of a the *jizya* tax. The ruler is legitimated by the people – he cannot claim power on any other basis. The ruler must uphold the fundamental tenets of the faith and the institutions of rule and government – the security system, taxation and so on – should be directed to these ends.

The community founded by the Prophet Mohammed in Medina established an important relationship, sometimes symbiotic in its nature, between religion and politics during an era when such relationships in other faiths were not unusual. In the seventh century religion and politics in the Christian tradition were also similarly located. Yet, the Medinan state has also come to represent an ideal that has influenced the subsequent development of Muslim thinking on the relationship between mosque and state, religion and politics or put more prosaically between the ruler and the ruled. The modern-day Islamist theorists who develop their ideas of the state around this Medinan model, however, generally articulate their ideas from an orthodox, rigid and conservative mindset, arguing that the problems which currently beset the modern Muslim world can only be resolved by a wholesale rejection of current approaches and thinking and with a return/revival of this fundamental state type. As Taji-Farouki observes, these theorists hold up the Medinan state type and the fixed rules of *Shari'a* law in resistance to 'the modernist project of the late nineteenth and early twentieth centuries ... [and as a] medium through which to articulate the rejection of the theoretical underpinnings of Islamic reform and a reassertion of Islamic authenticity'.[41] The difficulty behind such a project and theorisation of state type lies in the ability to measure the authenticity of the original project (of which there is relatively little remaining evidence) with the modern age – an act that in itself requires separation from the contemporary political arena. What emerges clearly from theorising and accounts of the first attempt at state formation under the banner of Islam was the objective of statehood and community in peace not conflict. Episodes of force maintenance and violence as defence were naturally part and parcel of this process. One has to hold such episodes up against the discourse on violence more generally and conceptualising about jihad specifically.

Caliphal authority

Caliphal authority from the seventh century onwards was marked as much by the personality of the ruler as by other dimensions of Muslim authority and politics. Modes of authority were diverse and divergent over important issues, such as the function of political leadership and the boundary with spiritual leadership. The maintenance of societies that were stable and peaceful, however, remained a constant feature of Muslim rule and leadership. Stability, according to historic epoch, was either threatened by internal elements of opposition that sought to depose or remove the leadership or by external enemies including the Europeans. Sometimes the threat was both internal as well as external. In this respect violence was present on the landscape – sometimes having a direct effect on the political realm. Violence, however, cannot necessarily be attributed primarily to the function of rule. Rather it is found in the realm of opposition – whether internal or external. Violence as characteristic of the Muslim state was translated and understood as part of the function or monopoly by the state over force. Indeed the development of a sophisticated military apparatus was key to the most successful and stable Muslim dynasties.

Before outlining this particular aspect of the state, however, it is important to acknowledge one of the most important internal conflicts in Islam, and that was the succession battle or 'civil conflict' which led to the schismatic chasm between *Shi'a* and *Sunni* Muslims. Yet, it should be noted that this conflict had as much to do with the vagaries of politics as a battle for the soul of Islam. In this respect politics can be interpreted as mattering as much as faith. Indeed, some argue that the roots of the *Shi'a* rift within the house of Islam lay in an attempt to use religious symbolism as a political tool in a competition for power and legitimacy. Subsequently, orthodox *Sunni* theorists promoted this critique – particularly in extension of the debate about the nature and framework for Caliphal authority; for from this division emerges, the *Shi'a* attachment to the notion of Imamate. Leadership through the principle and office of the Imam emerges a key feature of *Shi'ism*, both as a historical and revived and newly interpreted contemporary phenomenon. The state, therefore, emerges as a function of the Imamate. This perspective is not shared by *Sunni* jurists such as al-Iji who argues that the notion of the Imamate, held as fundamental by the *Shi'a*, is not a defining marker of Islam but rather an additional input organised by the adherents of the faith.

In the conflict that unfolded, the forces of Caliphal authority were sent to meet the opposition on the battlefields of Karbala. Against such a force defeat was inevitable and Hussain, the prophet's grandson met his death at the hands of the Ummayad forces. Saunders rather colourful account notes that the 'ultimate result of Karbala was to provide the *Shi'a* with a martyr and Islam with a mediator between God and man'.[42] The ruling state elite, despite its religious credentials, organised conventional military force in an attempt to meet a serious threat to its legitimacy. In creating a locus of peace, it became increasingly clear that order would only prevail once opposition had been met and contested. The acknowledgement that Ummayad power was linked to a developing and subsequently developed military elite, however, was a double-edged sword.

In this respect, developments under the succeeding Abbasid caliphate hint at the recognition of this factor and an attempt to legitimate such authority through ethical codification by the tremendously dynamic and influential corps of scholars and theologians that dominated the knowledge industry on a global scale at this time. Indeed, Abassid power was built on a rejection and revolt against the authority of the Ummayyads and yet, in practice, was itself diffuse in terms of authority and competition for power and authority across the Muslim realm. One attempt at codification is apparent in the work of Abu Hasan al-Mawardi, an eleventh century Iraqi scholar, judge and diplomat under the Abbasid and Baghdad-based caliphate of al-Qa'im (1031–75). A Basran born and educated scholar al-Mawardi's expertise was developed in the field of jurisprudence, political science and ethics. Deeply conscious of the complicated spin of contemporary politics and power, as well as the fluctuating and ultimate declining importance of the Abbasid caliphate based in Baghdad, al-Mawardi proved himself as a diplomat extraordinaire as he sought the establishment of peaceful and cordial relations between the old and the new ruling forces. It could be argued, however, that at the heart of his efforts lay a determination that the Caliphal authority should remain sacrosanct as divinely ordained. While it is true that he acknowledged the power of delegation, including military affairs, the Caliph was the source of ultimate executive authority in the same way that the office of President of the United States of America includes the designation of Commander in Chief of the nation's armed forces and the authority to declare war. The sheer practicalities of governance propelled any Caliphal authority to recognise that certain powers had to be delegated even if the symbolic authority of the state lay in the hands of one individual. It has been noted that such a development was apparent in succeeding caliphates with the emergence of 'three elements [of power]: that of legitimate succession to the Prophet, that of directing the affairs of the world and that of watching over the faith' which were not always necessarily functions determined by the same person but by as many as three groups of individuals or actors.[43] The recognition of such a diffusion of power is apparent in Mawardi's seminal work, *al-Ahkam as-Sultaniyyah* (The Laws of Islamic Governance). This work includes reflection on the conduct and rules of jihad as a form of defence within the Muslim community. Additionally the deputy role and function of the Princely states as a means and function of governance in Muslim polities is explored in this work. Regarding conflict and the principle of jihad – in this respect the rules, as they were applicable and relevant at that time, were theologically and ethically inspired. Thus, with regard to the issue of whether it is permissible to kill women and children during conflict, Mawardi, particularly compared to other issues, reflects an unequivocal position that is indicative of a tenor within the faith that has been lost in the mists of time:

> It is not permitted to kill women and children in battle, nor elsewhere, as long as they are not fighting because of the prohibition of the Messenger of Allah, may the peace and blessings of Allah be upon him, against killing them. The Prophet ... forbade killing of those employed as servants and mamlouks, that is young slaves. If women and children fight, then they are fought and killed, but only face to face, not from behind while fleeing. If they use their women and children as shields in battle, then one must avoid killing them and aim only at killing the men; if, however, it is impossible to kill them except by killing the women and children then it is permitted.[44]

Thus, in relation to wars conducted by order of the Caliphal or Amirate authority issues of conduct were explicit and well-defined. In this respect one wonders how al-Mawardi could ever concur with the argument advanced by the Islamic Jihad leader Sheikh Abdullah Shammi in defence of suicide attacks in which Israeli women and children have been victims:

> We are left with no choice but to answer Israel with martyrdom operations to let them feel our bitterness ... And with all of this we offered to stop killing civilians if the Israeli stop targeting our civilians and destroying our home and trees but they refused ... Now there are no martyrdom attacks but their tanks still kill our people sleeping in their houses, and why don't we hear loud voices saying they are criminals against humanity ... How come the Israeli can claim self-defense but we can't? ... Even when we attack their army we still get Bush on television calling us criminals and terrorists ... The Koran tells us we can return the same hurt to the enemy that they hurt us with but also that a punishment not be excessive ... These rules are a source to the mujahideen brothers to react against the crimes of the occupiers, they are not allowed to initiate the aggression but they may react using the same methods ... Throughout the 1980s we never targeted civilians (even if they used civilian cars) but martyrdom acts against civilians is a response to their acts.[45]

Additionally, distinctions were drawn between such conditions like war with the legitimate sanction of state force against an external aggressor and other forms of conflict including rebellion and revolt. Indeed, Ibn Taymiyyah addressed himself to this issue and pontificated on its portent and consequences for the established order and its ultimate relation to Islam. For Ibn Taymiyyah, 'no good' can come out of 'rebellion either for religion or for the world'.[46] In this respect, authority so long as it remains in God's shadow is more important than its legitimacy or other conditions. Indeed as one author notes, 'the most strange thing in Ibn Taymiyyah is that he nowhere discusses the problem of legitimacy of the deposition of the Imam ... it seems really sad that a free, democratic, critical and sublime spirit like that of Ibn Taymiyyah should have given his long hand of support to perpetual absolutism.'[47] Many western authors have seized on this issue as a means of illustrating their argument that under Islamic order oriental despotism centred on the political and through control of the armed forces combined with the predilection for violence and authoritarianism was the historical norm. In this respect, it is argued, 'it is not ownership of the means of production that determines who will rule; rather possession of military and political power determines who will enjoy the fruits of labour.'[48] Affirmation of a particular principle, as illustrated in Ibn Taymiyyah's view of rule and leadership, however, was not wholly monolithic and shared within or across the sects which explain the Muslim realm. Other voices did proliferate and in practice the challenges presented by such principles were not always easily adhered to.

Diffusion of power was inevitable as the banner of Islam was raised across the many realms by a variety of leaderships and not just by one. The framework for power included an acknowledgment that the ruler be made aware and reminded of his obligations to rule according to religious authority with a commitment to justice. The limits and constraints on force were important in terms of establishing a peaceful and harmonious society. In the *Sunni* tradition then violence should not be part of the character of society but society should be regulated and governed by the ruler according to the *Shari'a* including appropriate provisions for force, criminal justice and punishment.

With the decline of Abbasid power, the diffusion was inevitable and would characterise the Muslim world, including the Middle East, over successive centuries. Yet it is the diversity motif within the concept of Islamic governance and statehood that is also the key to understanding its survival, not only as a political phenomenon but also in so many other ways. This is where it is a mistake to reflect Islam as monolith. To do so means that it's historical relevance and resonance is lost. The correlation between monotheism within Islam and monolithic Islam has been historically determined making it even more difficult to comprehend that which is labelled and ascribed as representative of Islam in the present day. Usama Bin Laden has been labelled, and incorrectly, I would argue, as representative of the modern monolithic phenomenon of twenty-first century Islam in a way that creates dangerous pressures in the extension and characterisation of all other relationships within and between the Islamic realm and the rest of the world;[49] for if the foundational representation of Islam is accepted and promoted as a fundamental truth of the modern age, then the logic of enmity and revenge becomes seductive to policy-makers permitting them to fight fire with fire while at the same time abandoning the ethnical constraints that normally govern such relations. Here the import for principles of democratic governance count. As the father of a slain Israeli solider noted of his government's campaign in the West Bank and Gaza Strip, 'Ethics have to be free of vengefulness and rashness. Every act must be carefully weighed before a decision is made to see whether it meets strict ethical criteria. Our ethics are hanging by a thread, at the mercy of every soldier and politician.'[50] In this respect the mutuality of tension over ethical demands highlight not just modern-day conflicts that embrace Muslims but others was well.

Yet the diffusion of power within the Muslim realm is as diverse, if not more so, today as it was in the medieval period when the reach of Islam was felt across the globe and included Europe, Africa as well as the Middle East and Asian continent. Even the historic resonance of a figure such as Hassan al-Sabah, the 'Old Man of the Mountains' and head of the Nizari 'Assassins', is not necessarily easy to find in the modern-day representation of Usama Bin Laden and the al-Qaeda network. The place of violence as a mechanism of power within such realms then is difficult to generalise about; for violence, even in its political form, has many facets and perhaps more importantly belies many objectives and strategic agendas. The frontier between violence and force is reflected in a variety of contexts, with its presence felt in the historical and lived experiences of many societies, diverse cultures and communities with both urban and rural dimensions. The role of the state in this equation, particularly those states where Muslim rule occurred has traditionally been depicted by Western scholars as exhibiting a general propensity to violence as related to the despotic function and megalomaniac tendencies of the Sultan, Caliph, Wazir or Amir. This is understood as part of the concept of obedience that is central to Islam and invested through the *bay'a* (oath of allegiance) to the Caliph and considered divinely obligatory.

The jihadist debate

One traditional charge against Islam is that through the principle of jihad it exhibits an historic attachment to violence and bloodlust. It is alleged that this attachment creates bloody conflict or fault lines with other civilisations.[51] While other aspects of the jihadist debate in the modern era and particularly in relation to terrorism are explored in other chapters of this book, it is useful to the discussion here to explore the acclaimed historic link particularly as it relates to the expansion of Muslim empire. The notion that war in the name of Islam, jihad, is linked and connected to some kind of interminable relationship with violence has been contested. Kelsay, for example, notes that the linkage to such a concept creates limits and conditions on war. 'From the *Sunni* perspective', he argues, 'the religious aims of the jihad impose a certain set of means. The religious limitation of war is not only "at the front end", with respect to the *jus ad bellum*, where jihad is distinguished from *harb* [war]. It is also present "at the back end", with respect to the *jus in bello*. Notions of proper conduct in war follow from the religious purposes of jihad'.[52] Additionally, the classical doctrine of jihad was formulated and reflected on as part of a process of change and challenge within the Muslim domain and the outside world. Specificity of historical dimension is important in understanding the rules that were interpreted by the jurists. This process was not marked out by one dominant voice or position, for consensus would be difficult to discern in a series of perspectives and views that spanned the years. Such discourse, however, has been influential in informing modern interpretations as they relate to conflicts, occupation and other circumstances relating to the contest for power. An illustration of my argument can be made here. In reflecting on the classical *Sunni* arguments relating to the meaning of war, Kelsay cites al-Shaybani's reflections on the notion of 'repel[ling] force with equal force' in the context of battle with the enemy.[53] The same perspective or theological impulse is clearly behind the articulation of *Shi'a* politician and Hizbollah leader, Mohammed Fnaysh as he reflects on the present-day conflicts in the Middle East.

If the confrontation against oppression lingers, then human freedom is lost and people's role in this world is lost and Islam doesn't allow this. Islam says that the aggressor should be faced by equal aggression. Islamic law permits this saying: 'It is permitted to those who are attacked to retaliate because they are unjustly attacked.' There are basic rules for declaring fighting and for the tactics of fighting. After all, Islam is a religion of love, mercy, dialogue and acceptance of others and a religion that calls for wisdom, good advice and Allah does not like aggressors and all this.[54]

The consistency of the theme relates not to the generation of violence in the name of Islam for its own sake, or as a means of actively creating conversion to Muslim rule or the Muslim faith but about defence against aggression. The difference across the timeline lies within the territorial dimension of such discourse. For when Kelsay quotes al-Shaybani and we reflect on the works of others such as Mawardi or Ibn Taymiyyah, they have reflected on these issues from within the domain of territory under the control of Muslim leaders. In the modern day, it can be argued, the resonance of the debate is altered by the lack of territorial sovereignty enjoyed by a considerable number of cases where Muslims and Muslim leaders have advocated jihad. The question here is whether jihad is ethically and theologically apt outside the framework of Muslim governance. Certainly it would appear that Usama Bin Laden's assertions weaken in the face of such logic. For his critique of the al-Saud family and their autocratic governance of Saudi Arabia is not cause enough to engage or even encourage insurrection from within. Additionally, it could be questionable whether such actions related to a critique constructed by Bin Laden of the Saudi regime are truly grounds for the engagement of mujahidden in the pursuit of jihad as it is understood in the classical sense. By extension, the same logic would apply to the case constructed by Bin Laden against the United States of America. It is difficult to truly legitimate, according to theological sources, the claim that US armed forces stationed on Saudi soil – at the invitation of the ruling authority – are an occupying power. The legitimacy of such assertions is contested from both within Muslim discourse as well as outside it. Muslim discourse does not represent Bin Laden's claims as just but his sense of injustice against a variety of parties in part of a shared experience among Muslims across the globe. In the wake of 11 September the Iranian President Mohammad Khatami condemned Bin Laden's claims to Islamic credentials, 'I don't believe that his message really resonates strongly in the Muslim world. Public opinion in the Muslim world in general wants peace, security and stability and the right to defend their religion and their freedom.'[55]

Jihad as a means of religious conduct of war has thus been subject to the construction of rules and norms. The obligation of jihad, whom it is incumbent upon and in which circumstances it is used were identified through the primary sources of Koran and hadith as well as through the historical record that was built during successive centuries of Muslim rule and dominion. The notion, therefore, that Muslims might be motivated by some primordial connection to violence as a fundamental expression of attachment to a spiritual identity which in turn is constructed around an emotional experience is, given the evidence above, difficult to maintain as something core or innate to the religion. Jihad is an obligation or fundamental theme within the faith system. I believe that it can be argued that jihad[56] is not like the prayer, fast, hajj, zakat and profession of faith that makes a Muslim Muslim. These five fundamental keepers in fact say more about a fundamental attachment to peace than violence. Jihad, as a means of striving, propagation of the faith and ultimately defence in the face of an aggressor cannot be likened in a wholesale fashion to an equivalency with war. To date classical doctrines of war really fail to address this religious/cultural dimension as it relates to the Muslim domain. Nor do such doctrines recognise the environments in which Muslims find themselves located in as it relates to dimensions of war.

Monopoly of force

Successive Muslim dynasties, within the *Sunni* tradition, from the four rightly guided caliphs to the last caliphate of the Ottomans employed conventional force as a means of defending the state. As such a historic relationship was built between the state elite that included the military as well as other functionaries. A separation of power was apparent in the emergence of centralised authority within the state and the delegation of power to certain Emirates and later vilayets throughout the Muslim domain. The duty of protection, lay in the hands of the state with a state-funded regular army charged with the defence of the realm and its subjects. In this way the potential for violence as part of force was institutionalised and regularised as a state function governed by *Shari'a*. The imperative of the *Shari'a* did of course shape the functions, objectives and nature of military engagement and the use of force in such societies. Additionally, such powers would be subject to other forces once the centrifugal nature of the centre was weakened through sheer geographic expansion of the Muslim domain. The functions of law and order according to religious obligation became an increasingly state activity regulated by a bureaucratic establishment. A tradition regarding the conduct of military exercise, war and defence against the enemy developed as part of Muslim tradition. It did not develop, however, in a uniform fashion but has instead been subject to contested interpretation and practice, not just in terms of the *Sunni/Shi'a* divide but also between jurists within one schism or the other. Authority in terms of violence and its legitimacy is often considered a lynchpin in the discourse that has emerged in the Western philosophical tradition. For, as authors such as Guelke have argued, the symbiotic relationship between violence and legitimacy is in turn linked to the modern-day phenomenon of terrorism. In turn, terrorism is a charge that by the late twentieth century was laid more frequently than not at the door of Islam. Indeed, as Guelke asserts, 'it is easiest to establish in what context violence is generally perceived as illegitimate by considering how violence is normally justified. It is rare for violence to be glorified as an end in itself. The usual justification of its use is that it constitutes an effective means to a legitimate end.'[57] The justification then, in the historical context, has lain with the leader of the Muslim polity. The implication of this lies in the nature of leadership and authority to rule in the name of Islam. In this respect the schismatic difference did historically come into play in particular epochs in relation to spirituality and leadership of a polity from alternate perspectives. The notion of violence for violence sake is associated, by some authors, with *Shi'a* dimensions of Islam.[58]

Yet by contrast many Islamists argue that conflict and war, even in the name of Islam, was never something that was actively sought. Indeed within the verses of the Sura of the Cow, war is reflected on as a negative phenomenon:

> Prescribed for you is fighting, though it be hateful to you. Yet it may happen that you will hate a thing which is better for you, and it may happen that you will love a thing which is worse for you; God knows and you know not. (2:216)

The interpretation of such injunctions when combined with others, which permit war in pursuit of jihad, leaves the door open on this topic making it difficult to categorically assert, as others have done, that Islam disdains pacifism. Kelsay, for example, has argued that according to classical tradition a 'thoroughgoing rejection of war, was not an option for Muslim thinkers', although he admits that 'the Qur'an and the example of Muhammad gave them a means by which to discriminate between legitimate and illegitimate uses of force.'[59] Such a perspective, it could be argued, prevents a claim to a classical tradition of peace within Islam. This is particularly pertinent in terms of western debate and understanding of Islam's historical or traditional record as some form of marker and indicator of the modern phenomenon. In this way, Islam is judged by its past. This is a past in which ethical conduct and code inspired or guided by a form of religious inspiration is put on the margins. Such a perspective differs quite radically from the way in which such issues are understood within the Muslim domain itself by its modern-day adherents. Indeed, as Mohammed Fnaysh, a leader of Hizbollah, has asserted in relation to this question, 'Islam is not a religion of violence. Islam is a religion which gave its followers the legitimacy to resist the aggressors based on justice and preciseness.' He then quoted from the Sura 22:39–40:

> Leave is given to those who fight because they were wronged – Surely God is able to help them – who were expelled from their habitations without right, except that they say 'Our Lord is God'. Had God not driven back the people, some by means of others, there had been destroyed cloisters, and churches, oratories and mosques, wherein Gods name is much mentioned. Assuredly God will help him who helps Him – surely God is All-strong, All-mighty. (Sura 22:39–40)

'So.' as Fnaysh continued, 'this is a precise rule in justice because aggressors face those who are equal to them, not someone who is more powerful and I think this rule is a military, fighting and ethical one at the same time ... There is no meaning to human life, there's no value, there's no freedom for humans if we allowed the oppressor to carry out aggressions and there's no right of retaliation.'[60] In this respect then an interpretation of defence is understood as an ethical basis for war or resistance by forces which battle against an aggressor both in the name of Islam and for a sovereign modern nation. Such approaches highlight the deeply elaborate and major contribution within both the *Sunni* and *Shi'a* tradition to such issues. Yet in practice it appears that ethics are breached; hostages are taken, civilians are killed and order and stability disrupted through acts of terror and violent revolution.

Yet, the radicals of Hizb Allah do not represent an exclusively *Shi'a* perspective on this issue. Indeed such *Shi'a* inspired sentiments are echoed in the words of the leadership of the *Sunni* nationalist-Islamist organisation Hamas. The political leadership of Hamas believes in the justice of its actions and in the obligation to protect the Palestinian people. Hamas leader Ismail Haniyeh, argues, for example, in relation to Yasser Arafat's statement that suicide bombers were harmful to the Palestinian cause that:

> Abu Ammar is being obliged by others to make statements about martyr-dom operations ... He is addressing the outside world not the Palestinian people. Even if he makes those calls it doesn't stop Israel in assassinations and aggression. So we are left with no choice but to defend ourselves even with these martyrdom attacks. But at the same time we have no intention of harming civilians and we didn't initiate this process ... they [Israel] started it with Hebron and they've continued ... Which people who were subjected to this would not defend themselves?[61]

If taken seriously, do such statements throw up a dilemma about the red line between resistance and terrorism in its modern form? What do these statements tell us about cultures of violence in a modern era and their ethical dimensions?

Antecedents of Bin Laden?

The historical association with Muslims and terrorism, however, has been maintained and utilised as a way of making sense of what is termed as modern religious terrorism. Hoffman, for example, remarks in respect of modern-day terrorism that, 'the religious imperative for terrorism is the most important defining characteristic of terrorist activity today.'[62] For this author, and others, there is a proven historical connection between the past and present in explaining the compulsion within Islam toward terrorism – and in particular terrorism perpetrated as a form of 'sacramental act'. The logic of this argument, as it relates to international terrorism, is then extended in claiming a linkage between modern-day revivalism of religious movements – the resurgence phenomenon – and a concurrent rise in religious terrorism. Thus the past is cited as evidence of Islam's real intent to establish and expand Muslim rule across the globe by any means necessary in the present. One example of Islam's historical relationship to terrorism that is oft-cited is the Assassins (1090–1272). Yet to truly make sense of the Assassin phenomenon one needs to understand the nature of the state in medieval Islam and the tension between elements of Caliphal authority, the military, administration and tax-raising duties as well as the *ulama*. Without acknowledging these factors the Assassins represent nothing more than Hashish-taking religious fanatics intent on wanton terrorism.

> Et tu, Brutus? – Then fall Caesar! Liberty!, Freedom! Tyranny is dead! Run hence, proclaim, cry it about the streets. (Julius Caesar, Scene 1, Act 3)

In the wake of the attacks in America on 11 September 2001, elements of the media who tried to explain the motives behind al-Qaeda scuffled through Islamic history to lift out the example of the Assassin as symbolic of the Muslim attachment to aggrandising bloodlust and terrorism. The historical account and evidence, however, bears little resemblance to the violent wantonness presently associated with the label. While Bernard Lewis had labelled the Isma'ili *Shi'a* Assassins as the 'first terrorists', he drew on modern rather than historical sources to reach his conclusions.[63] There is considerable debate over the interpretation of the Assassin as the correct label for the small group gathered together under the religious leadership of Hassan Sabah, 'the old man of the mountains'. Their purpose was to meet a sectarian and political challenge in the wake of the imposition of military rule under the authority of the Fatamid caliphate. The strategy of violence adopted by this theologian of the Isma'ili sect was political violence rather than terrorism in the sense that it was a final route of defence for a beleaguered sect that was already considered heretical under the rule of the Fatamid caliphs of Cairo. Additionally, the intended target of the Assassins were political figures rather than ordinary Muslims. They drew their legitimacy from this distinction. The small group drawn around Sabah were not solely dedicated to violence but indeed embraced the Muslim obligation of *daw'a* (preaching) common to many thousands of Muslim organisations through time and to the present. In the same way that political violence was an established feature of the arena of power under Roman, Egyptian and Byzantine rule, the same was true of Muslim rule. It was more often practised within the circle of the elite than outside it. The Assassins, however, represented outsider forces and a threat from within the Muslim realm that signified the difficulties inherent in maintaining Islam as a unitary and organic project.

Dafarty explains this in the context of attempts to subsequently misrepresent and blacken this sect within a sect of Islam by the convenient use of the Assassin-terrorism tag. In this version of history the small group of followers who subscribed to Sabah's theological doctrine were in fact drug-crazed mercenaries hired to wreck havoc on the stable and orderly hierarchy of Islam. Indeed 'by the middle of the fourteenth century', argues Dafarty, 'the word assassin, instead of signifying the name of a sect in Syria, had acquired a new meaning in Citeian, French, and other European languages: it had become a common noun describing a professional murderer'.[64] This process obscures the sectarian and political dimension of the dispute that engulfed Sabah's followers who in turn engaged in a process of martyrdom-seeking. The objective was the removal of an unjust or illegitimate political or religious elite or leadership hostile to the Isma'ilis. Isma'ilis had been persecuted and subjected to state-ordered expulsion or elimination of entire communities. They were terrorists in that their acts of violence were unlawful. Their resistance took a bloody turn and condemned them to infamy.

The year, 1094 serves as a watershed of the Isma'ili experience with the emergence of Nizari Hasan Sabah and the establishment of the group that would engage in a dedicated defence (jihad) of their rights and commitments to Islam. They formed a cohesive and yet diverse community dedicated to the arts of science and literature, astronomy and theology and yet as authors like Lewis contend it was their 'terrorism' that marked them out and gave rise to successive black myths. Dafarty argues that these resistance fighters, however, 'did assign a major political role to the policy of assassination'.[65] In this respect, the violence perpetrated by the Assassin's can be interpreted in one of two ways: either as a form of jihad as a defensive act or as a political act during a period of great turmoil where violence contributed to the art of statecraft and politics in more than just the Muslim empire of the Ummayads. Indeed, the linkage between politics and violence is found as a contemporaneous phenomenon in the Christian fiefdoms of Europe and their Crusades. The bloody border between faith, politics and violence was perhaps more strongly associated with the Crusading adventurers as indicative of fusion and tensions between faith and politics in Europe. If senseless violence in the name of religion was to be discovered in the region at the time when the 'Old Man of the Mountains' and his dedicated followers sought to undermine the Caliphal claims, then it is not just to Islam that one must look but to Christianity as well. Indeed, when the Crusaders took Jerusalem from Muslim hands the city was literally awash with blood, a contrast with the noble commitment to spare life upon the eve of Muslim conquest previously. As Jones and Ereira remark, 'It is impossible to know what was going through the minds of the Crusaders as they rampaged through the Holy City – but it certainly was not the Sermon of the Mount.'[66] Deliberate desecration of holy sites, senseless bloodlust, pillage and violence were very much the hallmarks of Christianity. As Jones and Ereira assert, 'The fanatical blood-lust ... would never be forgotten.' But one is compelled to ask whose bloodlust? For both Crusader's bloodlust and the Assassins' are part of the cultural symbols that are recanted by contemporary sources on both sides of a divide characterised by suspicion and mistrust. Surely such assumptions should remain open to debate? In the Middle East, the Christian bloodlust is not forgotten in the collective memory of Muslim and Jewish and even Eastern Christian circles. That bloodlust, for example against the Jews, reflected the historical antipathy of Europe's leaders and its people manifest in centuries of anti-Semitism, pogroms and holocaust. The mutuality of misperception informed by historical myth that is manipulated by modern ideologues distorts the present. Hence, an Islamist leader in Egypt or Algeria gets away with peddling an ideological position against the West and more specifically an anti-Americanism that is rooted in the notion of historical myths a thousand years old. America is interpreted and sold to the followers of many Islamist organisations as the 'new Crusader' state. As one Islamist thinker declares, of the United States of

America, 'They are the new Crusader, the US support dictatorship, they are doing their utmost to exploit us and serve their interests. In this respect they don't differentiate between the past and present.'[67] Such ideologues on both sides of the divide refer to such events as if they happened yesterday – they are deployed to demonstrate the strength of their arguments – reductive, simplified myths that (mis-) lead followers and supporters into acts with profound consequences.

In the wake of the apocryphal images that the world witnessed on 11 September 2001, it was the bloodlust of Islam that was raised by commentators in echo of the power to motivate men to terrible acts of violence that hit the headlines. The tripartite relationship between Islam, Christianity and Judaism which, Armstrong argues, was born out of the crusades as a 'murderous triangle' implicating them 'in different ways in holy wars between them', in which 'the greatest tragedies and atrocities have occurred,' was not acknowledged in this respect.[68] If this perspective is advanced as relevant then there is an implicit assumption that the dynamic of history includes a propelling force that promotes and generates certain myths through the ages, including the modern secular age. These myths are subsequently interpreted as part of mainstream cultures and as relevant and helpful in explaining the motives of men who perpetrate evil and violent acts. Not only that, but Armstrong is urging her audience to acknowledge that we should be wary of labelling one religion with characteristics that exclude or ignore the others. Of course, this perspective encourages us to acknowledge that the religious remains relevant not just to interpreting the behaviour of those we label as religious but to others too. This is interesting because the labelling process does not translate as easily to the other faiths outside Islam. The Reformation and subsequent secularising processes that have interrupted Christianity and Judaism form part of a different historical experience to those in the Muslim realm. Nevertheless, this throws up an interesting conundrum if we reflect on the cultural dimensions of such processes. Historically, and even in the modern age the cultural dimension of Western societies have remained less conscious of its Judeo-Christian backbeat even to the so-called modern secularised discourse. Others argue that such a backbeat is thinly disguised but still not openly acknowledged as in the way it would be in cultural discourses emanating from the so-called Muslim realms (many of which feature secularised contexts).

A modern-day Mahdi?

Emerging from the myriad attempts to make sense of the scale of terror visited upon America on 11 September 2001 was the imputation of a historical correlation between Usama Bin Laden and the Mahdi in the Sudan in the late nineteenth century.[69] Such examples, along with those of the previously mentioned Assassins, have been brought into the public domain through the mass media. The example of the Mahdi perhaps appears, at first, more apt. Here was a figure who emerged to challenge both Egyptian and British domination over Sudan and to put an end to their power. At the same time the Mahdi and his followers attempted to establish a new political order based on Islamic principles. Here was a religious figure around whom a political and social movement coalesced to challenge the political authority employed by the governing authorities, and legitimated by their use of Islam, as well as the colonial force of the imperial power of Great Britain.[70]

Yet, Bin Laden and the al-Qaeda network cannot be described as a modern-day social and political movement with the same motives. It may well be true that Bin Laden and his associates were inspired or influenced by their experiences in the Afghan Mujahideen movement against Soviet occupation. Al-Qaeda, however, is not a social or political network similar to that of the Mahdists or the Muslim Brotherhood. The perpetrators of the acts of terror, which al-Qaeda are implicated in, were not old enough to have fought alongside its leadership in the Mujahideen resistance. Bin Laden's acolytes were middle-class, well-educated and had not experienced involvement in an Islamic social and political movement of the kind associated with the Mahdi. Mohammed Ahmed, although a Sufi by spiritual inclination, had a vision of Islamism in state form that drew on the early Medinan model of the Prophet Mohammed. Sudan had been subject to the conquest of territory throughout the nineteenth century, first by the Egyptians and then by the British. In terms of Muslim rule, it is interesting to note that Muhammed Ali and his Ottoman successors increasingly bypassed or demoted the local religious elite, including the important *Sufi* orders, preferring to install their own Egyptian-run clerical establishment as part of the state-paid *ulama*. This process, however, backfired and the obvious failure to co-op the previously dominant and locally organised Sufi orders gave rise to a movement of opposition. From one of the more important *Sufi* orders emerged Mohammed Ahmad with what in the late twentieth century have been described as a fundamentalist agenda. He, like others of his generation, had developed a *Salafi* approach to the faith urging his followers to reject the folkish practices that had grown up around the religion.[71] The popularisation of the faith through such acts as the veneration of saints and their shrines, or women attending and crying at funerals, were disdained as part of the backwardness of Muslim culture which contributed to its decline in the colonial age. And although it was Sheikh Izz-a-din al-Qassam in Palestine in the 1920s who had declared, 'As for holding funeral processions with wailing and praying loudly and making noise and visiting graves of prophets and leading men in the known procedure of touching and rubbing the tombs and committing sins and the blatant mingling of me and women and spending money in not the right and proper manner', he merely re-stated the known sentiment of the Mahdi who had trodden this path before him almost 40 years earlier.[72] The Mahdi linked his message to a call for a locally organised resistance against externally imposed rule. To this end the movement that was established around this powerful individual succeeded in deposing their Egyptian rulers and founded a new state system that was Islamic both in inspiration and practice. Of course it is the victory against the British forces led by General Gordon of Khartoum in 1885 that strikes the deepest chord in the Western imagination. Yet in terms of rebellion, violence and power, it is the transformation of this movement, in the wake of victory and the death of the Mahdi itself, which gives some indication of the acknowledged limits of violence once the resistance against foreign occupation had achieved its goal. The short-lived experience of the Mahdist state in Sudan demonstrated the same issues of power, force and violence that beset most.

There is, I would argue, little historical resonance if one examines the example of the Mahdi and his followers with Usama Bin Laden and al-Qaeda. Such a figure demonstrates the potential strength of Muslim mobilisation around a force that resists the apparent injustice at the heart of any act of occupation, historic or contemporary. Whether there is much to learn about the motives behind Bin Laden's political ambitions though is difficult to say, for surely there is evidence of violent intent at the foundation of Islam in every historic episode that touched the Western experience of this realm, if that is what one is looking for? But this ignores the other evidence of Islam in relation to the Western experience that is founded in engagement with Sufism, Muslim sciences, philosophy and arts that was not coloured by violent intent.

Hegel has declared that 'the first glance at history convinces us that the actions of men proceed from their needs, their passions, their characters and talents; and impresses us with the belief that such needs, passions and interests are the sole spring of actions.'[73] In many respects this quote sums up the ways in which history matters in the assessment of the relations determined between Islam and violence. This is enough to demonstrate a historical relationship and intertwined dynamic between Islam and violence that appears to colour and shape the present. Yet, Islam in political form endures and experiences cycles of revival and resurgence. Here is a paradox, for as Kaldor argues, 'Fear, hatred and predation are not recipes for long-term viable polities', yet Islam in its political form endures.[74] In the interface with the modern West, as we will discover in the next chapter, the tension appears at its strongest with a dynamic dominated by a fracture that is described as creating a collision course or clash in which only one side can emerge victorious.

2
The West's Terror of Islam

Whenever I think of Muslims I think of terrorists
Tom, Belfast 2002

Introduction

Many significant political actors or groups of actors in the West and among western democratic states currently contend that a new threat is posed to the system of government and rule which prevails in the post-Cold War order. That threat, according to defence department analysis, for many sections of the mass media, foreign policy strategists and intelligence agencies in Washington, Bonn and Paris, has emerged with a set of qualitatively different characteristics.[1] The new threat is increasingly religious (including cults) in nature, thus setting it apart from dominant political ideologies of secular-based democratic capitalism, communism or democratic socialism. As a form of terrorism, the threat is also different from that which was known and understood as part of a global pattern of international relations and politics which grew in the 1960s and dominated western attitudes towards political violence – as directed at its institutions, symbols and citizens – for so many decades. As a form of combating and countering terrorism, this new threat challenges prevailing traditions and conceptualisations about war and conflict that had dominated defence analysis and military/strategic thinking throughout the latter half of the twentieth century.

From a secular perspective the new threat, with its para-theological and populist approach, makes it more difficult to meet and organise a response to it. It requires a different perspective and understanding of the motive for violence in a post-modern era where scientific rationalism has banished the religious to the sidelines of the political realm and away from the battles for power that beset modern societies. While the logic of deciding upon a declining definitional force for religion is understandable, it is less than helpful when reflecting on how that which is defined and understood as 'religious' by others motivates them in the political arena as well as in other arenas as well. This is a manifestation of the force of the secular at the interface with the religious and the unresolved dilemmas that this creates. This interface, however, is larger than most might expect and where often the majority associated with the manifestation of religio-political activities may be found. Rarely in the twenty-first century are those who engage with the political realm from the religious vantage point divorced or ill-versed in the secular experience and the prevailing philosophical exegesis of rational modernism.

The tag put to this new threat in the past has been religion in general and Islam more specifically. In engaging in this process of signifying Islam through the prism of terrorism actors in the West, through cultural reference, politics, economic and diplomatic avenues, have established that Islam has the potential to serve as an apocalyptic threat of global proportions. Elements within certain Western policy-making circles demonstrate an increasing desire to create a distance from the threat that is perceived as latent within Islam. This perspective is realist in inspiration and though it has vied in circles in the United States of America with other multi-lateralist or Wilsonian perspectives, it has emerged as dominant. The creation of the distance or disconnection with Islam is cultural, philosophical, psychological and political, and can also be understood in terms of legislation and the immigration barriers that many, though by no means all, Western states erect to keep elements of Islam out and prevent its threat from undermining societies from within. Such a bald statement may seem unfair, and critics would say it fails to recognise the many bridges that have been built between Islam and the West. But my point here is not to ignore or denigrate such efforts but to examine the wider disconnection that exists and the way in which it is perpetuated in a variety of forums, for in terms of the realist perspective the Cold War is over, the United States of America has emerged triumphant and its current involvement in global affairs will vary depending on American defined national interest. Security concerns and threats are shaped by realist principles. Hence hegemony and a threat to this state of affairs are how security and threats are determined. International terrorism is understood and presented as the most significant threat. States that 'support' terrorism are put on the US target list, alongside the terrorist groups. This has drawn attention to the Middle East and other Muslim domains as the centre of the threat. Each contribution to this discourse then becomes a thread in a hitherto abstract tapestry of discord and antagonism. Indeed, this process runs in direct contradiction to the realities of the global age where new technologies challenge traditional concepts of national borders and boundaries in societies and between them, and clashes with the economic impulse behind such approaches. Indeed globalisation, when reflected in the realist perspective, may in part contribute to the proliferation of threat rather than its isolation.

Thus the issue as it relates to the West's fear and even terror of dimensions of Islam must be finely balanced by the geo-economic realities of dependence in hydrocarbon societies on the oil and gas of Muslim populated entities and polities whose leaders and citizens challenge the ideals of corporate approaches to global development. In addition, the growing dimensions of transnationalism and the impact this has on interfaces involving Western and Muslim actors needs to be addressed with particular attention paid to the seeming paradox of transnationalism and its linkage to the phenomenon of terrorism and political violence in the modern era; for one outcome or threat from the emerging globalised international order is the issue of 'the excluded', as Lieven calls them – 'Those numerous social and ethnic groups who, for whatever reasons of culture, history and geography, are unable to take part in the world banquet.'[2] Lieven, identifies the Muslim world as 'the greatest victim' and that it's fundamentalist 'pathologies have assumed their greatest and more dangerous forms'.[3]

Clash of academy

A few words of caution should be sounded before the discussion progresses further. Throughout the 1990s an awful lot of academic attention was paid to the so-called Islam versus West debate with a factional approach emerging from those contributions. On the one side stood a faction that acknowledged and even defined this new interface and which formulated an approach to it. They emerged with a collective thesis that stressed the dangers in ignoring the perpetual threat posed historically and in the modern era by an Islam, ascendant and rampant. In the context of the present discussion one faction or party to this debate, I contend, believes that the fortress mentality is the best way to deal with the problem that Islam poses to modern secular societies.

The second faction organises around a totem which has many faces to it and is emblematic of their recognition that the notion of an Islamic threat to the West can be misleading, conflating that which is Islamic with a monolithic all-embracing movement with a fundamental anti-westernism at its core. Members of this faction seek to 'disentangle' that which is myth and that which in fact explains a set of relations currently underpinned by invented memories of the past alongside specific and slanted impressions of the present. In so doing it is not always clear what the objective of this task may be. Yet the 'fortress mentality' faction has interpreted such activities as akin to an act of apologia for Islam and its terrorist tendencies. Part of the problem with the message relayed by this faction is related to the access it has to suitable forums and a receptive audience. The other downside of the many-faced totem faction lay with its apparent difficulty in translating or being able to use their ideas to persuade others to translate such thinking into new policies on counter-terrorism which protected freedoms and saved lives at the same time. The problem with the other faction was that by overgeneralisation they couldn't see the wood for the trees and they still didn't stop the bad guys (whatever their religious impulse) when it mattered.

Perpetual threat

The importance of the perceived threat, on both sides, has failed to diminish and in the light of the events on 11 September 2001, the war on terrorism and the continuation of acts of Muslim inspired and perpetrated terrorism it has only grown in stature to become a number one national priority for many governments of the contemporary globe. Terrorism, for example – of the Muslim variety – has come to dominate the American popular imagination in a way that was hitherto unknown. As Harvard Law Professor Alan Dershowitz has decried, 'The greatest danger facing the world today comes from religiously inspired terrorist groups ... that are seeking to develop weapons of mass destruction for use against civilian targets.'[4] Relatively untouched by domestic-based terrorism the events of 11/9 have altered the landscape for analysis in this area. Suicidal terrorists undertaking 'poor-mans warfare' have been visited upon a variety of locations. Similarly in Australia, in the wake of the Bali bomb, the national political elite and citizens of the state were compelled to formulate a response to the attack, which was later labelled as 'barbaric'. Australians were forced to come to terms with the dawning realisation that the war on terrorism would perhaps need to be fought closer to their own doorstep. In the United Kingdom, where the British had been habituated to acts of terrorism carried out by the Irish nationalist republican movement, the whole of society has been compelled to look – perhaps for the first time – at the Muslim communities that they live and work among.

Many commentators argued that such a change could well make such governments more sensitive to the kinds of debates about terrorism and political violence that had characterised public discourse in countries like Israel, Spain and the United Kingdom. Without a doubt, it is not difficult to discern the parallel that Ariel Sharon drew in October 2001 when in a speech he made in the wake of the killing of three Israelis in Northern Israel, he declared 'I call on the Western democracies, and primarily the leader of the Free World, the United States – do not repeat the dreadful mistake of 1938 when Europe sacrificed Czechoslovakia. Do not try to appease the Arabs at our expense ... Israel will not be Czechoslovakia. Israel will fight terrorism'.[5] The issue here then is whether in their attempt to meet the feeling of 'terror' that Islam is perceived as posing to western governments and cultural values, legislators and policy-makers are undermining the universal values of freedom which so many hold dear in the face of so-called terrorist threats?

The new fear factor

> The fear factor ... there is a new feeling of mistrust and anxiety in the world
>
> 'A World of Difference', *The Guardian* – G2, pp. 2–5

The statement above was the caption for a photo that appeared in a newspaper. The photo itself was dominated by an image that covered three-quarters of a whole page of a dark masked man. In the background a crowd of bearded Muslim men and a fuzzy image of Usama Bin Laden completed the picture. This photo formed the centrepiece of a major broadsheet reflection one month after the bombings of 11 September 2001.[6] Its potent imagery dominated and partially obscured the sober and diverse reflection offered by authors, poets, journalists and business people that appeared on subsequent pages. In this context the image is mightier than the word. The image and the caption reflected and demonstrated a western interpretation of Islam in the wake of one of the most significant acts of political violence in the past 50 years. The caption spoke of 'fear' ... 'a new feeling of mistrust' and 'anxiety' in the 'world.' The worldview that represented in the image had the dark veiled and hidden force of Islam in the centre stage, flanked by the Muslim mob. There was nothing else in the image save the blurred outline of a building. It is obvious from the photo where the source of the fear emanates and that is the Muslims represented exclusively in this picture.

The threat is most significant and manifest in the guise of things referred to as 'Muslim', 'Islam' and 'Jihad.' Indeed, even when the threat against that which is representational of the West is a western-based phenomenon, it is still signified in terms and concepts associated with Islam as something understood to be external to the dominant political culture, norms, values and institutions of a particular nation state. Even the term jihad itself becomes associated with negative imaging and fear. There is evidence aplenty to attest to this process, 'jihad is itself a dialectical response to modernity', writes Benjamin Barber, reflecting an 'ongoing cultural struggle' that further signifies the clash and dissonance raised in Huntington's thesis on Islam and the West.[7] Barber re-writes jihad and squeezes it through a conceptual mangle producing something that fits the threat profile yet is contorted in the process. His rendition of Islam as Jihad and Islamic fundamentalism is represented as a set of values shared by all Muslims. These Muslims, Barber asserts, 'make war on the present to secure a future more like the past'.[8] But in Barber's account of Jihad I would argue that Islam is inadequately known and no line appears to serve as a method of distinction between, for example, Islamic fundamentalists and other Muslims. Barber represents Islam as fundamentally at odds with democratic values and, therefore, an embrace of anti-democratic principles and practices including violence and terrorism 'nurtur[ing] conditions favourable to parochialism, anti-modernism, exclusiveness and hostility to others'.[9] Here the structuring of the new discourse against Islamic fundamentalists and Islam more generally would appear to elide with old discourses about the threat inherent in the communism or the old Arab Nationalist Movement. Indeed, as Nielsen has contended, while the terms have changed it is questionable whether the structure of the discourse or those that are designated enemy and those that are not (the goodie-baddie distinction) has.[10] When Barber distorts jihad into something that moves beyond the boundaries of faith and territory its import is also increased. Jihad as a form of culture is presented by Barber as a phenomenon waging war on the modern nation state. He echoes Bernard Lewis in the explanation of rage associated with the symbols and faith of Islam. Lewis points out that Muslim antagonism to the West lies in the emasculation of Islam in the contemporary era. Lewis contends that 'Fundamentalist leaders are not mistaken in seeing in Western civilization the greatest challenge to the way of life that they wish to retain or restore for their people'.[11] Islamist movements, leaders and groups act as the conduit for Muslim ire against the West. According to Lewis, they have 'given an aim and a form to the otherwise aimless and formless resentment and anger of the Muslim masses at the forces that have devalued their traditional values and, in the final analysis, robbed them of their beliefs, their aspirations, their dignity, and to an increasing extent even their livelihood'.[12] The threat is presented as significant and as Lewis asserts, 'it should now be clear that we are facing a mood and a movement far transcending the level of issues and policies and the governments that pursue them. This is no less than a clash of civilizations – the perhaps irrational but surely historic reaction of an ancient rival against our Judeo-Christian heritage, our secular present, and the worldwide expansion of both.'[13]

Of course the notion of Islam as a threat, as discussed in Chapter 1, has its well-documented historical roots and in the modern era was revived in the wake of the Iranian revolution; for there was a fear expressed by some Western actors that the *Shi'a* theocratic establishment would manage to broaden its schismatic appeal to a wider *Sunni* audience. This in turn would promote Islamic revolution with the end goal of a region of the globe dominated by Islamic states under clerical rule. Thus, while in the first half of the twentieth century, Islam was largely understood in the West as a spent and defeated force – the Ottoman collapse symbolising this – in the latter half of the twentieth century and particularly in the wake of the ending of the Cold War between the West and the Soviet East, Islam was perceived to be emerging as a new strategic threat. Of course, in some quarters no excuse was needed to revive or make explicit the latent anti-Muslim mores of many Western and other societies.[14] These mores stem from a variety of ideological impulses including radical liberal and left thinking to right-wing racism. Indeed the racist foundations of the phobia expressed against Muslims and specific perceptions of what the faith system stands for are found in a variety of forums. Indeed it is true that the sight of a veiled woman can incite the most vociferous of racist views from otherwise seemingly western liberals and leftists. The hostility stems from what they perceive to know about Islam; their knowledge of this most 'backward and barbaric' of faith systems and its adherents is a form of power which largely remains unquestioned. What they know is that Islam is a threat and Muslims are warriors willing to engage in terror, to create fear and kill, and that this is evidence enough for counter-hostility and rejection.

In some respects to identify elements of Islamism as representing a threat is not without merit. US discourse reflects the fact that since the end of the Cold War there has been a global growth of both anti-Americanism and resentment at US involvement in Asia, Latin America, Europe, the former Soviet Union and the Middle East.[15] In this respect Muslim hostility and the branding, by the late Ayatollah Khomeini of America as the 'Great Satan' is just one facet of a global phenomenon that in essence reflects a refusal to quietly succumb to the objectives of US national interest refracted through its foreign policy. Authors such as Robert Kaplan reflect this back in American discourse as proof of Muslim hatred of America and the democratic values of liberty and capitalism that it represents. In explaining why al-Qaeda attacked America, Kaplan declared, 'the real cause of the attacks is that the terrorists have an existential hatred of the modern technological world, even though they use its toys. And that hatred exists because they see our world as the real challenge to Islam in a way that communism never was ... We really are a challenge ... And our popular culture has the ability to suck up their new emerging middle classes ... Because it's an informal culture, anyone can join it, and it becomes very enticing. And that's the threat.'[16] Kaplan pulls out an interesting thread in the debate that once again puts culture not ideology and power politics in the mainframe. He argues that Muslims want 'blue jeans and coca cola' not democracy and plural political systems. Muslims are uniform in their envy of that which they do not command. Their envy appears to drive them to violence.

Bernard Lewis identifies the threat posed by Islam in the modern age against the West. He sees Islam as a force motivating terrorism that reflects a 'lack of concern at the slaughter of innocent bystanders'.[17] Lewis, then, narrates a history of political violence in which the Arab 'both in defeat and victory' has 'pioneered the methods later adopted by religious terrorists'.[18] Yet in reality the methods Lewis refers to are neither exclusive to the Arabs nor religious terrorists but common to the manifestation of ethno-national conflict as a modern phenomenon. This explanation, for example, fails to take account of 'a lack of concern at the slaughter of innocent bystanders' in the acts of terrorism perpetrated by the bomber of the Alfred P Murrah Building in Oklahoma in 1995, the Phalangist perpetration of terror in the Palestinian refugee camps of Sabra and Shatilla in 1982, the Hutu and Tutsi genocide of Rwanda, and the Omagh bombing in 1998. In some respects, Lewis impugns Muslims and Arabs in the modern era in much the same way that in the past the Irish people were impugned for their propensity for violence.[19]

Explain the pain

If an explanation for this kind of terror and violence is needed, and indeed it does, then Wright's notion of 'representative violence' which he defined in explanation of conditions of conflict and violence in Northern Ireland does appear to have relevance. This approach has much resonance in seeking an explanation the motive behind political violence perpetrated by Muslims and others too. He argues,

> Very few people in Northern Ireland today ... would try to claim that the victims of violence are chosen because of their individual characteristics; they are attacked because they are identified as representing groups of people ... Everyone might be a target for reprisal for something done in their name and without their approval ... Even if few aspects of the representative violence enjoy widespread support of the kind that could only be established by opinion polls, it is only necessary for people to *understand* what is happening for it to create a generalised danger.[20]

The relevance of this notion lies in a correlation between treating the problem or issue that motivates such violence differently. Counter-terrorism measures that reflect a range of responses towards the perpetrator as well as the victim have some degree of saliency and this has been acknowledged in some circles. This in turn contributes to the construction of approaches that reflect a more holistic appreciation of the range of measures needed to tackle such problems.

What many in the policy-making community are stuck with, however, is a tradition of cultural antipathy that results in the exclusion of other perspectives and approaches. This cultural antipathy is not exclusive to policy-making communities in the West but is reflected, as Sardar and Wyn Davies highlight, in the most significant transmitter of culture and identity in the modern era: the television.[21] The reliance on a historical narrative that posits the cultural antipathy and perceived violence and murderous intent of Islam as central to a religio-political impulse will ultimately only serve the interests of the ideological phalanx it represents. The problem here is when this antipathy fails to elide with national interests or the interests of the majority. For Wright's reflection that 'Everyone might be a target for reprisal for something done in their name and without their approval' works both ways and is a better explanation for the cause of terrorism than the belief that constructed 'pasts' mixed with present injuries explain the motive.

Of course cultural antipathy is not the preserve of any one party but what it does do is build on and feed the perceived dissonance and prevalent belief in many Muslim circles that anti-Islamic sentiments do have a history and, in turn, influence discourse and attitudes in the present. In this 'blame game' the accusations of racism and historical aversion emanate from both sides. In an open letter from the eminent and influential Saudi-based theologian Safar al-Hawali to President Bush in the wake of the 11 September attacks on America dissonance against America is palpable. From this Islamists perspective emerges a language that reflects on the key vocabulary of hostility.[22] His anti-western sentiments are at the foundation of many of his sermons, broadcasts and writings. His interpretation of the present-day woes of Saudi Arabia and its failings as an Islamic polity lies in both the moral corruption that beset society and the impact of the West in the Middle East. 'Do you think that the West came to this region to defend us?' he asked in a broadcast in 1990. 'By God, No! They haven't ever wanted any good to happen to us ... They want the humiliation of Islam and the subjugation and destruction of the Islamic movement ... This militarism is directed against their enemy Islam. Now is their chance to destroy the enemy.'[23] This particular reading of western involvement in Muslim and Islamic polities is suffused with a reaction based on conflict rather than resolution. As Hawali reminded his listeners, 'Brothers, the war against Rome – the West, and the US in particular – is not going to be one year or ten. It is going to be a long war and it will require a faithful nation that abides by Islamic law. We need to live according to the teachings of the Koran. And then we prepare for war.'[24] In this case the myopic anti-Westernism and anti-Semitism is as strong as myopic anti-Muslimism as expressed in some influential quarters in the West. Al-Hawali reflects a series of views and perspectives that are common in quarters of Islamist discourse. Islamist ideologues also recognise that for the majority of Muslims in domains such as South Asia and the Middle East, the globalisation process has generated a sense of further impoverishment, insecurity and a sense of remaining on the margins of global development. They have identified the United States of America as playing a significant role in this state of affairs. America is perceived as dominating global organisations like the World Trade Organisation (WTO), and radical Islamist ideologues blame such organisations for the pitiful state of economic crisis that besets many Muslim polities. Their emasculation is blamed on the outcome of American policies. 'It's not Americans that we hate', opine radical Islamist leaders, 'but their policies, their injustices against our people' that is the core of the issue. Such views reinforce the perception, on both sides, of a timeless enmity that has remained fixed and immutable over the centuries. For al-Hawali and his Western opposites like fundamentalist cleric Franklin Graham, only the means of conflict, the resources and technology at their disposal have changed. Theological fatalism appears to steer the discourse on both sides only serving to emphasise difference. Such discourse attains an added fix when the debate turns to the state of Israel and its place in the regional order of the Middle East.

Israel is the West?

Islamist discourse about Israel is also significant.[25] Much discourse on Israel is an expression of anti-Westernism in terms of its outcomes for domains where Muslims are a demographic majority. Israel dominates radical literatures found for sale from Jakarta to Jerusalem, and Bosnia to Birmingham; it is a focus of Islamist and Muslim concern. The issue of Israel and conflict with its Arab neighbours animated secularist and leftist as much as Islamist discourse, and in this respect much that is represented in such discourse is not necessarily Muslim in tone. There are some dimensions of Islamist discourse that have adopted what I would call a religious overtone. Foundations of analysis of the conflict between Israel and the Palestinians are understood and presented for consumption through sermons, recordings, pamphlets, books and articles as religious in nature. Israel is portrayed as a Jewish political and religious entity. In contradistinction to the politicising of religion argument on the issue of Israel, elements of the Islamist fold are religicising the political conflict. In some respects the phenomenon is almost as old at the conflict itself. In the 1930s the Palestinian Mufti of Jerusalem, Hajj Amin al-Husseini was compelled (for a variety of reasons) to add a particular religious dimension to the unfolding conflict between Britain, the Zionists and Palestinians.[26] In more contemporary time, it was once common in Hizb Allah rhetoric, to conflate Israel and the West into one. Israel was understood as a product of the West, a symbol of its impact on the Middle East. In the 1980s, Israel from the perspective of this movement was the West. The policy of Hizb Allah towards the West included Israel in the equation. Hizb Allah viewed its relationship with Israel from a dual perspective. The first perspective increasingly emphasised the particularly religious nature of the dispute between them and the state of Israel as a Jewish homeland. The first viewpoint is particularly Levantine in origin, placing modern-day political systems within the realm of the religio-geographic location of the Holy Land. The second viewpoint perceived Israel as the 'West', a signified political label through which all other views of the West were filtered. From this perspective the group believed that the West acted as a unified forum against Islam in its quest for domination in the Middle East and control of resources. The principle source of this hostility lies in past and recent history, which is constructed to objectify the enemy as 'colonisers' past and present. For Hizb Allah, the Israeli invasion and subsequent occupation of Lebanon (1982–2000) was evidence of the expansionist project inspired by its founder Herzl and at the heart of Zionism.[27]

Constructions of present strategic and political positions rest on ideological 'givens' about the nature of Israel and its relationship with the West. This view is illustrated in the words of the commander of Hizb Allah's resistance, Sheikh Nabil Qa'ouk. Interviewed on the eve of Israel's withdrawal from Lebanon in May 2000 he pronounced on the issue of Israel,

Firstly, there is the historical context which we must be aware of. The problem of Lebanon and the conflict between Lebanon and the Israelis was established before Hizb Allah was established. This problem has a history ... the legacy of the role that the colonial powers played here. They also lie with the British state that issued the Balfour Declaration and favoured the Jews. Later it was the same, the Jews were given undue influence by both the British and the Americans as they carved up the region.[28]

This perspective does indeed appear to endorse the notion of some form of 'clash of civilisation' between Islam and the West. From this perspective Israel as a Jewish state was the primary lens through which Hizb Allah assessed, analysed and developed their policies towards the West. Israel was variously described as 'America's spearhead in the Middle East', 'America's cancerous and artificial entity' and 'the first foothold for American ambitions in the region'. In addition America's involvement in the region and more specifically Lebanon is explained in terms of its relationship with Israel. Grievances against the United States of America are based on the United States of America's support of Israel's continued occupation of the West Bank and Gaza Strip, its invasion of Lebanon in 1982, its failure to urge compliance of UN resolutions 242 or 425 and the perceived 'double standards' of the United States of America in its support of Israel in the Middle East. While the West, to include special reference to the former colonial powers of Britain and France, is identified as a hegemonic force, it is still headed by the United States of America. In Nasrallah's 'Open Letter to the World' the act of Israeli occupation, it was argued, was part of a plot spearheaded by the United States of America designed to undermine the position of Muslims and promote Phalangist hegemony in Lebanon.[29]

From this particular Islamist perspective the bilateral relationship between Israel and the West emphasises western support of the Zionist cause in the region. Here Zionism is promoted as another version of colonialism and imperialism emphasising the goal of subordination of a native people to a Western economic, political and cultural agenda. Israel is the West because from this perspective Israel is an instrument of Western expansionism, strategic, territorial and economic ambition. This perspective presents an image to its followers of an empowered Israel that would be nothing without the West. Israel is understood as empowered by a coalition of Western governments who seek to use Israel as a spearhead for their own national interests and ambitions in the region. The Islamists project their emasculated body politic and leaders into their assessment of Israel as the West bestowing this tiny nation state with superpower status on a global stage. Muslim empowerment is hence achieved when Israel is defeated. As such they are guilty of acceding to a form of myopic Occidentalism that creates myth, stereotype and endows modern nation states and their political leaders with power that ignores real strengths and weaknesses. Thus, in one sense it can be contended that an emasculated Islam constructs an image of Israel as the West, which is signified as superhuman, technologically advanced, relentlessly successful and militarily mightier than anything or anyone else in the Middle East.

Israel, however, through the dual perspective remains the primary target of hostility. In the early 1990s a diffusion of perspective did begin to emerge in certain quarters of the movement as a result of Hizb Allah undergoing a process of 'Lebanonisation' and drawing away from the theatre of direct conflict with western states such as France and the United States of America.[30] It is in this context that Deputy Secretary-General Naim Qassam was quoted as declaring that 'While Hizb Allah sees itself capable of having relations with the West in the future, it cannot envisage such a possibility with Israel.'[31] While some may have seriously doubted the ability of the organisation's pragmatists, 'who favour[ed] suspending Hezbollah's active campaign against the West' in Lebanon, the evidence that emerged throughout the decade supported the contrary conclusion.[32] Hostages were released, assassinations, raids, bombings against western targets including Western military personnel, all but ceased. The strategy of resistance was reviewed and resistance re-interpreted on cultural and political rather than military levels emerged as an important feature of Hizb Allah rhetoric. In one respect the 'war with the West' has been over.[33] Only a major conflagration within the region involving United States of America and other Western forces in somewhere like Syria, Lebanon or Iran would be likely to spark military action and political violence from Hizb Allah against the West. As Hizb Allah leader Naim al-Qassem has asserted, 'we should distinguish between two things: between the ideological and practical position regarding the conflict', and here there is evidence of a meaningful distinction between a critique and a strategic threat to the West over a ten year period.[34]

In this respect there is evidence of a careful delineation emerging between what might be termed as Hizb Allah's intellectual critique and hostility to the West categorised as an immutable element of Hizb Allah's philosophical configuration and recognition of the limits of political violence in its confrontation. This was indicated by the leader of Hizb Allah's parliamentary bloc, Mohammed Raad in addressing the issue of resistance and solidarity on the Palestinian issue, 'We Lebanese may not fight the Israelis in Palestine but we can extend our support for the Palestinians ... But international law does not permit us to take up arms against them [Israel]. We don't want to break international law ... There may be a disagreement in cultures between us but we do believe the Europeans have a civilisation and culture aspects of which we respect.'[35] Here it appeared that the rules of the international system were being explicitly recognised and regarded as valid. What has emerged, however, is the persistent claim that throughout the duration of the second Intifada Hizb Allah (through agreement reached with the PLO – Palestine Liberation Organisation) has supported operations in the West Bank.[36] The assertions underscore the importance attached to the opposition to Israel as a western construct embedded by religious arguments against the acceptability of a Jewish state on Muslim territory. Anti-Westernism, therefore, is a multi-faceted phenomenon. It centres on the outcome of Western military, strategic, economic, cultural and political policies and actions in Muslim domains that are understood as impeding Muslim development, Muslim prosperity, Muslim security and freedom. These actions and their outcomes have generated a belief that America, in its quest for global domination, loathes the Muslim world. The loathing is also suffused with fear of the bearded clerics and their armed followers that appear to dominate contemporary cultural and media imaging of modern Muslim domains.

Fear and loathing: insecurity on the margins

The locus of anti-westernism, and more specifically anti-Americanism, in radical Islamist discourse has been debated and located in domains that have experience of what they believe are the outcomes of the forces of American power. Such threats were traditionally perceived as being at one removed from the West as a geographic entity. So long as the symbols of the United States of America came under attacks in Tehran, the US flag was burnt and trampled in Peshawar or chants of Death to America echoed after Friday Prayers in Kabul, there was a sense that the threat could be contained, managed and even turned to the strategic or political advantage of US ambition in far flung places.[37] Viewers of TV and film, readers of newspapers and other media in the United States of America were thus always encouraged to believe in the superiority of its democratic principles, its state-of-the-art armed forces and formidable overseas intelligence network. Throughout the late 1980s and the most part of the 1990s, popular culture uncritically represented that sense of superiority in the face of the so-called Muslim threat. One dimension of stereotyping of cultural attitudes, however, was the growth of hostility to Muslim communities within the West as well. By the late 1990s Islamophobia was a term coined to explain the 'reality of unfounded hostility towards Islam. It refers also to the practical consequences of such hostility in unfair discrimination against Muslim individuals and communities, and to the exclusion of Muslims from mainstream political and social affairs'.[38] The attention paid to Islamophobia or 'anti-Muslimism' as Halliday terms it, reinforced the historicised and culturally acceptable notion that there is that within Islam and always has been that which is essentially anti-western.[39] 'Despite centuries of invasion and strife' asserted a headline for a synoptic history of Islam in Europe, 'the faith has left an enduring legacy of art and learning'. According to this banner-line, it was the 'centuries of invasion and strife' that defined the experience of Islam in Europe. In one sense what is most interesting about these polar-opposite discourses is that they both reflect the same thing: an attempted hegemony of the dialogues of the elites that are fed back to the masses. These are the discourses that now play a large part in shaping international relations in a significant number of areas in the globe, including the Middle East, parts of Africa, the former Soviet Muslim states, West Asia and parts of South Asia too. This discourse begins to shape the foreign-policies of say the 56 members of the OIC (Organization of Islamic Conferences) even limiting the manoeuvrability of conservative pro-western regimes in policy decisions that relate to notions or discourse of western engagement and policies in their regions.

Hence, we are presented with a less-than-simple picture of anti-Muslim bias which however ironically is fixed in reductive and simplistic assumptions about Muslims and what they think and how their actions should be interpreted. Such a discourse is not only reflected in Western strategic or security debates but permeates other encounters in discourse on gender, human rights, economy, globalisation, violence, conflict resolution, arts and so on. In the course of this rendition of Islam as a threat even the specific characteristics of those elements that establish and set themselves as a threat are represented without meaningful account of distinction, difference or dichotomy of approach.

This raises an interesting dimension to the debate, whether there is a distinction drawn in Western circles between a critique of the West emanating from subaltern voices and sources globally including Muslim polities and communities and anti-Westernism as a form of prejudice and racial discrimination. Indeed, I would assert that it is the very prevalence of representing Islamist critique of the policies of the West as something rigidly anti-Western rather than as a variety of voices, perspectives and views reflecting theocratic, political and lived experience in various parts of the globe that perpetuates the kind of myths that currently abound about Muslim warmongering and blood-thirst for Western targets. By failing to delineate between critique that is valid, perspectives that reflect logic and experiences which are unjust whichever way you read them, policy-makers, strategists, intelligence experts, academics and the media, all contribute to the demon myth that characterises the encounter, the reflection of what is known as Islam. The current perspective only contributes to the fixing and immutability of a set of battle-lines that are increasingly drawn, on both sides, around the 'other' as a reductive unit. If the threat to the West lies with Muslims rather than the domains that experience outcomes of Western inspired policies that are less than favourable, then the sense of threat is further heightened; for if the threat is from Muslims themselves and their 'innate and historically embedded' sense of hostility to that which is the West, what then of the millions of Muslims who are citizens of western states in the modern era?

Legislating to protect against the threat

There are a variety of mechanisms open to any nation state as it seeks to defend itself from both internal and external threat. In preparing any form of 'homeland' security, modern democratic states are likely to encourage the introduction, reading and passage of legislation that enables the state to meet the challenge posed by existential threats while working within the rule of law. To move outside the rule of law leaves such states vulnerable to the charge of state-based terrorism or violence, which is almost impossible to defend. Ultimately, acting outside such principles undermines the principles and claim to democratic credentials and the legitimacy that is tied to it. The eternal struggle in such societies is balancing the principles associated with human rights, individual protections and freedoms with the demand to 'protect' the state and its citizens from perceived threats. In democratic states where terrorism has been a recognised domestic phenomenon, the legislative channel has been actively employed to create legal routes for the state to continue its defence and protection obligations to its citizens. At the same time the courts legitimate processes and paths for its armed forces and intelligence communities to meet and combat the threats posed to it. In the past, in the United Kingdom the threat to the state had been understood and located with the armed elements of the Irish republican and Loyalist paramilitary movements. In some, though by no means all respects, the nature of that threat was altered in the mid-1990s onwards when both the IRA (Irish Republican Army) and the Loyalist paramilitaries in Northern Ireland signed up cease-fire agreements and their political representatives progressed to peace talks and a political agreement with decommissioning elements built-in. The nature of the threat to the British state was altered by such historic events, and the raft of legislation and legal landmarks – including major miscarriages of justice – seemed part of a historical epoch that might pass from British shores forever. Of course, even with the threat in decline some degree of legislative vigilance would be retained in order to protect the state and its citizens. There was, however, a real sense of optimism that the constraints on liberty to ensure freedom imposed by the parliament and upheld by the courts might be loosened.

From a legislative point of view, however, the outcome was not quite what the United Kingdom's liberal elements had anticipated, and the changes to the Prevention of Terrorism Act (PTA), the introduction of the Terrorism Act and other legislative rules mirrored the eruption of such restrictive legislation in the United States of America under the Clinton administration in the wake of the new threats being discovered.

Indeed, in the field of national security, immigration and terrorism one of the most interesting aspects of American legislative alteration in the 1990s was the emergence of new laws that reflected ideological and political agendas based on perceptions of Muslim threats. Anti-terrorism legislation proposed by President Clinton and passed (albeit with a lot of Republican foot-dragging) by the Republican-controlled legislature in 1996 was reactive in terms of meeting and responding to the single most significant terrorist atrocity of that time. In curbing rights to the individual outlined in the American constitution and with a legislative slant that profiled terrorists as Muslims and Arabs, the response to the Oklahoma atrocity a year earlier confounded some observers. The new legislation would promote the extension of government control in areas of American-cherished individual liberty and freedom. The context of the new legislation mattered in terms of the domestic considerations of the Clinton administration which needed to be seen to be 'tough on terrorism and tough on the sources of terrorism' in the wake of Oklahoma. The new legislation disturbed the liberal wing for two reasons. First, the new legislation appeared to tip the balance between state and individual in favour of the state security agenda and at the expense of individual rights. Second, the new legislation also reflected a deep-seated attitude towards America's Muslim migrant population and the Muslim community abroad, which has been interpreted as deliberately prejudicial and reductive.

The new legislation met the fears of elements in America that believed that religiously motivated terrorism, particularly of the Muslim sort, was a major threat.[40] Leaders of Muslim migrant communities, along with others, however, interpreted the new legislation as prejudicial and a major restriction of the freedom of speech. The new law would entail provisions for deportation of any foreigner suspected of supporting any activity (terror or otherwise) of a state-designated terrorist group. In addition the US courts convened for the purpose of hearing such cases enshrined the principle of the acceptability of evidence in secret on the grounds that it would maintain national security.[41] This had the potential to empower US enforcement agencies such as the FBI (Federal Bureau of Investigation) to submit secret evidence to a court that even the defendant and the defendant's legal representative was denied access to. Designation of terrorism was (and remains) a Presidential or State prerogative and, therefore, a matter of subjective distinction, which in the past has included the ANC (African National Congress) and the IRA.

Clinton's Anti-terrorism and Effective Death Penalty Act of 1996 (Public Law 104–32) empowered the state and its law enforcement agencies in its battle against new terrorism – funding was increased, legal jurisdiction extended including the realm of immigration, fund-raising and designation of terrorist activity. The FBI at last appeared to emerge from the long shadow of extra-judicial abuse and constitutional violations perpetrated during the Hoover era with new powers to undertake its task. Under the new legislation Clinton's FBI would be freed from such constraints to meet the challenge posed.

The legislation reflected a fear that the warriors of Islam were on the war path with sovereign American territory firmly in their sights. Warfare, as traditionally understood, was being challenged by a domestic phenomenon hitherto unknown in the American experience. The targets weren't military, the war waged both from within as well as without by migrants and their supporters who had claimed to find succour and support in a state that enshrined rights and freedoms after they fled societies where such rights were largely absent or abused. The new threat from within was linked to the threat from without by religious rather than national or tribal ties. The threat could no longer simply be defined in terms of a breakdown of relations between states over ideological or economic issues, but was increasingly presented as non-state, amorphous, multi-faceted, ever-present, a transnational web transcending national borders and boundaries representing a democratisation of the tools of terror with worrying consequences.

The belief that if the nature and tools of terrorism had changed then so too did the counter-terrorism effort of the state prevailed. In essence, I would contend that the rights of ordinary Americans were traded in the belief that such measures would prevent another World Trade Centre or Oklahoma attack. In the wake of the new law many in America's migrant Muslim community prepared themselves for the kind of state-orchestrated offensives that had taken place during the McCarthy era where support for communism was deemed unlawful and punishable. The law, therefore, represented the state's attempt to criminalise a range of activities including welfare and humanitarian assistance – that many thousands of Muslims and other migrant communities in the United States of America had traditionally supported as part of the obligations and support function of the diaspora network. This tactic, as Guelke has pointed out when employed by the British government to counteract political violence in Northern Ireland in the late 1970s while 'initially quite successful' backfired spectacularly in 1980 with the cumulative effect of the counter-protest hunger strikes by IRA prisoners and popular Catholic support and disorder.[42] The lessons of history served in the example of the McCathy era and the attempt at criminalisation in Northern Ireland were clearly not absorbed as the Clinton administration faced political pressure to act quickly. There was certainly no guarantee that in the proceeding years that as Muslims were arrested, subject to trials and hearings with secret evidence and deported, the threat posed and symbolised in the attacks on the World Trade Centre and in Oklahoma and Atlanta, as well as the threat of terror exposed by the Unabomber would counter terrorism in a substantive manner that would make the constitutional sacrifices worth it.

The question here is whether America's freedoms were further sacrificed on 11 September 2001 as Bin Laden's bombers appeared to be the undoing of all the counter-terror work of the previous five years? The new legislation had failed to stop the employment of a weapon of such massive destruction. Intelligence efforts, increased funding and the so-called effective tool of profiling had failed to stop the perpetration of the single most devastating act of domestic terrorism in the history of the United States of America. Profiling, for example, would have worked had the bombers shipped up with their beards, Korans and Kalashnikovs from Kabul, Gaza, Cairo or Beirut, but it just didn't turn out that way. In the wake of the attack profiling was still the primary principle upon which the government ordered the immediate detention of thousands of mostly Muslim American residents or immigrants who matched the Muslim/Arab profile.

By the end of December 2001, the US Attorney-General John Ashcroft revealed that hundreds were still being held in detention in connection with investigations into the events of 11 September. Human rights organisations such as Human Right Watch criticised 'new US anti-terrorism measures that authorise military trials of those accused of terrorism, permit prolonged administrative detention without charges, enable the government to monitor communications between federal detainees and their attorneys', as fears over new security regime and its import for human rights grew.[43] The argument that such efforts undermined the American constitution were strongly rebuffed by Ashcroft who declared that, 'To those who pit Americans against immigrants, citizens against non-citizens, to those who scare peace-loving people with phantoms of lost liberty, my message is this: 'Your tactics only aid terrorists for they erode our national unity and diminish our resolve ... They give ammunition to America's enemies and pause to America's friends. They encourage people of good will to remain silent in the face of evil ... Our efforts have been crafted carefully to avoid infringing on constitutional rights, while saving American lives.'[44]

Events that followed including the controversial opening of Camp X-Ray in Guantanamo Bay, Cuba for detainees (including children) flown out of Afghanistan, the turn in US public opinion in favour of torture of suspects in American detention, the construction of a criminal case against the alleged '20th bomber' Zacarias Moussaoui and the designation of the label 'enemy combatant' against US citizens, contributed to what appeared to be an emerging security-led government agenda towards its Muslim migrant community. As US legal expert Patricia Williams noted in the wake of 11 September 'Americans suddenly seem willing to embrace profiling based on looks and ethnicity, detention without charges, searches without warrants, even torture and assassinations,' yet none of these measures guarantees that national security will be achieved or reflect the failure of such approaches to prevent the domestic terror phenomenon in the first place.[45] The legislative route followed since 11 September has given rise to a significant erosion of the rights previously extended. Profiling, nationwide interrogation, detention without trial, and an explicit linkage to immigration laws in respect of Muslim and Arab nationals have undermined group and individuals rights within this community. The passing of the Patriot Act, argues David Cole, 'imposes guilt by association on immigrants, rendering them deportable for wholly innocent non-violent associational activity on behalf of any organisation blacklisted as terrorist by the Secretary of State. Any group of two or more which has used or threatened to use force can be designated as terrorist. This provision in effect resurrects the philosophy of McCarthyism, simply by substituting "terrorist" for "communist" '.[46] The state in the United States of America has increased its powers in important spheres and this process of encroachment of liberal values largely went unchallenged. It can be anticipated that it will not be easy to win such freedom back from the state, particularly under the political helm of such a right-wing administration. As one African American cab driver in Washington DC explained to me in the Spring of 2004, 'Everyone seems to have forgotten how hard people like me struggled for those rights ... now they have gone in the blink of an eye and do we feel any safer?' Similar debates about racial profiling emerged in the United Kingdom in the wake of the suicide bomb attacks of July 2005. Although government officials were encouraging the British police to engage in 'stop and search' campaigns that publicly cautioned against racial profiling, there were still widespread media reports that young Asian and Black Muslim males were being stopped in disproportion to other groups. Supporters of government policy counter that the Bush administration is not engaged in a war on Islam but in a war on terrorism. They argue that Muslim countries have joined the international effort to end terrorism and that President Bush went out of his way to call on his fellow Americans to desist from attacking their fellow Muslims in the wake of, 11 September 2001. Yet, a divide in opinion appeared to open in the Western alliance with actions as well as the choice of words interpreted even most Muslim quarters as a sign that Islam was being singled out for American ire, while some European actors sought to distance themselves from the prospect of a 'clash of civilizations'.[47]

The extension of the remit on the war on terrorism to other geo-strategic frontiers in the year following the September atrocity, including the Arab arena and the Palestinian–Israeli conflict further undermined the sense of security that Americans have previously enjoyed. In terms of Muslim and especially Islamist opinion such actions also undermined the credibility of the argument that the war on terrorism was not a war on Islam. Increasingly it became difficult to read it as anything else. Such views were bolstered by the cultural hostility explicit in arguments forwarded by authors such as Huntington and Fukuyama and in the growing suspicion across the Muslim domain that actions speak louder than words – everything pointed to the singling out of their faith system. As one prominent Islamic Jihad leader remarked, 'All we see from America is enmity ... the US gives itself rights which they deny to others ... and although we have suffered from their enmity we didn't bring the war to their doorstep ... Its totally wrong to sweep 11 September 2001 as the sum total of Islam.'[48]

Fukuyama in an attempt to re-fashion his approach in the wake of 11 September 2001 labels Islamic radicalism as a new form of fascism unique and peculiar to the religion only in the twenty-first century. Perhaps more surprisingly, he pronounces that the cultural difference between Islam and all other 'world cultures' is that it has 'repeatedly produced significant radical Islamist movements that reject not just Western policies, but the most basic principal of modernity itself, that of religious tolerance'.[49] Such assertions are worth reflecting on for their sheer lack of understanding about the development of religious revivalism and the additional phenomenon of anti-Americanism/anti-globalism as a late twentieth century phenomena that characterise almost all cultures and societies rather than one. In asserting that Islam alone has repeatedly produced radical religious movements that exhibit hostility to other cultures and other faith systems, Fukuyama appears to be forwarding an argument from a sanitised secular bubble that floats above the reality of modern religious phenomena that has emerged in modern secular contexts such as Japan, Northern Ireland or the United States of America.[50] In Northern Ireland the phenomenon of religious intolerance that has rendered deep divisions has nothing to do with Islam. How then does Fukuyama's argument tally with Juergensmeyer's contention that Christian 'religious warfare exists in the most modern of twentieth-century societies' proving that there is no cultural or geographic boundary to a phenomenon that is intolerant, bigoted and prejudiced.[51] Such warriors have been intolerant of Jews, Muslims, Hindus, and Blacks in equal measure, but they are not held up by Fukuyama and others as evidence of a 'culture' different from all others in its intolerance to plural traditions seemingly associated with secularism. Nor, is a 'rejection of Western policies' something than can be laid exclusively at the door of the cultural essence that is known by Fukuyama and others as Islam. Such a perspective does not explain the rise of the anti-globalisation movement nor the hostility to what is perceived as aggressive Western-inspired interference in economic, political and other spheres of the developing world in Asia, Latin America and Africa.

In the American-led war and occupation of Iraq the religious warriors are perceived as forming battle lines on both the Iraqi and Allied side. The American-led coalition has found itself in contention with Islamist forces in Fallujah, Baghdad, Najaf and other cities in Iraq where previously there were none. Islamist warriors have emerged as a direct result of the western occupation of Iraq. Many Iraqis and Islamists across the globe speak of the American-led war to topple the regime of Saddam Hussein and the consequent occupation of Iraq as another example of the religious war that America has launched against Islam and its followers. As a statement issued by the Islamist group *Hizb ur Tahrir* highlights,

> the West in general and America in particular, do not want a rule in the Islamic region where the people elect their rulers by choice and consent. In other words, the West does not accept representative government, as called for by Bush. The reason is that the West knows that had the people of this region elected their rulers then Islam would have come to power and the rulers would have been those who are sincere to their Deen and Ummah, and the Khilafah Rashidah would have returned once again.[52]

It can be argued that it is too simplistic to cite consumerist aspirations of the Western kind or as evidence of a global embrace – Islam excepted – of the West in the twenty-first century. This is not to say that radical elements of a variety of political hues aren't part of the Islamist spectrum; they are. This is not the same, however as representing them as defining and shaping and dominating the manifestation of the faith and politics of the 'Muslim culture'. Such an argument allows certain elements to get away with the fifth column perspective about Muslims wherever they are found and fails to acknowledge the context in which Muslims find themselves.

It also asks us to reflect on the kind of mainstreaming of opinion in Western discourses since 11 September. When shortly after the attacks on America, Italy's Prime Minister Silvio Berlusconi asserted that the war on terrorism was at heart a clash of civilisations, a major controversy emerged in Europe over his remarks. During a visit to Berlin he proclaimed the supremacy of Western civilisation and urged the leaders and people of Europe to build on its 'common Christian roots' in the forthcoming battle against Islam. He, like Fukuyama verbalised a perceived linkage between 'Islamic terrorism' and the anti-globalisation movement as enemies of a Western civilisation. Like Fukuyama, Western civilisation for Berlusconi is characterised as supreme for its 'discoveries and inventions, which have brought us democratic institutions, respect for the human, civil, religious and political rights of our citizens, openness to diversity and tolerance of everything ... This respect certainly does not exist in the Islamic countries'. Such remarks, taken along with the infamous 'crusade' remark by Bush, were condemned as exceptional and unrepresentative, yet in the cold light of day and out of the heat of the immediate storm it would appear that they have in fact formed the foundations for a sustained intellectual wellspring underpinned not by a knowledge of Islam and an acknowledgement of its diversity, but in a half-knowledge of Islam that is fixated with dangerous consequences for future national as well as international security agendas of many western nation states in the twenty-first century.

Too much too late

The legislative route for addressing the new threats implicit to Muslim radicalism was also in evidence in the United Kingdom in the late 1990s. As laws on terrorism were changed to reflect a growing domestic preoccupation at governmental levels with the 'new Muslim threat' while the historic threat of Irish terrorists appeared to go into relative decline, important legislative changes were afoot. Under 'emergency/crisis' contexts and through the legislative route, the British government like its counterpart in the United States of America has been able re-define terrorism in the absence of significant and major public discourse about what this means for the rights of citizens and citizen-seekers. Once again it was amongst the most vulnerable elements of society that the new legislation would have import. The migrant community, including those seeking asylum from regimes of abuse, were to feel that the new legislation put them in the sights of a hostile state and they could find themselves guilty of terrorism, even by association with the general principles that so-called terrorist organisations adhered to.

In December 2001, after fierce debates and a U-turn from the Home Secretary, emergency anti-terror legislation (The Anti-Terrorism, Crime and Security Act – ATCSA) was passed in the UK Parliament. The Bill had proposed detention without trial, a further tightening of the definition of terrorism to include those found guilty by association and further restrictions in the fields of immigration appeal and disclosure of information – including information held by ISPs (International Student Programs) – all of which appeared to signal a uniquely British departure from European conventions protecting human rights. Critics of the new law argued that 'immigrant and refugee communities in particular will feel the full force of the new law that implicitly makes them suspect'.[53] Almost a year after the 11 September atrocity and while certain sections of the UK government had admitted that there was no direct threat to the United Kingdom from Bin Laden-type terrorism, the legislative route still indicated that there was a preoccupation (in certain quarters of the government and British security establishment) with the Muslim threat. Throughout 2002, non-UK nationals who had been arrested in the wake of the 11 September security crackdown in the United Kingdom remained in indefinite detention, without charge or trial, under the terms of ATCSA. Suspected of involvement with or being international terrorists, non-nationals arrested in security sweeps were subsequently held in high-security prisons as Category A prisoners.[54] The Act empowered the Secretary of State to order such detention if there was a belief that non-nationals were a threat to national security and suspected by government security services of terrorism. Additionally, a legislative route was made available for the provision of secret evidence to be put before the Secretary of State. Like US legislation such evidence does not have to be put before the person detained. The other significant actor in the UK arena on this issue is the Special Immigration Appeals Commission (SIAC) which, in conjunction with the Secretary of State has the authority to end the detention of suspects.

In an acknowledgement that such legislative strictures could contravene European Law on Human Rights on enacting the new legislation, the UK government derogated its responsibilities claiming that the emergency context compelled them to temporarily ignore such important human rights provisions. Amnesty International, in opposing the detentions without charge or trial noted that 'The UK remains the only country that has derogated from the ECHR in the aftermath of the 11 September 2001 attacks in the United States of America' and urged the government to release those who were not going to be charged with terrorist offences from British jails.[55] Additionally, a variety of aspects of ATCSA came under the scrutiny of the legal and human rights community raising fears of breaches as they relate to many hitherto assumed rights to fairness and justice under the UK legal system. For example, while denied proper access to legal counsel the new legislation does make provision for what are referred to as Special Advocates 'to represent appellant's interests'.[56] Significantly, however, the notion that certain sections of the Act had been devised to meet the exceptional 'emergency' circumstance experienced in defence, intelligence and other governmental agencies in the wake of 11 September is reflected in the provision in ATCSA where sections 21–23 which deal specifically with 'certification of suspected international terrorists, deportation, removal and detention'.[57] Under the terms of the Act these would fall into abeyance and will be subject to review 15 months after the date of the passing of the Act. In reality, however, the contradictions of the Act as they relate to the protection of human rights have been exposed on more than one occasion.

By December 2004 non-nationals were still being detained in UK prisons, but a specially convened committee of law lords ruled that the policy of detaining foreigners without trial under emergency anti-terrorism laws broke European Union legislation of human rights. In issuing the ruling the law lords described the anti-terror legislation as 'draconian' and 'anathema' to the rule of law. It was reported in one newspaper that, 'One of the law lords, Lord Hoffmann of Chedworth suggested that the act itself was a bigger threat to the nation than terrorism.'[58]

One case in particular generated controversy. In the late 1990s a Palestinian refugee called Mahmoud Abu Rideh was granted asylum by the British authorities. In the wake of 11 September he was arrested and detained under the provision of section 21–23 of ATCSA. With a documented history of mental illness (as a result of torture claims) and self-harm, Abu Rideh was held as a Category A prisoner in the notorious Belmarsh Prison in London. In July 2002, as news emerged that Abu Rideh had in addition to acts of self-harm gone on hunger strike, moves were made to appeal to have him moved to a low-category prison. He had been denied bail to a low-security mental hospital, and while doctors at Broadmoor Prison Hospital had recommended such a move the Home Secretary overruled the recommendation counter-charging Broadmoor with responsibility for such a prisoner. The Home Secretary obfuscated the debate on the real issues at the heart of this case. First why was a British national with asylum status being detained without trial on the evidence of Britain's security agencies at a time when by its own admission Britain was not facing a threat to national security by al-Qaeda elements of radical Islamism? It was reported that the doctors at Broadmoor had subsequently accused the Home Secretary of 'unprecedented political interference' by ignoring their professional opinion on a vulnerable individual.[59] The continuing detention of someone like Abu Rideh undermines the efficacy of such legislation in meeting the demands of national security in the wake of 11 September. In theory, if such individuals were engaged in acts consistent with a threat to national security then the evidence should have been put on charge sheet and placed before the Crown Prosecution Service. Instead it was placed in a secret file for viewing by a limited number of UK officials. The case, as it is currently known in the public domain, appears that Abu Ridneh may be suspected of terrorism by association. Such charges are always difficult to bring – particularly if the case involves a mentally-ill torture victim granted asylum and residency rights in a democratic state such as the United Kingdom.

An indication of the implicit suspicion can be illustrated in the example of a further individual. In December 2001 an asylum-seeker living in the north-eastern city of Newcastle-upon-Tyne received a visit from the Special Branch at the modest terraced house he shared with other asylum seekers from Afghanistan and Iran. The man had arrived in the United Kingdom in April of the same year; a Muslim, probably of Arab origin, he like many others arriving in the United Kingdom's ports of entry that month claimed asylum and refuge from the UK authorities.

He was subsequently charged under the 2000 Terrorism Act, section 11, with being a member of a proscribed organisation, professing membership of the proscribed organisation and intimidating a witness. The prosecution case, which drew extensively on Special Branch interviews and investigations against the defendant, was built on the belief that the defendant was a member of the radical Islamist organisation Hamas Izz-a-din-al-Qassam Brigades and that he was willing to carry out attacks against targets, including a pub, in the United Kingdom. The case would be the first prosecution in the United Kingdom since 11 September 2001 under the Terrorism Act 2000.[60] The visitors to his house in December 2001 were Special Branch officers who subsequently arrested and charged him with the offences outlined above. When the charges were finally brought to court in Newscastle-upon-Tyne in May 2002, the judge moved to direct the 11-member jury to clear the defendant, Adnan Abdelah of the main charges relating to terrorism against him. The case was dismissed and there were calls for a top-level probe of the Special Branch investigation and the intervention of the Attorney General with a view to this test case having implications for future charges brought under the Terrorism Act.

In bringing its charges and the allegations of criminality against the defendant the Crown Prosecution Service (CPS) began in court by relying on an expert report and witness testimony that was designed to play on preoccupations (post 11 September 2001) with suicide-bombings, the extent of transnational financing and organisation of Islamist terror networks in the United Kingdom as well as intelligence assessments from the Israeli military. Indeed it is interesting to note that national public broadcast coverage of the trial played on these same associations. The BBC in a piece entitled 'Hamas suspect supported bin Laden' – with two images dominating the coverage of the opening days of the trial: one of Usama Bin Laden and the other of hooded and armed Islamists allegedly from the Hamas Izz-a-din-al-Qassam faction – reported the allegations against Abdelah. This included that of Prosecuting QC Hedworth, who told the jury that the defendant was, among things, 'multi-lingual and associated mainly with Middle-Eastern males'.[61] On this kind of 'evidence' the Crown felt it had enough support, in a particular climate of fear, to arrest and bring charges.

The jury was also told according to the Special Branch and CPS investigation that Abdelah had told of being trained by Hamas in 'bomb-making and terrorist techniques and supported Osama bin Laden'. The judge himself, however, referred to the defendant as a 'Walter Mitty' or 'Billy Liar' type character. It was also clear from the transcripts of his police interviews that Abdelah knew as much about 'bomb-making' and 'terrorist techniques' as anyone who had ever watched an episode of the BBC's Spooks programme or a James Bond film. Nevertheless, the will to prosecute in the wake of 11 September appears to have outweighed such considerations. The trial also exposed the issues inherent in the Terrorism Act 2000 as they relate to 'freedom of speech' and European legislation on this issue. The trial continued but the BBC coverage did not. The trial illustrates, albeit in an extrapolated fashion, the kinds of issues faced by Muslims migrants and asylum seekers – citizens and citizen-seekers in Western states.[62] The recourse to legislative measures in response to the terror threat posed by Muslims in the West, however, has become a primary tool in the domestic management of the war on terrorism. The extent to which justice will be utilised in the protection of national interest has become open to pressing political pressures.

The enemy within?

Since the Second World War the migrant communities of many European and North American states have swelled and morphed altering the domestic landscape of these nations – particularly in its urban guise. These migrant communities have included Afro-Caribbeans, Turks, Algerians, Palestinians, Chinese and Cambodians. Some communities have been formed as a result of the demand by industrialising states for labour and others out of refuge from the horrors of tumultuous conflicts, which have been defined as shaping the international order. Some communities reflect a consequence of a colonial entanglement and the difficulties inherent in re-making new relationships between the dominator and subordinated. All communities have contributed, not only to the economic vibrancy and wealth-making of modern capital economies, but contributed in major or minor ways to re-shaping culture, identity and community relations. Amongst this number Muslim migrant communities are to be found in Italy (1 million), Germany (3.2 million), Sweden (130,000), France (5 million), the United Kingdom (1.8 million), the United States of America (5 million), Canada (650,000) and Australia (300,000). In many of these communities a sense of threat had emerged from within and distinguished one generation from other in relation to the place, the potency and the function of Islam in the individual and collective life of the community.

Muslim migrants have now played their part in shaping the development of some locales in the West. The economic, religious, cultural and political profile of the United Kingdom's second largest city, Birmingham, for example, is unimaginably different in the twenty-first century to how it was in the wake of the bombed out devastation scarring this industrial heartland of England in 1945. The influx of a large migrant community from the Asian subcontinent to, ultimately, assist in post-conflict reconstruction and generation of prosperity included a sizeable Muslim element (15%) whose citizens have subsequently represented the community in local as well as national politics. The growth of Britain's Muslim community largely went unnoticed. In wider society's perception they were not visible in the British multi-cultural landscape. When such communities, whether they are in Britain, France, Germany or the United States of America are noticed or recognised, it is in the context of tension, conflict, dissonance and as a problem. Even minority Muslims in Asian states such as the Philippines and India hit the headlines across the world, and fall into the public consciousness when there is strife. This phenomenon and its important consequences in terms of the 'threat factor' is explicable through reflecting on the 'lived' experiences of these minorities and the cultural and historical baggage they are perceived as bringing with them. Muslims experience discrimination in these contexts. In the United Kingdom, for example, British Muslim Bangladeshis and Pakistanis are 'two and a half times more likely to be unemployed than the white population and three times more likely to be on low pay'.[63] Without the protection of laws against religious discrimination these minorities experience hostility and exclusion. In France, the law was interpreted by the state in the mid-1990s to restrict religious symbols in schools (proselytising) including a subsequent and well-publicised decision by the French Minister of Education to prohibit the wearing of *hijab* (headscarf) by Muslim schoolgirls. In addition some *hijab*-wearing schoolgirls were expelled from their schools. The media in these contexts have reinforced marginality in their stereotypical representations of such citizens as threatening a shared vision, perpetrated by the non-Muslim majority. Muslims are understood by the non-Muslim majority in these contexts as a challenge and threat to the state and pre-existing order. They are perceived not as part of society, integrated and organic to the whole but undermining it as part of a transnational fifth column whose partisans will perpetrate revolution and the rise of the green flag of Islam in the capital cities of Western Europe and North America.[64] Symbolic of this perceived threat and the response to it was the exclusion of former pop sensation Cat Stevens (who converted to Islam and is now known as Yusuf Islam) from the United States of America in 2004. The plane he was travelling on was diverted and he was subsequently deported back to his home in the United Kingdom. Although an outspoken opponent of terrorism, the American authorities had put Islam on a 'no-fly' list contending that the former pop singer had links with Muslim terrorist organisations. In meeting this perceived challenge the state has embraced a number of control strategies including legislation, social and economic exclusion and in extreme circumstances attempted hegemonic assertion through ethnic cleansing. Such responses do not seem set to change.

In meeting the challenge posed by Muslim minorities the state has found itself accused of many crimes, some racially-motivated and experienced by other minorities, others unique to the migrant and minority experience of Muslims. The state and its non-Muslim citizens can be seen to reflect 'uneasiness' at Muslims who 'front it out'. Las Vegas, set in the Nevada desert is the modern American Mecca for gambling, drinking and pleasure. Its neon strips, marriage chapels, luxury hotels and shopping malls represent the dedication to secular pleasures and consumerism at its most garish and provocative. It would not be unfair to claim that Las Vegas is as much a symbol of America's global status as the Pentagon or New York's World Trade Centre. In April 2001, one of the most important younger personalities of the Muslim world raised a gloved fist in Las Vegas at a tumultuous and repetitive call. As the young sportsman entered the auditorium, loudspeakers conveyed the muezzin's declaration of *'Allahu Akbar'* (God is Great). This young Muslim, world famous, an icon to thousands of young men, declared to the gathered audience 'Who else can I fear apart from Allah? I can't fear any human being.' With these words the Sheffield-born boxer known as Prince Naseem Hamed entered the ring in a momentous bout with Mexican fighter Antonio Marco Barrera. The boxing event involving a devout Muslim taking on an opponent in the Las Vegas jarred and felt incongruous to those that viewed it.[65] Indeed, the tenor of 'Prince Naz' in exhibiting his devotion to his faith was portrayed as nothing more than part of the 'hype' that belied the base competition between two pugilists as they faced each other off on the canvas floor. Prince Naseem's declarations of faith, his interpretation and understanding of Islam threw confusion into the ring along with his punches. Indeed it was noted that with that interpretation of faith and entrance, Naseem's approach 'went down badly' with the fight crowd. Generations earlier, the infamous Muslim pugilist Cassius Clay had also stunned the world and made his fellow citizens of America writhe in uneasiness as he declared his conversion to Islam and changed his name to Mohammed Ali. Ali – 'the most recognised human being on earth' – converted to Islam and used his faith as a potent badge of identity.

Yet the difficulties inherent in Muslim demands and difference are that the state and its policy-makers interpret them as an attempt to undermine the 'sacred' secular order while failing at the same time to acknowledge the Judeo–Christian context out of which this norm grew and is maintained. The Muslim demand, say, for legal control over personal status issues or for religious schools of their own is interpreted as a major assault on secular state principles and further evidence of the Muslim conspiracy to establish the abode of Islam (*dar al-Islam*) in the West. Such demands appear to promote controversy. In January 1998 following persistent request, rejection and even a High Court ruling, the British government gave the go ahead for Britain's first two state-funded Muslim schools. The Muslim community had had to apply consistent pressure on the state for the same recognition given to other faiths. While state funding was already given to Anglican, Roman Catholic, Sikh and Jewish schools in the United Kingdom, it had been denied until that point to the Muslim population of the United Kingdom. Parents at one of the schools, the Islamiyya in East London, had had to threaten to sue the Government following persistent delays (over a 13-year period) in their application to join the state system.[66] Such victories from the state were obviously hard-won and did little to diminish the perception that the state behaved differently to Muslim demands. Such demands have further been interpreted as evidence of innate hostility to an integrationist agenda promoted by the state at the helm of post-modern multi-cultural societies and are employed as evidence by the sceptics in their case against Muslim minorities in their midst.

The cultural representation of such minorities in non-Muslim cultures also contributes to the environment of suspicion and fear surrounding them. If good relations take place, as they do in certain urban neighbourhoods of the United States of America, it is against the odds and as a result of persistent attempt. Good relations and co-existence is not perceived as the norm. Instead the norm is found in the extreme fringes and elements that exist in Muslim migrant and minority communities. Muslims through history to the present are brought to non-Muslim consciousness in cultural settings depicted as alien. The historical cross-fertilisations of cultures and cultural influences over the centuries of interaction and contact are entirely lost. There is no acknowledgement of the Muslim contribution to the cultural life of such societies, whether in the form of the most popularly consumed foods or sports. Instead Muslim culture is hidden or if public, shaped through reductions. This exaggerates the sense of a divide and the confrontations that take place over that divide. The images and words that cover their story convince that they bring their own problems and are to blame for their plight. And in addition, if that plight is shared (through transnational networks and notions of community (*umma*)) then the threat posed by Muslim militants in Chechnya or Afghanistan has the potential to transfer to other locales through association and support. This may explain the current preoccupation with Muslim networks – funding and fuelling Muslim antipathy through terror. In 1996 for example, the Daily Telegraph in an article entitled 'London fatwa backs suicide bombers' alleged that a respected and Charity Commission-registered charity, Interpal, was a sponsor of Hamas terror and suicide-bombing. Subsequent press reports, particularly a number appearing in the wake of the 11 September bombings in the United States of America resurrected the claims against Interpal. This was in an attempt to give credence to the notion of a major European and North American conspiracy by Muslims to fund suicide-bombers. Such reports ignored Charity Commission investigations which cleared Interpal of such allegations in the late 1990s and the conclusion that instead Interpal was carrying out 'important work in a part of the world where there is great hardship and suffering'.[67]

When the politics of Kashmir and the Middle East are still subject to internationalisation as a result of the global clout of Western powers, it is Muslim minorities who are regarded with suspicion. They are treated with suspicion because they connect with and some express political opinions about the effects that such interventions might have.

New wave terrorism

In the absence of dialogue and trust and in the presence of a threat, the need to eradicate it through the form of profiling emerges. By trawling for the trouble-makers using technology instead of human contact and communication to weed out the threat from within and without only serves to heighten the sense of so-called division and threat. Such approaches do underscore anti-Muslim and anti-immigrant tendencies and give support to anxieties as they are expressed either in concern at migration or as a result of internalising external security threats to national assets and interests abroad. The development of a discourse on the latter aspect allowed the spotlight to fall on Muslims in the early to mid 1990s. Elements of the western media, policy-makers and public had been alarmed as they struggled to make sense of violence in the post-Cold War era where peace and security were supposed to be guaranteed. The response to this new context, where the old Red menace was replaced by a growing fixation with the 'green peril' had been manifested in a variety of ways. This included the Hollywood depictions of Muslims as the 'bad guys'. The Kurt Russell and Steven Segal film of 1996 entitled Executive Decision, for example, was premised on a plot in which ringleaders of a notorious Muslim terrorist organisation hijack an aeroplane. The American heroes of 'the President's Crisis Management Team' rescue the aircraft's '400-plus American passengers'.

Additionally, a large number of books and articles including an Associated Press feature, 'Jihad USA' and the 1994 documentary 'Jihad in America' also reinforced the negative stereotype encouraging real fear of and hostility to Muslim minorities in the West. The chief architects of the discourse on new wave terrorism were, to a certain extent, the counterparts of Kurt Russell and Steven Segal. They emerged from right-wing think tanks and were employed to provide government and legislative committees, lobby groups and the media with an explanation. This explanation tended to rest on the opinion that a new threat to global security lay in Muslim hands. In America in the early 1990s the sense of a threat from Muslim violence did not correlate with the facts. 'Terrorism in the USA' had been an almost exclusively 'home-grown' phenomenon. Federal Bureau of Investigation (FBI) figures for domestic terrorist incidents from 1990–94 cited 28 incidents, of which only two were identified as acts of international terror. FBI 'Bombing Statistics' issued in 1996 cited 2577 incidents, none of which were committed by Muslims.[68] The perpetrators of such acts of political violence were not mostly Muslim. Yet the threat remained, heightened by attacks in Europe and the World Trade Centre (WTC) in New York in 1993. The attack on the WTC had been planned by radical Islamists, and their ambition had been to end thousands of lives. Ramzi Yousef who had led the conspirators in the attacks was part of a radical Muslim cell with the United States of America in their sights. The investigations and allegations following the attacks and the discovery of others like them highlighted the weaknesses within the American intelligence structure and how poorly co-ordinated the effort to protect national security at home and abroad was. As security officials later admitted, the 1993 attack 'should have been a wake-up call for America ... We simply didn't see it as an international conspiracy to destroy our society.'[69] For most Americans the idea that the United States of America was being targeted as a source of terrorist rage was difficult to grasp.

In part, the idea that Americans didn't see themselves as a target is explicable by what Sardar and Wyn Davies describe as 'knowledgeable ignorance'.[70] This, I would argue, was knowledgeable ignorance not just about the rest of the world but the ways in which the rest of the world experienced and saw America. Public confidence in the wake of the 1993 WTC attack was also restored by the seemingly quick identification and apprehension of the perpetrators. Charges of conspiracy were also brought against others, including the Egyptian cleric Sheikh Omar Abdel Rahman. With the 'bad guys' brought to justice and put behind bars a sense of safety was restored. The trail eventually led to Ramzi Yousef and the connection with Afghanistan and Bin Laden was established. The import of the connection for America, however, did not appear to hit home. In one respect the wood could not be seen for the trees. With so many Muslims purportedly threatening the West; with old alliances, with some radicals and fundamentalists muddying the waters; with the sense of threat abroad increasing in the explosion of conflicts in so many Muslim domains; with weaknesses in threat assessment grading, as well as a reliance on the politically-motivated intelligence of other allies and parties; and with a clarion call resounding in right-wing circles that Muslims themselves and their faith system were the threat, surely Americans can be forgiven for not predicting the unthinkable?

Whither Muslims and the West in the West?

In the wake of the attacks on America and other Western targets across the globe it does appear that the gap between Islam and the West has opened into a chasm that appears to confirm Huntington's hypothesis that the 'fundamental source of conflict in this new world will not be primarily ideological or primarily economic ... The great divisions among humankind and the dominating source of conflict will be cultural ... the clash of civilizations will dominate global politics'.[71] The attacks by al-Qaeda appear to underscore such a hypothesis. The emasculation of the Muslim people and their leaders is a reality when compared to early historical epochs. The source of that emasculation is Western, first Europe in the eighteenth and nineteenth centuries and then an ascendant United States of America in the twentieth. The Iranian ideologue Ali Shariati, ironically influenced by Fanon's work, urged Muslims to 'abandon Europe' and end the impossible task of acting as intermediaries between them and the forces at work in the colonisation project.[72] In this respect Muslim consciousness in Asia, the Middle East and Africa echoes and reflects the development of Third World consciousness and a growing resentment at the outcomes of current and historical episodes of western involvement and interaction. The growth of Muslim transnational networks, built on global interconnection and migrant population movements, acted as an intellectual vehicle for growth, exploration and generation of discourse of protest against the West. This has been coupled to the resurgence phenomenon and it's accompanying political agenda for change. Islamism has emerged as a modern phenomenon in relation to its critique of the West. In contradistinction to Huntington, however, I would argue that the Islamist agenda is mainly founded on an ideological and economic experience and issues. It is in terms of these issues and debates that Bin Laden has been able to exploit and represent his vision back to the Muslim mass. Islamist leaders, when they opine against the West, do so because there is a genuine sense of grievance at the outcome of Western involvement and interaction with their domains. Where the house of Muslim unity falls apart, however, is in the extent to which an Islamist critique of the West demands have the same strategies of response and resistance.

When groups of Muslims struggle against injustice and for their rights, the fear that such struggle will perpetuate disruption and instability has led Western government policy-makers to ignore such demands.[73] Instead of supporting Muslim rights and demands for justice, the Bangladeshi Muslim citizens of Britain, the Algerian Muslim citizens in France, the Turks of Germany and the Palestinians of Chicago, ill perceive their states as hypocrites who stand by when oppression, humiliation and occupation takes place against beleaguered Muslim minorities in Kashmir, the West Bank and Gaza Strip and Bosnia. Slings and arrows are thrown at British, American and French Muslims who speak out about their support for the struggles of their Muslim brethren across the globe while their government's join in alliance to prosecute war or support states which continue in such oppression. Such dilemmas and distrust surrounded the American declared war on terrorism in the Autumn of 2001. During the war on Afghanistan a Guardian/ICM poll of Muslims revealed the extent of divided loyalties and identities. While 54 per cent considered themselves to be British Muslim, 66 per cent disapproved of the British role in the war in Afghanistan. It is clear from the poll that British Muslims were very concerned about the impact of the war on ordinary Afghan Muslims. Furthermore the place of Islam in British culture was perceived as marginal: 69 per cent of those polled believed that non-Muslim Britons do not see Islam as part of mainstream British culture. Such dissonant perceptions were exacerbated by the furore surrounding the highly publicised accounts of British Muslim mujahideen taking off to fight on behalf of the Taliban/al-Qaeda forces in Afghanistan. The news that British Muslim youth from cities and towns such as Luton and Birmingham were 'prepared' to fight British forces gave rise to the notion of a threat from within and was read in conjunction with the polls and well-publicised demonstrations organised by anti-War protesters and Muslims to create an impression that the loyalty credentials of these citizens would be called into question by the majority. Such popular perceptions are underscored by media exploitation of fictional/factional storylines about Muslims sitting in Mosques and plotting suicide bombs not prayers. In reality those enraptured by the extremists of al-Qaeda and *al-Muhajiroun* are small in number. The danger is that the beliefs of a few Muslims being represented as indicative of the entire Muslim community temporarily passed. The diversity of Muslim opinion, however, tends to remain lost and the diversity of Muslim identity ignored by the majority of non-Muslims in the West. The nuances of broadsheet opinion pieces and analysis are lost on the majority who either read tabloid presses or nothing at all. The complexities of holding many identities but one nationality failed to emerge from the picture. Relations between Muslims and the West are perceived as deteriorating.[74] Identity itself is not fixed and immutable but subject to all sorts of pressures and turns. Identity is not something that is one-dimensional but instead can represent the vagaries of the modern soul and the environment it is located in. Yet, as Maalouf reminds us, 'The fact is, it's difficult to say where legitimate affirmation of identity ends and encroachment on the rights of others begins. Did I not say that the word identity was a "false friend"? It starts by reflecting a perfectly permissible aspiration, and then before we know where we are it has become an instrument of war.'[75] The question here is: Whose identity is threatened?

There is a perception that the threat from Muslim violence is pervasive and both a source of fear within and from outside modern western secular societies. It also betokens a fear of faith revived against the modern secular order. It represents a picture of immense magnitude for policy-makers, security experts and specialists if they are to generate policies that thwart the threat and prevent its manifestation from undermining national and global security. Many of the difficulties in meeting this threat arise from a disharmony of actors, views, perspectives and an ever-present clash with the associated principles of rights and values that are supposed to define and shape such modern entities and mark them out as models for others to emulate. The generation of a unified vision of what the threat is or threats are, who represents the threats and which threats actually undermine national security to the extent that it is worth sacrificing hard-won and cherished rights for has proved, on the one hand, easier to determine so long as the Muslim moniker appears in the equation. On the other hand, by presenting the threat in such general and major proportions it has exposed inconsistencies, promoted unnecessary tensions and encouraged the empowerment of state agencies that undermine the general sense of freedom, which citizens of such societies expect to enjoy.

It is important to remember that the generation of such debates creates new borders and barriers, which are fixed within modern multi-cultural societies across the globe. They cannot be geographically fixed and have implications for the generation of debates about culture, norms and values and the secular project in the post-modern age. Islam is in the West and this is not a new phenomenon, the West is in Islam and each must be understood as diverse, divergent, deeply penetrating and important. Islam tends to be essentialised and the distinctions that in practice are evident in real politick are often ignored. There are transatlantic differences in these relationships as they are expressed as part of the discourse of modern nation states and differences within and between regions like Europe or North America or Australia. The establishment of a notion of a Muslim threat within France, for example, has manifested itself in a variety of spheres, some of which are different from the way in which the threat is perceived in Italy, Germany or Ireland. In some of these states the discourse over multi-culturalism and religion in secular societies has emerged as distinct, reflecting the concerns of old states re-organising themselves and coming to terms with their own colonial pasts. These pasts include intrusion and interference in Muslim domains, as well as the economic determinism associated with developing economies and the demand for migrant labour. These relationships with multi-cultural migrant communities forged out of the colonial relationships of earlier and darker eras are not necessarily recognised nor reconciled in the right-wing intellectualism that has emerged to dominate certain policy-making agendas and nor do they adequately reflect on the difficulties inherent in essentialising specific cultures in multi-cultural societies but not others.

In the post 11 September environment, there have been serious and sustained attacks on Islam and the West and in many cases the dissonance of competing hate claims has dominated news agendas and reflected on the images by which communities are understood and labelled by ordinary people. How similar the hate claims are – the same reductive characterisations and failure to reflect on an emerging world order in which empires are unsustainable and borders rendered increasingly meaningless. Yet the discourse that dominates can be criticised for rigidity. In this context, can the threat only be understood and exterminated through the prism of militaristic jingoism shaped by chauvinistic agendas by men in uniform and the fatigues of insurgents and martyr seekers? Certainly there is evidence of an asymmetry of influence in important policy-making circles in many Western states. The prominence given to those who proffer advice while wearing the uniform of the state's armed forces or sitting in the chair of the defence contractors' board gives definition and form to the asymmetry. As such this underscores the dominance of the realist doctrine of international politics in which the Hobbesian state of war is the philosophical mantle and armour of states that appear to fall under the target-sights of the so-called martyr seekers.

If the realists dominate the discourse and analysis of the threat and how to meet it, then it does have consequences for any society founded on principles and claims to liberal, plural, democratic credentials. As opinion polls consistently reflect, while world opinion may be turning against America and other Western states, the principles that define those states are still accepted and admired, even in Muslim domains. As a Pew poll summary revealed,

> While the ... poll paints a mostly negative picture of the image of America, its people and policies, the ... survey shows wide support for the fundamental economic and political values that the U.S. has long promoted. Globalisation, the free market model and democratic ideals are accepted in all corners of the world. Most notably, the 44-nation survey found strong democratic aspirations in most of the Muslim publics surveyed.[76]

Muslim perceptions and opinions have to enter the equation and be exploited and changed if terrorism of the Islamist variety is to be successfully undermined and the relationship between Islamic communities and Western communities improved. As Robinson highlights, 'If we act so as to alienate, or sustain the existing alienation of, that public opinion, we might just begin to have a real clash of civilization.'[77] In the long term it is necessary to seek repair and reinforce existing relationships while acknowledging that they are forever tainted by the legacy of the past. The duty lies with all.

3
Islam and Violence

No arts, no letters, no society and which is worst of all, continual fear and danger of violent death; and the life of man, solitary, poor, nasty, brutish and short

Thomas Hobbes, Leviathan pt I, ch. 13

Introduction

There are a series of deep issues associated with Islam and the debate about force and violence. As such the debates set out in this chapter will focus on power and authority as they are understood from a theological viewpoint. Schism in attitude will also be reflected along doctrinal lines. Emphasis on dynamic interpretation rather than the commonly portrayed 'immutable' givens that are held as fundamental tenets of the faith will be evident throughout this analysis. Current orthodoxies as they relate to war, terrorism, foreign policy and international relations are found wanting in respect of the debate as it relates to Islam. Forms of force and violence will come under scrutiny. By this I mean that issues such as the sanction or condemnation of force or violence against distinct groups of actors by other actors, such as between the sexes and between adults and children, those of the community and those outside, those accused of transgression and subject to *shari' a* justice will be delineated. Public and private violence that may well also focus on the taboos of this particular dynamic of power within the faith will also be debated in a variety of contexts to test the saliency of either doctrinal difference or traditions of interpretation (*ijtihad*) and innovation (*taqlid*). Indeed it is through an examination of these issues as religious articles and the attempt to distinguish them from cultural patterns of power and domination through violence that I intend to further push at the boundaries of this particular debate.

The thread of human history

There have been periods of history in which episodes of terrible violence occurred but for which the word violence was never used ... Violence is shrouded in justifying myths that lend it moral legitimacy, and these myths for the most part kept people from recognizing the violence for what it was. The people who burned witches at the stake never for one moment thought of their act as violence; rather they thought of it as an act of divinely mandated righteousness. The same can be said of most of the violence we humans have ever committed.

Gil Bailie[1]

There are important distinctions that need to be drawn between Islam, its adherents and the ways in which the tenets of the faith are accepted, interpreted and made relevant to force, violence and the contest for power. There is obvious tension and dissonance in these understandings and perceptions of the faith system both within and without the Muslim body politic that are worth exploring. There are many that contend that the violence that is perpetrated by Muslims as a means of regulating the faith system, managing relations outside the system with other actors and finally as a way of ensuring the primacy of the faith system over other faiths and ideologies is more lethal. In this way the potential and power to de-stabilising their own societies as well as the international order is interpreted as the greatest threat since communism. As such this poses difficulties in terms of accommodating a faith system in which violence is not just something associated or represented by an enraged rabble manipulated by a few to use Islam as a vehicle for protest. Instead, violence is also interpreted as part of a culture of regulating Muslim governance in modern nation states. Thus violence is understood as something implicit to the faith that is reflected in other realms; including the cultural. Violence is like a thread that runs through the faith and it ties its adherents to particular types of behaviours.

A further issue is whether a debate about Islam and violence should start with the present and reflect on Muslim practice and discourse as it is currently known and represented? Or should one start with a literal exegesis of religious text starting with the Koran and hadith and working through the contributions of Muslim scholars to such debates throughout the centuries? In this case, one might need to take into consideration not only the primacy of the fundamental texts but the preference given to some religious opinion over others. If, however, one accepts the maxim that actions speak louder than words, then not only does the historical record need to be taken into consideration but the modern context of actions and consequences also need to be taken in as well. Indeed, debating the definition of violence has been notoriously difficult in a variety of cultures and traditions. Such debates themselves form a corpus of work that embraces the economic, philosophical, psychological and political as well as other factors.

Such discourse reflects the power-centric aspect of violence particularly as it relates to the contest within societies for political power. Thus there is value in acknowledging the place of, for example, Weberian definitions of the state in relation to the monopoly of legitimated physical coercion otherwise known and understood as violence. Indeed for Weber the value of the 'modern nation state' lay in the ability of its structures and institutions and those who run them to prevent the past disorder of societies where constant war and violence was present. Although Weber still recognises that 'force' remains within society he also admits that 'force is a means specific to the state ... the state is a relation of men dominating men, a relation supported by means of legitimate violence'.[2] Nevertheless, the value of such definitions in the context of reflecting them on Muslim polities must inevitably be constrained by issues of relativism and interpretation of past and present examples. Weber's contribution, for example, is altered and re-shaped in this debate if one acknowledges that there is significant evidence to suggest that his own engagement with and 'interpretation' of Islam and reflection of the faith system was subject to inconsistently applied 'methodological and philosophical principles' which can be said to have misrepresented aspects of this particular religious phenomenon.[3] One particular aspect of Weber's work, as it reflects on the 'warrior'-status of Islam shall be discussed later. If, however, we return to the force-violence debate there is ample opportunity to encounter discourse and interpretation in the Muslim realm, which also reflects on these issues. As such the ideas and discourse that unfolds and the contributions that are assessed demand a template to this debate that becomes all the more valuable.

Template for debate

This template is important because of the types of Muslims that are associated with violence and the labels employed to explain violent acts perpetrated by such people have enormous consequences for the ways in which Westerners in particular understand such acts and how they are related at home and abroad. Violence, as Hobbes and others have implied, is a norm that can be recognised as present in all cultures and societies. It is impossible to deny that violence, particularly in its political manifestation, is also signified in terms of power, authority and its associated structures. In modern societies violence is dominant in many cultures, whether this is acknowledged or not. Its presence shapes societies and leads to demands for responses from the state. Illegitimate violence, that which is not sanctioned by the state as force, demands a reaction as it is viewed as a challenge. Such violence is linked to the contest for power and is considered a subversive threat to the system. In such contexts violence – particularly its political variant – is part of an expression of opposition to the state and the exercise of state power. The emergence of political violence in such contexts is identified with a group of forces, or groups of force that seek to alter, fracture, break and sometime re-make the state or secede from it altogether. This is explicable in terms of understanding one dimension of the

Basque-Spanish conflict. Here the Basque minority of Northern Spain in its attempts or struggle to gain independence have utilised violence in campaigns against the state as well as Spanish citizens. Such campaigns symbolise their cause and undermine the power and authority of the state demonstrating its vulnerability in its duty to protect its citizens.

The challenge is clear and demonstrates the complexities of ethno-national rather than religious demands in the modern international order of nation states. In the Philippines, moreover, political violence against unarmed civilians has not been subject to the monopoly of one party over the other. From the early 1970s to 1980, Muslim separatists engaged in a major campaign of violence against a violent state. The consequences of this separatist campaign included thousands dead, over a million internally displaced persons and thousands of others becoming refugees. The Philippine Muslim minority of four million out of a total population of 14 million developed separatist tendencies in the 1960s against a backdrop of an emerging military state ruled from Manila by President Ferdinand Marcos. Following the imposition of martial law the separatist movement gained momentum representing periphery ethno-national demands for independence. This movement, as I have already stated, is labelled and identified as Muslim first, separatist second and although the nationalist dimensions of this campaign are identified, they are not the primary signifier for the state over which there is contest. External elements – such as Western state actors – often have interests in maintaining such a state and may consider those caught up in the violence as necessary collateral damage. These so-called Muslim separatists were motivated by a sense of injustice at inclusion in a post-colonial modern nation state system foisted upon them. This movement of disparate linguistic groups and ethno-national solidarity was motivated as much by the demand to exercise the right to self-determination as a Muslim philosophy of something commonly understood as jihad in the modern age. Separatism in this case was more a reflection of a failure at nation-building in modern states where multi-ethnic and religious minorities are encountered. The failure of the state to accommodate such demands has, in the case of the Philippines, led to the emergence of radical Islamist elements from the Muslim separatist constituency.[4] Such elements, including the smallest of these, Abu Sayyaf (Father of the Sword), have employed domestic terror tactics of bombing, assassination and high-profile kidnappings of foreign tourists in furtherance of their campaign. The emergence of such an element is further complicated by the internationalisation effect of politics in South Asian states such as the Philippines. Additionally transnational elements of radical Islam in the form of the Afghan veterans are also cited as helping to explain the emergence of such elements in the early 1990s.[5]

A similar pattern emerges in the Indonesian context where in October 2002 Islamist elements were blamed for a bomb attack in Bali, which killed over 200, mostly Australian, tourists. As initial speculation focussed on the chain of international terror attacks allegedly perpetrated by al-Qaeda, they paid relatively little attention to the domestic context in Indonesia itself. In the past Indonesia was considered to be a tolerant and plural society where the majority of Muslims played their part in the largely secular political context of governance. Although conservative Muslim elements (some with separatist demands) did exist, they were not considered representative of the mainstream Muslim population. Radical elements, motivated by some external Muslim elements, emerged in the period of instability that gripped the state and political system following the fall of Suharto, the removal of President Wahid and the eventual ascension of President Megawati. Non-state Islamist actors emerged to partially fill the vacuum that the disruption at the level of the central authorities caused. Muslims who had been involved in the Afghan theatre of conflict returned in the early 1990s and influenced and inspired the internal elements and contributed to the construction of a critique of the regime and in particular the perception of its close alliance to the United States of America. Religious resurgence whereby Muslims were seen to demonstrate observance of their faith in what was considered to be a new and conventional 'Arab' fashion did not translate, however, to a significant popular-based challenge to the power of the governing authorities.[6] Indonesia's Muslim leaders were compelled into the political arena by the collapse of the old order with smaller radical elements also emerging and posing a significant threat. Thus, while the prospect of Indonesia becoming an Islamic state is undermined by the weakness and lack of unity among pre-existing Muslim political parties, the emergence of radical elements undermines the important strategic relationships that the government's elite has forged with external actors. This was evident in the way in which the issue of the 11 September attacks in America by al-Qaeda were also expressed as part of the internal discourse of politics. Like other locales, the internal debate – particularly among Muslim elements – established anti-Americanism as a key factor in local responses particularly as it related to Afghanistan and American involvement in the Israeli–Palestinian conflict and the position of their own President in relation to the Bush administration. As the Indonesia cleric Hasyim Muzadi warned,

> Proving the evidence is important to distinguishing which is Islam and which is terrorism. After it can be proven, attack the terrorists. Without the evidence … (retaliation) cannot be justified. If it does happen, the case for an attack will fade and be replaced by a war between Islam and Christianity. If the U.S. attacks and innocent civilians become victims, a global catastrophe will happen. And even a country as big as the U.S. will not manage to cope.[7]

The issue was whether such developments and indications should have alerted the Indonesian authorities and other actors in the region to the threat that Islamic radical elements posed.

In the wake of 11 September 2001 and as part of its global war on terror the government of the United States of America despatched over 600 US troops to the southern Philippines in an operation described as opening a 'second front' on Muslim terrorism and against Abu Sayyaf in particular.[8] Any key strategic and political issue facing the counter-terrorism experts was always going to be related to determining a proportionate and effective response to the threat posed by Islam. The US government sought to contain and reduce a tiny radical fringe element of Muslim separatism with a response perceived locally as 'disproportionate.' This was seen, in no small measure, as further serving to radicalise local Muslim elements that identified with the separatist cause rather than its violent methods. This perspective is highlighted by Crenshaw who has argued that, 'the outcome of terrorism affects the future of terrorism. For example, terrorism can provoke government [even foreign ones] repression, which in turn stimulates further terrorism, which provokes more repression ... the effects of terrorism are rarely limited to the state in which terrorism occurs. Terrorism vividly demonstrates the global interdependence of nations'.[9] The cycle of violence is explicit in the Philippine context and also demonstrates the interrelatedness of issues as they pertain to political demands in failing democratic polities.

All this notwithstanding the function of violence as employed by Abu Sayyaf and the other movements such as the Moro National Liberation Front can be interpreted as fundamentally for the same cause as the Basque movement in Spain. Separatism as expressed by an ethno-national minority lies at the heart of the Basque and Moro cause and political violence – against the state, against agents of the state, against civilians and between rival factions – is common to both. Yet, there is sufficient evidence to suggest that in reality such political violence as perpetrated by the Philippine-based separatist movement is interpreted by others as Muslim in nature. Somehow by articulating a vision of terror that is implicit in Muslim identity the nature of violence, the manifestations of violence and the means by which such violence is met and combated are significantly altered.

Additionally other forms of violence involving the struggle for power and control, even in democratic societies, may be identified as 'representative of the community from which it emanates, so that it seems reasonable to make members of that community accountable for it', as experienced during deep inter-community conflicts such as that in South Africa under the Apartheid regime.[10] Yet such forms of violence have been used to characterise Islam as a violent faith system, founded on violence and maintained by a violent impulse at its centre. There is evidence of this argument, according to Turner, in Weber's accounts and scholarship on early Islam under the leadership of the Prophet Mohammed. In this important interpretation of Islam, for western consumption, the motif of violence as a means of force is central to the Weberian discourse. Indeed the symbols for this new faith, as established in seventh-century Arabia, are the warriors of Arabia. The warriors are represented by Weber as the dynamic for the new faith. Weber is quoted as arguing that the warrior vehicle of Islam as determined by its founder 'was oriented almost entirely to the goal of the psychological preparation of the faithful for battle in order to maintain a maximum number of warriors for the faith'.[11] In this context violence is institutionalised or naturalised through the religious belief, built into its original message and recognised and represented as a transmitter for the doctrine of new values that it stands for. Through this process the violence, as warfare, is altered and through an interpretation of legitimacy shaped into the function of force. This perspective on force is reinforced in some Islamic discourse. Iranian author Nasr argues that force is a necessary element within any Islamic-based order related to concepts of justice and equilibrium. 'All force', he states, 'used under the guidance of the divine Law with the aim of re-establishing an equilibrium that is destroyed is accepted and in fact necessary, for it means to carry out justice'.[12] Force becomes present and thus dimensions of violence are admitted into the equation of faith and power or the political. Like orthodox theories of contemporary terrorism the acknowledgment of violence as terrorism is addressed as well as fear within the Muslim domain. Terrorism threatens the quest for order and harmony, rules and codified norms that give Islam its character. This fear of internal violence, terror and *fitna* (disruption) is significant and orthodox discourse would view it as damaging to Muslim order. Revolution has been the provenance of radical Islamists such as Qutb or Mawdudi as a means of addressing injustice. This stands in contradistinction to the orthodox antipathy to Muslim revolt, violence and terrorism; for resistance is permitted but treachery baulked at;

> Assuredly God will defend those who believe; surely God loves not any ungrateful traitor. Leave is given to those who fight because they were wronged – surely God is able to help them – who were expelled from their habitations without right. (Sura of The Pilgrimage, verse 39)

Resistance must be perceived as just, particularly when generated against elements from within. In this respect the act of revolt is not endowed with sacred meaning. Many hadith and Muslim jurists outline arguments against dissension and terrorism within the Muslim domain. Revolt is also generally considered against the character of Islam. Legitimate grievance should be given due process. Government should command respect and legitimacy obviating the demand for revolt against injustice, terrorism and assassination. Conflict avoidance within the Muslim fold is advised as the prospect of disorder (*fitna*) is considered a greater threat to Muslim order. Dissent is considered un-Islamic in terms of malicious backbiting within the community: 'Woe unto every backbiter, slandered who has gathered riches and counted over them thinking his riches have made him immortal.' states the verse of the Backbiter in the Koran.[13] Yet the historical reality is that schism, dissent and disorder has occurred within Islam as disputes over justice, leadership and succession have emerged. On the other hand, it appears that orthodox scholars and jurists have looked to the early schisms within Islam as an important lesson learned and one that has exacted a very high price.

Violence within, enemy within

The emergence of the schismatic break between Sunni and *Shi'a* Islam following the death of the Prophet Mohammed and the succession battle between the Rightly Guided Caliphs and Ali is represented as indicative of the kind of inter-community violence which has characterised Islam from its earliest period to the present. The presence of conflict and violence within the abode of Islam represents a stain on Islam that, it could be contended, many Muslims deny and ignore. The schism between Sunni and *Shi'a* is often the taboo within Islam that is regarded as of historic rather than contemporary evidence that conflict and violence is present within Muslim domains and as such demands Muslim liability. In the present era, schism and conflict within Muslim domains has resulted in terrorism wrought by Islamist elements that have wrought a climate of fear in areas such as Pakistan, Algeria or Afghanistan. Muslim militants, Muslim governments and Muslim clerics have been responsible for the deaths of thousands of their own co-religionists (as well as of others) across Asia, Africa, the Middle East and beyond. Terrorism has come to affect dimensions of daily life across the Muslim domain. As Sardar opines, 'Saudi Arabia, Indonesia, Algeria, Bangladesh, Lebanon, Iran – there is hardly a Muslim country that is not plagued by terrorism. It goes without saying, then, that the bulk of victims of terrorism are also Muslims, 11 September notwithstanding.'[14]

Nevertheless, a historic impression has been left that the martyrdom of Hussein as a result of battle against those from within the Muslim fold 'alerts us to the tradition of conflict within Islam'. Additionally, Hussein's martyrdom is interpreted as symbolising the tradition or norm of martyrdom and thus, by extension again, violence. In this respect the Ashura commemorations of Hussain's martyrdom under the *Shi'a* banner are interpreted as having institutionalised violent death and self-sacrifice as emblems of the faith. Indeed, one Iranian author suggests that 'Shi'ite funeral ceremonies [symbolising the dead as a martyr and the tradition of 40 days mourning] were instrumental in mobilising Iranians against the Shah's regime.'[15] Mourning, a tradition associated with the martyrdom of Hussein, becomes understood as a vehicle for modern-day political mobilisations. In the case of Iran in 1978, such events are represented as the catalyst of a revolution that brought down the Shah and led to the establishment of a theocracy led by Ayatollah Khomeini. In Lebanon Ashura rituals are a highpoint in the calendar of *Shi'a* resistance and political movement Hizb Allah. The symbolic import of sacrifice, martyrdom and faith politics on the battlefields of Karbala in the seventh century are given added resonance in the remarks and speeches made by leaders of Islam in the twenty-first century. In March 2003, for example, the Ashura in Lebanon was marked by Hizb Allah organised gatherings in Beirut and Bint Jubail in the south of the country. Hizb Allah leader Nasrallah used the occasion to address the theme of foreign occupation on Muslim lands and the implications and obligations incumbent upon all Muslims in such circumstances. Nasrallah, addressing crowds of over a hundred thousands in the Hizb Allah stronghold of Harat Hreik in Beirut declared with regard to a US occupation in Iraq 'We tell them that they will not be met in this region with roses, flowers, rice and perfumes. They will be met with rifles, blood, arms, martyrdom and martyrdom operations.'[16]

Subsequently such interpretation are employed as further evidence that the template of Islam is one shaped by violence and behaviours associated with motifs of violence. Similarly, in the twenty-first century the Palestinian context is increasingly represented as an environment dominated or coloured by the 'Muslim' hue of violence exhibited by the suicide bombers. Muslim violence symbolised by the phenomenon of suicide bombs alters the way in which the nature of the Palestinian–Israeli conflict and its dynamic is understood and responded to. One casualty is the 'legitimacy' of the Palestinian cause, as recognised by the international community, in the face of Muslim inspired acts of violence that are understood as morally and ethically unacceptable behaviours. The leadership of Hamas and Islamic Jihad argue that they do have a legitimate right to meet Israeli force with Muslim force. They believe that their faith system allows them to engage in acts that they term as 'defensive' and a response to what they perceive as Israel's policy of targeting of civilian or unarmed Palestinians. As Slim highlights, the introduction of the civilian concept into the discussion of violence, particularly in the Palestinian–Israeli context is problematic. Slim declares that, 'the high profile of civilians in this conflict has arisen because the idea of "the civilian" is a deeply contested one in both Israeli and Palestinian society. Several groups on both sides of the conflict reject outright or find it so ambiguous in the context of two "militarised" societies as to be virtually meaningless'.[17] Such ambiguity or rejection is apparent in Islamist quarters in Palestinian society. Hamas leader Mahmoud Zahar when questioned on the issue of suicide operations declared,

If Israelis are killing Palestinian civilians then why we are not using the same means? An eye for an eye ... None of them are civilians ... they say they are a military society and in civil uniform. The second point is – that it is not about civilian or military ... what we say instead is: is it right to accept occupation as legal or illegal? If it is illegitimate then every means to end that occupation is legitimate ... it is justified. So don't waste your time in Europe discussing is it civilian or not ... This is a dirty war ... in what sense can we make these distinctions?[18]

Although making a political point, Zahar employs a lexicon that belies the religious interpretation given to the notion of humanity and immunity. His conclusions (along with counterparts on the Israeli side who view all Palestinians, Arabs and Muslims as enemies) belie a very real dilemma facing many Muslim communities in conflict across the globe.

Such an interpretation is also deployed as a theological weapon by Christians who seek to contrast the righteousness and peaceful character of their own faith system against the contrasting character that they ascribe to Islam. This is transparent in the fundamentalist bent of Gerry Falwell and Franklin Graham, among others, in the United States of America. As a theological weapon, antipathy and hostility to Islam leads to a representation of Islam that is fixated with its violent past and present. Such positions might not be quite so important were it not for the fact that that conservative Christian coalition in the United States of America has wielded important influence and pressure on contemporary politics and sees itself at the vanguard in protecting Israel from the ambitions of Palestinian statehood. In other words, the views and opinions expressed by Graham and Falwell cannot be dismissed in the same way that hostile antipathy and hatred exhibited by the Nation of Islam's Louis Farrakhan towards another faith system can be. These are not views from the margin but representative of mainstream conservative thinking with a demonstration effect easily discernible on the American political elite.[19]

Of course there is logic in a post-modern age to identifying the most evil manifestations of wrongdoing and terror to the irrational forces of religion with their ancient bloody rites and cadences. For in a rational age, it is argued that such terrible terror – as experienced by the citizens of the strongest state in the contemporary globe – can only be explicable through association with the subjective expression and adherence to faith and belief in a transcendental force. Enlightenment and post-Enlightenment thinking allows little room for faith as linked to politics. What better demonstration of the dangers inherent in the irrational attachment to faith – whether Jewish, Muslim or Christian – than to identify and catalogue the modern phenomenon of post-Cold War terror as religious terrorism. The application of the label, the divination of religious motivation and inspiration behind terrorism touches a very raw nerve in many societies but particularly those that are understood as secular. In facing an enemy that seeks to destroy the edifice of society built on a foundation of rational secular principles in which faith is admitted only in a strictly regulated and usually privatised fashion, the conventional methods of defence are perceived as being weakened. Is it thus a question of religious violence containing within its realm a 'ferocity' that undermines and weakens notions of security (state or individual) that were previously un-experienced?

I would contend that having witnessed and experienced a range of acts of violence, which others would commonly describe as religious or otherwise, it is almost impossible to draw such distinctions. When bombs destroy clubs, buses, cafes and pubs, people are killed in sectarian tit-for-tat campaigns, targeted assassinations, mortar fire, tank rounds and bulldozers, violence and conflict are experienced in the same way. Why such violence is distinguished as religious or not is a distinction that is often hard to understand. The template for the debate then, needs to be very carefully constructed and the context of discourse must be acknowledged. The discussion above demonstrates that not all political violence is terrorism and not all violence carried out by those who are labelled as 'religious' is terrorism. Violence, however, has its place in relation to faith even if that faith makes claim to peace as its ultimate goal. The violent expressions of faith as politics within modern Hindu nationalist ideology, for example, disturbs the pattern of peaceful equilibrium traditionally associated with such a faith. The image of Hindu fundamentalist violence in India against the Muslim population jars uneasily with the previously stronger image or symbolic import of Mahatma Gandhi with his message of non-violence and civil disobedience as the principle behind political challenge. Indeed Christianity has its Martin Luther King and Hinduism its Gandhi; the perpetuation of these faith systems as non-violent has been celebrated in advancing the human cause as its relates to a rights-based discourse of universalistic proportions throughout the twentieth century.

With Islam the link between faith and peace is altered. Apparently Islam has no Martin Luther King or Gandhi only its nemesis in the form of Usama Bin Laden. In Western interpretations of Islam its bloody past and present are not usually filled with examples of Islam's peaceful character. Indeed the seismic challenges and shifts of the past few decades in the Middle East and Asia as well as parts of Africa and other locales led by Islamist organisations and movements, determined to challenge and alter systems of governance not of their own making, have further imprinted the dual nature of Islam and violence on the common consciousness of the West. This explains why a man who lives in a society fractured by decades of violence, terrorism and conflict, like Northern Ireland, still thinks of Islam as a more bloody and violent force. Terrorism becomes increasingly aligned with Islam its chief characteristic in the consciousness of many in the Western milieu.

Juergensmeyer defines terrorism by starting with the Latin origin of the word 'to cause to tremble' and then by explaining that it is not the motive but the interpretation of the act that makes and defines it as terrorism. He speaks of 'we' the witnesses and 'our' public agents as those who 'affix the label on acts of violence that makes them terrorism',[20] yet he also acknowledges the difficulties inherent in applying the label to any faith system per se or to all its adherents. Indeed the need for nuance and subtlety is overwhelming if the citizens of the globe are to feel truly protected. In the wake of 11 September 2001, however, and the decision to spearhead a war on terrorism in which a significant number of adherents to the Islamic faith system believe that they are being singled out, it would appear to be even more difficult to engage in such a task. If the template applied to the Muslim faith and its adherents is one-dimensional with a rigid baseline then it is inevitable that all violence that takes place within this dimension will be understood as terrorism. Such terrorism is not just implicit, as many authors argue; it is in other religions with their dark attachments to norms of pain, violence and suffering, but in the case of Islam is explicit. It is also represented as an eternal (both ancient and modern) unchanging feature of the Muslim dimension.

More than one dimension

The point worth highlighting here is there is a need for more than one template and to establish some points of comparison and reference that put violence as a multi-faceted factor or experience in the Muslim dimension. In this way the relationship between power and violence is acknowledged and can be used as a means by which to explain what appears to be the current explosion of that which is referred to as Muslim violence and terrorism in the current era; for it should be acknowledged that throughout the 1990s terror analysts increasingly identified the phenomenon of religious violence in the explosions of intrastate low intensity ethno-national conflicts that gripped major regions across the globe. By the mid 1990s, the Clinton administration in the United States of America, for example, was already identifying terrorism, with a particular religious dimension, as the most pressing issue facing the US government. President Clinton declared in his address to the United Nations in November 1995 that such acts of violence were part of an 'a world-wide phenomenon. No one is immune – certainly not Israel, but neither is Egypt or Japan; France, Britain, or Germany; Turkey, Saudi Arabia, Argentina, or Algeria. And, unfortunately, neither is America, where terrorists have struck from lower Manhattan to Oklahoma City'.[21] The religious impulses behind such new forms of terrorism were acknowledged and linked to the revival of faith as fundamentalism that had been ascribed to the increasingly public profile given to religious movements that grabbed the headlines of global media. As such the phenomenon was often presented as one-dimensional and linked to the fundamentalist discourse of the postmodern era. Oftentimes such analyses were divorced from or failed to pay enough attention to the context in which such acts of violence were perpetrated and, just as importantly, against whom. Context in terms of the socio-economic, political and historical milieu in which modern fundamentalist movements had arisen should have generated multi-faceted insight into the complex and mostly political issues and contests for power that animated these groups in opposition to others who controlled the state.

Power and authority

Normative discourse on violence acknowledges and centres on the key function of power and its use and abuse in a variety of substantive to insignificant encounters or relationships. Power, and authority – with its function legitimated through divine or popular sovereignty – lies at the heart of governance as it is experienced in any society past or present. Violence as a concept in this context is subject to a rainbow rather than a monochrome definition. Violence can be construed to be evident not only in societies rendered unstable by internal and external threats and conflict but even in relatively stable societies where such violence is perceived as regulated by the state and transformed through the coercive functions of force. Priestland, writing in the mid-1970s reflected that in its distilled form violence may be defined when 'physical power is deliberately employed with the ultimate sanction of physical pain and little choice but to surrender or physical resistance'.[22] Such a definition of violence is recognised within many Sura of the Koran. Violence is regarded as something to be avoided and its physical dimension is acknowledged: 'If two parties of the believers fight, put things right between them; then, if one is insolent against the other, fight the insolent one till it reverts to God's commandment. If it reverts, set things right between them equitably, and are just. Surely God loves the just.'[23] Yet like the discourse evident in current western philosophy the vexing rainbow dimensions of violence are also acknowledged in Islam, and the temptation to violence under the rubric of conflict is acknowledged. In an invocation to 'recite thou to them the story of the two sons of Adam truthfully', the futility of violence is set out for the Muslim believer. 'Yet if thou stretchest out thy hand against me, to slay me, I will not stretch out my hand against thee, to slay thee; I fear God, the Lord of all Being.' And when Cain committed the act of violence against his brother, the Sura maintains, 'and he slew him', it is acknowledged that he 'became one of the losers ... and he became one of the remorseful'.[24] The negative power of violence is explicitly acknowledged and its consequences acknowledged in a way that echoes the moral debates about violence within historic and contemporary cultures.

More importantly to the discourse, however, is that the force-violence dilemma or conundrum is also acknowledged. If, as McFarlane reminds us, 'violence is the capacity to impose or the act of imposing one's will upon another where the imposition is held to be illegitimate,' and force the same but 'held to be legitimate,' then the same paradox is reflected in Muslim discourse and theology.[25] This is reflected by Nasr who recognises a distinction between violence and force, in which force is acknowledged as within the Muslim realm and subject to a parallel function with the Muslim concept of justice (*al-adl*). Force as described and interpreted in this context is something that is utilised as a means of control against the prospect or actuality of internal disorder (*fitna*) in society, '[a]ll force used under the guidance of the divine Law (*Shari'a*) with the aim of re-establishing an equilibrium that is destroyed is accepted and in fact necessary, for it means to carry out and establish justice.'[26] This concept of force is thus linked to justice and injustice. If injustice is perpetrated or found there is a tradition within the faith system that obliges believers to defend and struggle (jihad) on behalf of those who are oppressed, wherever they may be. In this context, jihad is a tool of social justice and liberation and can be achieved through a variety of means. This perspective is relevant when reflecting on the role of militant organisations such as Hizb Allah in relation to the Israeli occupation of Lebanon and other Muslim/Arab territories. As the Deputy Secretary-General of the organisation Hajj Naim Qassem remarked in 2000, 'For jihad there is only one concept ... to strive with the soul to achieve submission to God. This directly affects everything we do. In order for justice to prevail we must face injustice, unjust occupation, even if it is with arms and the death of the victim. When we fought Israel we were fighting injustice and aggression'.[27] A very important linkage, therefore, emerges between the concept of justice and, if necessary, the employment of force, in modern Muslim doctrines. Such thinking is not only confined to a *Shi'a* interpretation with its acknowledged traditions of resistance, but in *Sunni* schools of thought as well. As Hashmi contends, 'justice may be seen without oversimplification to be the core value of Islamic ethics, for it runs like a binding thread throughout the Koran and the Prophetic traditions.'[28] Force then is interpreted as a tool for restoring peace and order under the divinely revealed Islamic framework. Force is not related to compulsion for other reasons. Force can be defined as but one expression of a jihad for justice, which Schliefer believes is 'the instrument of sacralisation of the social-political order in Islam.'[29] For example, force is not to be employed in the name of the religion for the sake of the religion. It is declared that, 'No compulsion is there in religion' and those who come to the religion must do so freely and 'not because circumstance or others compel them to it in an involuntary fashion'.[30] Power is related to authority as a means of justice and not tyranny.

The power of violence though is acknowledged. Violence against unjust rule and governance is admitted when other non-violent means fail. Indeed political violence and its justification in the context of injustice and cruelty as experienced by the greater number and as a means of ending repression is prevalent in modern Muslim discourse particularly at the radical revivalist end of the spectrum.[31] In this locale repression is perceived, as expressed for example in Qutb's writings, as man-made and in deliberate ignorance of God's authority over humankind. Force is employed to remove obstacles in the relationship between Islam and the individual. Qutb is direct about the function of jihad in this context, 'It was a movement to wipe out tyranny and to introduce true freedom to mankind,' he asserts. Indeed he advocates a proactive agenda and outlines a radical critique of the traditional notion of jihad as the defensive doctrine.[32] Similarly Abdullah Azzam embraces the Qutbian perspective regarding the employment of force as a means of advancing Muslim rule in lands that are governed and ruled by 'the enemies of Islam'.[33] Palestinian Abdullah Azzam was a veteran and vanguard of the jihad movement in Afghanistan. He became a prominent figure among the Arab Afghans and is credited with influencing Usama Bin Laden. Azzam advocated jihad in the context of Afghanistan with a particular emphasis drawn on his own experiences of the mujahideen struggle against the Soviet occupation of the country. As Azzam declared, 'we believe that Jihad in the present situation in Afghanistan is individually obligatory (*fard ayn*), with one's self and wealth as has been confirmed by the jurists of the four schools of Islamic jurisprudence, without any exception'.[34] Azzam is explicit that by jihad he means combat against the enemy. What is notable in Azzam's most significant publications is that there is no attempt to draw the debate about jihad to include a critique against pre-existing Muslim ruled regimes. He does not address the theme of *jahilliya* and in this respect in can be argued that Azzam's approach, as a result of this omission, is about the obligation of jihad as a reactive force in contexts where Muslim territories are subject to foreign or *kufr* rule and domination. As he argued, 'if the *Kufr* infringe upon a hand span of Muslim land, jihad becomes *fard ayn* for its people and for those near by'.[35] In this respect the perpetrators of the 11 September 2001 atrocity were the living embodiment of the perspective on jihad as a means of violence advocated by thinkers and Islamists like Azzam. Azzam, as a scholar of Ibn Taymmiyah, emphasised the obligation on Muslims to evict foreign 'occupiers' from Muslim lands and the ultimate goal that centred on the re-establishment of the caliphate. Azzam and Bin Laden practised what they believed through active involvement in the Afghan conflict. They recruited Arabs to the Afghan cause by promoting jihad by means of combat as the sole response to Soviet occupation. Azzam, who had been educated in Egypt, was receptive to the radical Qutbian discourse that proliferated in the literatures and sermons circulating the Muslim world at the time. Other radical Egyptian figures, such as Ayman Zahrawi, would also become prominent in the body of men that later surrounded Bin Laden. Azzam, killed in a car bomb attack in 1989, remains a significant influence on the ways in which jihad is conceptualised as a form of force and violence as it relates to radical discourse in this realm. Yet al-Qaeda took the 'frontline' to western states as well as western targets in Muslim and non-Muslim domains. They brought their dispute to the doorstep of the modern hyper power, the United States of America as a direct challenge to power and authority in the contemporary globe.

Within the amorphous coalition that was established by Bin Laden in the wake of Azzam's death and known as al-Qaeda (The Base) the legacy of Azzam is discernible. The vanguardist nature of al-Qaeda plus its Islamic infrastructure – including a consultative council head by Bin Laden – attests to the further manifestation of a jihadist organisation that was anti-Western as well as posing a major threat to Islamic-inspired and ruled regimes in Muslim domains that were identified as heretical or apostate. Theological justification for the employment of violence through the mechanism of jihad was apparent in Azzam's discourse with support from elements of the clerical establishment and the issuing of fatwas in this area.[36]

The al-Qaeda leadership has employed the fatwa as a means of justifying their calls and creating a sense or perception of incumbency on all Muslims (*umma*) rather than individual supporters or followers of Bin Laden. Although in principle a fatwa is an Islamic decree or judgement on a topic issued by the legal authority in practice, the publicity attached to certain fatwa issued in the contemporary era as they related to individuals such as Salman Rushdie or non-Muslim states; has established a sense of authority and importance in alternative fatwa-issuing Muslims.[37] This was evident in the fatwa issued by Bin Laden in 1996 entitled *'Declaration of War against the Americans Occupying the Land of the Two Holy Places'*.[38] In this fatwa the American presence in the Gulf state of Saudi Arabia is perceived as un-Islamic,

> Ignoring the divine *Shari'a* law; depriving people of their legitimate rights; allowing the American[s] to occupy the land of the two Holy Places; imprisonment, unjustly, of the sincere scholars. The honourable Ulema and scholars as well as merchants, economists and eminent people of the country were all alerted by this disastrous situation.

The obligation of jihad is considered – after belief – the most important obligation facing Muslims, 'If there [is] more than one duty to be carried out, then the most important one should receive priority. Clearly after Belief (Imaan) there is no more important duty than pushing the American enemy out of the holy land.'

In this visioning of jihad, violence is the mechanism for liberation. Violence becomes manifest and stays at the heart of the enterprise not necessarily because of its representative value in the name of Islam. Yet how binding is such a fatwa on the Muslim community? To what extent do such views reflect common consensus among Muslim scholars in the modern age? Here the debate within the Muslim realm rages; for there is no evidence of universal agreement on the binding nature of fatwa such as those issued by the leadership of al-Qaeda or other radical Islamist organisations such as the Jihad movement or Abu Sayyif. Indeed it is the un-representative schismatic or cultic nature of Bin Laden's enterprise that goes further in explaining the dominant presence of violence and terrorism legitimated as 'jihad'. Violence is a common feature of religious cults and in this respect Islam cannot be considered as exclusive. In fact, cults represent a significant challenge to mainstreaming of faith in the modern age. Their theological bent is rooted in radical departures and challenges to the prevailing religious orthodoxy and its associated establishment. From this perspective al-Qaeda has more to do with David Koresh than the religious establishment of many *ulema*. The theological impulse at the root of Bin Laden's advocacy of jihad does represent a new way of interpreting Islam that is unorthodox. The Afghan Arabs did exhibit cultic characteristics that went some way, I would argue, in terms of defining it as a new religious movement within the Islamic spectrum. Within orthodox Islam, cults and schisms have always been regarded with the deepest suspicion and scepticism. The historic memory of past schisms in Islam sustains the fear of further internal division and dispute. More importantly, the way in which such cultic associations have tapped into mainstream popular antipathies against the established order has heightened the threat presented by such groups to political elites established and legitimated by orthodox Islam and its leaders. Here we can see a direct relevance to the al-Saud ruled and *Wahabbi* legitimated regime that has dominated modern Saudi Arabia and they way in which it has been seriously undermined by the popular adherence to the critique at the heart of Bin Laden's attack on this regime. This critique privileges 'primitive' anti-Americanism and is reflected in polls conducted in Saudi on attitudes towards the United States of America.[39]

Violence and struggle

> The naked truth of decolonization evokes for us the searing bullets and bloodstained knives which emanate from it. For if the last shall be first, this will only come to pass after a murderous and decisive struggle between the two protagonists.[40]

Norms, as they have been developed through the tradition of interpretation, are challenged here by the advocacy of a radical philosophy that mirrors much of western radical notions of violence. In this respect it would not be too far fetched to suggest that Qutb, Azzam and Bin Laden have much in common with Franz Fanon and Jean-Paul Sartre as their intellectual counterparts elsewhere in the Muslim world. For they, like them, are drawn to the conceptualising of violence and advocacy in practice for the purposes of regime overthrow and revolution. 'Violence', Fanon declared in his influential text, *The Wretched Earth*, 'is a cleansing force. It frees the native from his inferiority complex and from his despair and inaction; it makes him fearless and restores his self-respect'. Sartre, in the preface to the posthumously published book, pointed the finger of blame at the West, 'To shoot down a

European is to kill two birds with one stone, to destroy an oppressor and the man he oppresses at the same time.'[41] In addressing race and decolonisation through the vehicle of absolute violence, Fanon stresses his Manichean understanding of the world – a perspective that is obvious and pertinent to the radical foundation motivating Bin Laden and his supporters. This Manichean perspective of the world, although dualist but religiously rather than Marxist in foundation, is more than apparent in Bin Laden's epistles and fatwa. He preaches a Muslim-based Fanonist perspective of the world for a new generation.

The discourse on power here is not difficult to either define or discern. The authority of God and his power is acknowledged as the primary signifier around which all other relations orbit. In this respect the authority and regulation of violence is also present. Violence is acknowledged as a phenomenon that afflicts society and is abhorred for the chaos that it threatens to bring with it. The state is obliged to eliminate such violence, particularly if it threatens the society of believers and the laws that govern them (*Shari'a*). The Islamic state governs according to the consensus of the believers in fulfilling their duty and respect of God's power and authority. The state is charged with governing fairly, justly and according to the divinely inspired *Shari'a*. Transgression is dealt with according to the full authority of the state. In the modern era this conceptualising of state authority has had limited function. Many modern nation states exist across the globe that contain Muslim majority populations. Many such states are bound and legislated for, through some form of *Shari'a* but not in a consistent or uniform pattern. In some Muslim polities only certain activities in society are regulated by Islamic law and in others nearly all or all are regulated in this fashion. States with a claim to authority through theocratic convention are to be found in polities such as Pakistan, Saudi Arabia, Iran and the Muslim northern-states of Nigeria. The regulation of force and the management of violence between the state and society in such contexts are varied.

Yet a correlation may be drawn from the radical-fundamentalist-moderate spectrum in assessing the tensions that occur and their foundation in such states. Additionally, it can be contended that in such modern states the policy of central authorities in pursuit of a monopoly of power, force, coercion and authority is perceived by Islamists as indicating an absence of opportunity for contestation from below. In the absence of dialogue, access to power and the decision-makers, many Islamist thinkers have contended that the state resorts to force or violence as a primary means of containing the citizenry. It is questionable in these contexts, therefore, to claim to rule with the authority of God yet suppress discontent that focuses on the interpreted deviation from that which is understood as a truly Islamic polity and the functions of the state. The Muslim response to this state of affairs has been mixed. For as Ghannoushi remarks, 'There is no consensus among Muslim today on the most appropriate methodologies of change. And the issue is not confined to differences about the degree of legitimacy or the propriety of using force as a means of change, or to determining the legitimacy of existing Islamic states.'[42] What remains immutable, however, is the degree of discontent in evidence in a variety of Muslim domains as a response to the appropriation of power by state elites who are perceived as undermining Islam from within while it is also undermined from without.

Seedbed of discontent

The revelation in the wake of the 11 September attacks in America that the al-Qaeda bombers were well-educated and well-off young men, the majority of whom originated not from the teeming refugee camps or urban shanties of the Arab world, but the relatively wealthy states of the Gulf, surprised many observers in the West. In the initial minutes and hours of the events that unfolded that day, media pundits the world over were encouraged to initially focus on the discontented and dispossessed Palestinian radical elements and not the motives that lay behind the blind ambition for martyrdom contained in the hearts of a corps of young Arab men inspired by a radical leader holed up in Afghanistan. Even as the link to Usama Bin Laden was drawn and revealed and the death toll and dust clouds rose in Manhattan, the linkage between a dispute over Muslim authority and power in Saudi Arabia and the consequences of western involvement in such lay at the heart of those who directed and order the suicidal mission that day. Bin Laden's action in relation to his political ambitions simply confounded the West. In this respect, US counter-terrorism official Paul Bremer pointed out there was little point in looking for the kind of root causes that had been identified in the past, a means of explaining political violence carried out by other groups Islamist or otherwise.

> But I would say in the case of people like bin Laden, there's nothing we can do politically to satisfy him. There's no point in addressing the so-called root causes of bin Laden's despair with us. We are the root cause of his terrorism. He doesn't like America. He doesn't like our society. He doesn't like what we stand for. He doesn't like our values. And short of the United States going out of existence, there's no way to deal with the root cause of his terrorism.[43]

The official making these remarks made them some three years before the al-Qaeda attacks of 11 September 2001. So even if, as far as Bin Laden and his supporters were concerned, misrule, authoritarianism, corruption and injustice were the ill-disguised features of the Kingdom established by the al-Saud family in 1925 in alliance with the fundamentalist tendency of *Wahabbism*, for experts like Bremer this is not the point. There is saliency to the point, however, that it is some of the gulf states of the Middle East where the radical

Islamist phenomenon in the twenty-first century has potency. Such forces were waxing not waning throughout the 1990s. While in Egypt and Algeria and other locales in the Levant the full thrust of the radical Islamist movements had reached their apex in the mid to late 1990s, the same could not be said for a modern Muslim state like Saudi Arabia. In Saudi Arabia radical *salafiyya* support has emerged in an environment where plural politics and opportunities for formal participation fail to feature in the political system. The state in Saudi Arabia is Islamic, yet Fandy asserts that 'interaction between the state and Islam [in Saudi Arabia] brought about certain adjustments to Islam rather than the other way around ... Islam was adjusted to support the state'.[44] In this context, the *ulema* functions to support the state and its maintenance under a distinct form of family rule based also around the principle of *Wahabbi* Islamism. Fandy argues then that 'the function of the *ulema* is thus to establish the hegemony of the ruling Amir and his family'.[45] Radical *salafiyya* support in the country comes in the wake of sustained and increasingly prolonged tensions between the Saudi regime and elements of its clerical establishment. In suppressing even those clerical voices considered to be moderate yet critical of the political or social agenda of the state, a vacuum emerged in which more radical personalities dominated. The focus over the late decades of the twentieth century for discontent against the Saudi regime was symbolised among many Saudis and particularly those drawn to Islamist discourse by the continuing presence of foreign troops in the Kingdom. The presence of American troops, although at the invitation of the leaders of the state, to protect its sovereignty following Iraq's invasion of Kuwait and sabre rattling on the border with Saudi Arabia had turned into a prolonged presence of over a decade. In this respect, Bin Laden before he was compelled to exit the Kingdom and subsequently stripped of citizenship struck a chord of complaint in the hearts of many. Indeed his famous 'Declaration of War against the Americans occupying the land of the two holy places' may be interpreted as significant in terms of its rebuff of the state elite in Saudi Arabia that is criticised for governing the country in an unjust manner and creating the circumstances in which violence enters the power equation; 'Why is it the regime closed all peaceful routes and pushed people toward armed actions?!! Which is the only choice left for them to implement righteousness and justice', Bin Laden opines.[46] The Islamic credentials of the Saudi state, as it attempts to co-exist in a modern secularised global order, are subjected to thorough criticism in Bin Laden's statement. The power and authority of the regime is actively contested, 'Through its course of actions the regime has torn off its legitimacy: suspension of the *Shari'a* law and exchanging it with man-made civil law ... the inability of the regime to protect the country', are identified as contributing to a crisis of legitimacy that, it is argued, is further exacerbated by the 'crusader forces [who] became the main cause of our disastrous condition'.[47] The experience of frustration and perception of injustice, while living in one of the richest states in the world, proved fertile ground for the extension of ideas of contestation and action which later marked out Bin Laden's followers and his supporters.[48] In the face of deepening discontent and an ever-growing questioning of sacred, legitimate and just authority of and by the religious-establishment that had hitherto been wedded to the al-Saud family, the focus of Bin-Laden's apparently outlandish appeal began to make sense. In response to perceived unresponsiveness and intransigence by the ruling elite to re-think the consequences of the Muslim-inspired claim to legitimacy when a foreign presence was maintained in territory considered the holiest in Islam Bin Laden's criticism of the regime gained currency among Saudi and other Muslims who embraced a discourse on Muslim power and authority that was not mired in a reality shaped by allegations of corruption, disparity and injustice. It may also be argued that for some, if not many, who have contributed to this particular discourse on Muslim power and authority in the modern age, reform or revolution of existing state structures, including those that profess Islamic credentials, are criticised as a fiction or unjust representation of Muslim rule. I would contend that elements of such discourse reflect a possible acculturated visioning of Islam as power and authority which is cognisant of the passing force of the monolithic and instead recognises the necessity in the modern age for more plural constructions of power, authority and rule in the name of the community (*umma*). The difficulty with the modern discourse, so far, lies in the inadequate formula for conversion into practice. In reality there have been very few opportunities to embark on new eras of Islamic rule in the wake of the total decline of the old regime, and in the majority of cases reform or change from within has created new dilemmas and problems for the motivated minority.

State force or violence?

If we return to the state as the locus of power and authority enjoying the monopoly on force but not violence, it is not difficult to discover that across a variety of Muslim domains in the modern age the line between force and violence is regularly transgressed. It is transgressed even by those states that claim to rule in the name of Islam. The consequences of such transgressions are the kinds of disorder that are so abhorred in orthodox Muslim discourse. The state becomes the source of violence and the object of it at the same time. Those who claim to establish *dar al-Islam* (the abode of Islam) in the midst and as opposed to *dar al-harb* (the abode of war), where divinely inspired and interpreted conceptions of justice, peace, power and authority touch every member of the community (even those of other faiths under Muslim rule), are exposed through their actions in persecuting, repressing and denying rights to their citizens and contributing to state of fear that prevails in so many of these polities. In such states violence has the potential to be politicised and Islamicised by both state and non-state actors. The resort to force and violence establishes new pressures on the state and society. State and society in this context must be seen as tied to each other, as Ibn Khaldun remarks, 'a state is inconceivable without a society, while a society without a state is well nigh impossible, owing to the aggressive propensities of men, which require restraint ... The two being inseparable, any disturbance in either of them will cause disturbance in the other'.[49] In such a circumstance terrorism becomes a feature of such contexts. In this respect, Sardar comments,

> Terrorism is a Muslim problem for some very good reasons. To begin with, most of the terrorist incidents actually occur within the Muslim world. In Pakistan, for example, terrorist violence is endemic. Marauding groups of fanatics ... have spread terror throughout the country ...[50]

The notion that Muslims are victims of terrorism and state terror is not, however, widely debated. Yet the old dichotomy of blame emerges untouched. Opponents of the state are terrorists and the state has to resort to force to protect itself. Yet, when violence appears to underscore the relationship between state and society as a form of two-way traffic, the prognosis is poor. The list of victims continues to grow so long as the address to legitimate grievance remains neglected by the power-holders in society. In this context the role of faith – as a means of legitimating the state – calls into question the delicate symbiosis that Ibn Khaldun refers to as a prerequisite for Muslim state and society.

In Islam, like so many other faith system and ideologies, authority and power is centrally located in the spiritual not the temporal realm. Ultimate authority is divine and lay with God. In the first instance this can be read and understood as the essence of Islam on the issue of power and authority. God is omnipotent humankind is not. Islam, in the modern context, however, reflects and refracts and is open to many interpretations on the issue of power and authority. Conceptually and empirically that which is described and recognised as part of a Muslim realm reveals an array of interpreted and legitimated approaches to the subject matter. Interpretations and empirical practice as they relate to this theme are subject to schismatic fracture with, for example, a pronounced series of differences, theological, historical and politically empiricist demonstrated in *Sunni* and *Shi'a* doctrine on the subject. As Esposito reminds us, since Islam lacks a centralised teaching authority or organised hierarchy, there is no obvious answer to the question, 'Whose Islam', nor for that matter 'Which Islam' one should read in relation to the meta-motif of violence.[51]

On issues of power and authority, one is compelled to ask which Islam or Islams, past or present should be addressed and through which prism should the inquiry be conducted? The motive behind such an endeavour ultimately alters or re-shapes the outcome. If, for example, the inquiry is predicated on a one-dimensional economic approach, it will inevitably be shaped by such considerations. If the inquiry is from within rather than without, it may well bring with it dissonance, dissidence, challenge and be perceived and even predicated on an attempt to undermine or disrupt the prevailing norms as they relate to power and authority. This is demonstrated in a close examination of Usama Bin-Laden's discourse against Muslim power and authority invested in the ruling regime of Saudi Arabia as well as in his vehement antipathy towards the 'Great Satan' of the United States of America. Bin Laden's challenge, his dissonance, his self-appointed right of interpretation vis-à-vis Muslim divination on sources of power and authority in society were among things a direct challenge to the prevailing authority of the al-Saud family and its *Wahabbi* interpretation of rules on governance and Islam over the *umma*. Bin Laden read the outcome of such religiously-inspired rule as unjust cruel and despotic. Echoing Qutbian discourse on the crisis that beset Islam under *jahilli* rule Bin Laden condemned the Saudi regime and accused its leaders of abandoning the principles of Muslim law, and 'refusing to listen to the people accusing them of being ridiculous and imbecile'.[52] This is just one of many examples within the *Sunni* Muslim experience where the tradition of rule, power and authority in the name of Islam as divinely revealed by the Prophet Mohammed and sourced through textual reference to the Koran and other holy literature is subject to a challenge or contest.[53] The examples are both historical and contemporary, the most interesting aspect of such examples is the response and outcome to such challenge. In this sense, the response and outcome reflects the rainbow not the monochrome vision and experience that Islam represents to its adherents. Can Muslim and Islamic states, however, be responsive to such demands without recourse to force or violence? How do such states police their citizens and legislate for opposition? These questions reflect a real dilemma that much discourse fails to adequately address. Yet in neglecting the topic the acceptance of norms as they relate to revenge, sacred duty, proportionate response and reaction with respect to the rule of law and human rights leaves Islam open to accusations of intent to terrorise, a disrespect for human rights and norms of proportionate response that are supposed to animate international relations theory in the twenty-first century.

An eye for an eye?

In the modern era there have been a variety of responses to the challenges outlined above. Some responses lead to conflicts which are nevertheless resolved through non-violent methods and others not. In the context of violence no one side to the conflict can be declared to have a monopoly. Such conflicts are not about making 'war on the present to secure a future more like the past; de-pluralized, mono-cultural, unskepticized, reenchanted'.[54] Barber appears to deny to Muslims their own ambitions to live in modern societies in their own locales (rather than someone else's) where the promotion of power and authority are fair, just and cognisant of the diversity and plurality of modern Muslim societies. Such ambitions are illustrated in a variety of Muslim locales. In Indonesia, which is the largest Muslim majority country in the world, conflict over power and authority in the modern era has been about the acknowledgement of the tension between that which is interpreted and reflected as secular in realms of governance and public society and that which is Muslim. Yet, according to Hefner, the challenge to power and authority in this Muslim context is not radical, fundamentalist or violent but represents 'an intellectually vital and political influential community of liberal or civil pluralist Muslims' who perceive secularisation as a vehicle 'to realise the ideal of tawhid'.[55] This is not to deny the import behind fundamentalist or violent Muslim elements but the degree to which they can be ascribed a representative character of the Muslim milieu in an ethnically plural society such as Indonesia. The mainstream Muslim challenge has not, by and large, resulted in violence but made accommodation and compromise, albeit difficult and tense. The same may be said of Malaysia where the modern nation state, a state of many nations, went some way in accommodating the demands of a politically diverse Muslim constituency by embracing a state-led process of Islamisation as an attempt to displace the challenge to power and authority that the organised Muslim constituency posed. It did this while attempting to maintain balance with the demands from other constituents at the same time.

In other modern Muslim locales, power and authority are vested in religious personages that sit atop a state structure that is labelled as Islamic and theocratic. Ayatollah Khomeini played a significant part in shaping the amorphous social forces behind the revolution in Iran in 1979 and Islamifying the whole project. The establishment, post-revolution, of the Islamic Republic in Iran was largely due to Khomeini's *Shi'a* based but unique interpretation and vision of Islamic statehood. Khomeini's blueprint for Islamic government has remained distinct from other viewpoints held by figures like Mawdudi, Qutb or Taki ad-din al-Nabahani – it results from a distinct marriage of ideas drawing from Islamic tradition and jurisprudence and interpretation (*ijtihad*) and yet emerging with a unique notion of the state.

Khomeini's vision of power and authority as leadership of the Islamic state is quite different from that expressed, for example, by Mawdudi. Khomeini was explicit in his outline of this Islamic state system 'It is not dictatorship: the leader must rule according to divine law not his own will. It cannot be an elected system in which representatives of the people can legislate, nor a popular republic that makes people their own rulers. It is the rule of Divine law as interpreted and applied by the Just Faqih – the duty of the people is to obey in accordance with the Koran.'[56] From these general principles the Islamic republic was established and the religious elite dominated political rule shaping the republic's constitution and appointing Khomeini as ruler. The *ulema* controlled the cabinet, the parliament and *Shari'a* became state law – the Islamisation of the political system was the goal post-revolution. Khomeini's vision of Islamic government was subsequently and successfully institutionalised throughout the 1980s. The death of Khomeini in June 1989 did not immediately trigger a change in ideological direction within the Islamic republic, but internal power struggles within clerical circles between traditionalists and modernists have resulted in what Ehteshami refers to as the Islamic republic's second era and a ideological change which has filtered from the bottom up in the absence of a strong charismatic figure to guide the masses – through fear, Islam or other means – in Khomeini's inimitable manner.[57] For Khomeini, the emphasis and locus of power and authority lay not with the community but the charismatic leader. His doctrine of *Vilayet al-Fiqh* focuses on the issue of leadership underpinning the state – linked to *Shi'a* traditions of *Imamate*. In his lectures on Islamic government Khomeini argued that 'Islam as a religion must include a governmental system' – according to Zubaida he believed that the 'functions which are integral to the Islamic religion require a government'.[58] The head of this state, in the absence of the Prophet or Imam is a significant religious leader – the *faqih*. The power and authority invested in this position was subsequently cemented through the revised constitution of 1989 in which not only did the Fiqih serve as spiritual leader of the state under which all other offices and the citizens remain accountable to, but it also included significant powers as head of the states armed forces, powers over the President, as well as other public offices including the judicial system, the council of guardians and state media networks.

The nature of opposition to this state of theocratic rule is diverse within Iran and includes the religious scholars (its reformist element), students and the women's movement. The growth of opposition located deep within important social forces and actors has been a warning sign that significant problems lay in the body politic. Regime response has been heavy-handed and disproportionate. Nevertheless, the inexorable force of opposition calling for reform and greater democratic leverage in Iran remains inexorable. New voices have a vision of Islam and democratic forces in harmony in Iran, and this is perceived as a challenge to the theocratic framework of the state and its political system established post-revolution. Thus far the state struggles between the forces of responsiveness or repression to a new generation of Iranians who wish to change the regime from below.

The reassertion of *vilayet al-fiqh* as a structure for theocratic power and political authority is also evident in the Lebanese context. Here it flourishes as an internal regulatory force within Hizb Allah, subordinated to the Iranian-based political leadership. The principle of *vilayet al-fiqh* has been adopted on the basis of the Iranian model. As an internal mechanism for structuring power and authority, it has been described as one of sacred primacy and stands in stark contrast to the wider-political context of consociational democracy that characterises modern Lebanon. Indeed, it is remarkable how this resistance movement has engaged in a process of Lebanonisation that has witnessed its active participation and representation in a secular system of governance based on principles of power-sharing and segmental autonomy through full parliamentary life, while at the same time regulates its internal structures and organisation through principles of leadership and rule unique to a theocratic system of modern governance. Saad-Ghorayeb contends, however, that this notion of authority and power is not an inhibitor on Hizb Allah: 'the generality of the *Fiqh's* proposals leaves the party with a wide space for decision-making. His authority is confined to strategic issues such as jihad, political rule and the classification of "friends and enemies" '.[59] I believe, however, that this principle actually does imply and result in considerable political authority and when reflected into the locus of the state has implications vis-à-vis coercive functions and the use of force, as will be discussed in a later section of this chapter. Political authority and power legitimated by the people in their religious elite has implications for the locus of power as violence and violence as power. Although the contemporary example is limited to relatively few cases such as *Shi'a* Iran and *Sunni* Sudan there may be something to be learnt from reflecting on the very real dilemmas this presents.

In the *Sunni* tradition, the absence of a singular principle of political authority invested in the *ulema* does not necessarily imply the absence of any investment or relationship between those who rule and engage in governance and the religious authorities of any given political entity in a Muslim locale. Under Ottoman rule, the links between the state and the clerics was regularised and seen as important to the legitimacy of the ruling agent. Hourani contends that the creation in the late Ottoman period of an official clerical class ('*ulema'*) in 'parallel with the political politico-military and bureaucratic corps; [established] an equivalence ... These official '*ulema* played an important part in the administration of empire'.[60] Yet there was no monopoly of power extended to the *ulema* (even in this formal arrangement), for the Sultan established and maintained the right to determine and shape rules by issuing his own edicts and rules (*kanun* or *firman*) that were administered and upheld by the *ulema*. In the modern era, the political authority of the *Sunni* ruling classes has been willingly and sometimes less willingly legitimated by the religious and political establishment implying a balance between the theocratic demands of Islam as a faith system which does not distinguish, in principle, between the sacred and the temporal and the pragmatic realities of governance and power in modern nation states that arose from the ashes of a moribund and deceased caliphate. In Iraq the establishment of a new state by a British force of occupation, mandated by the League of Nations to tutor the country to independence, was partly centred on the realisation by some British actors that the structures of the new state would survive better in the old *ulema*, and religious elite were incorporated into the British devised structures of the new state.[61] One such example is the extent to which the al-Ghaylani family (one of the most notable of the *Sunni* ruling classes) was embraced by the British – with both negative and positive consequences.[62] It is the loss of the caliphate – a political and military institution of leadership with the principle of religious authority placed in the collective hands of the *ulema*; however, that accounts for a major disruption and growth of tension in the modern era around notions of power and authority in Muslim-based polities. This issue is also reflected in the emergence of the Asian Muslim states of the former Soviet Union in the 1990s where power and authority is contested and subject to radical as well as reformist pressures. One arena where the contest for Islam's moral core and influence over the political system is found is that of gender. By this I mean that the issue of force (and thus by extension, violence) in public and private in many Muslim domains has in the modern era revealed a particular focus in relation to women and their rights and responsibilities as variously interpreted within Islamic discourse.

Private violence/public violence

> Men are the managers of the affairs of women
> for that God has preferred in bounty
> one of them over another, and for that
> they have expended of their property.
> Righteous women are therefore obedient,
> Guarding the secret for God's guarding.
> And those you fear may be rebellious
> admonish; banish them to their couches,
> and beat them. If they then obey you,
> Look not for any way against them;
>
> Sura 4: 35

A hitherto neglected dimension of force/violence debate and discourse within the Muslim realm is that which takes place within the private sphere but is acknowledged and legislated in the public as well. In this respect there is a specific value in examining violence that is sanctioned against others within the circle of spiritual life that Islam, as both a contemporary and historical, legal and cultural phenomenon represents. Indeed it is the cultural dimension to this aspect of violence that provides the most valuable platform for examination. In this context there is evidence that violence is 'sacrilized' in the broadest sense of the term, and a strong correlation to the culturally dominant framework of patriarchy can be demonstrated. By patriarchy here I mean quite simply the system of rule and order by men and the tradition within Islam that the interpretation of the faith can only be undertaken by men. In this sense Islam appears with a patriarchal character but one that is contested from within. As Zainah Anwar asserts, the monopoly, however, must be broken,

> What I and my sisters are actually guilty of is asserting that there are deep differences between the revealed word of God and human (read: male) interpretation of the message. For centuries, men interpreted the Koran and codified Islamic rules that defined for us what it is to be a woman and how to be a woman. The woman's voice, the woman's experience, the woman's realities have been largely silent and silenced.[63]

This makes for a contested notion of patriarchy, but I believe it is a useful foil in the debate as it pertains to the sanction of force by public bodies.

The themes addressed in this section are controversial and hotly-contested both from within and outside the faith system. For those outside, particularly in the liberal West, where feminist interpretations of violence have begun to impact culturally and legislatively to alter the 'acceptability' of violence as a form of behavioural regulation as well as an expression of power and authority in the private realm that which is understood as 'Islam's position' is considered inhumane and unacceptable. The debate within Muslim societies centres on the force-violence distinction and the continuing interpretation of Koran and hadith not only by traditional male scholars but also by a small and new generation of Muslim women as well. In some Muslim locales women have also disputed the force-violence distinction through the public realm of the courts, which have, in turn, also prompted debate in some Muslim legislative and other forums. There is, however, limited evidence of a state-led address or discourse on the acceptability, of, for example, due protection to victims and punishment for the perpetrators of honour crimes. In the West Bank and Gaza Strip, under the rule of the Palestinian Authority since 1994, the political exigencies of occupation have also meant that even if there is a limited will to offer state-assistance to women victims of violence, the conditions on the ground prevent it.[64] Yet, as Kandiyoti has observed, 'Governments that granted women new rights frequently proceeded to abolish independent women's organisations while setting up state-sponsored women's organisations that were generally docile auxiliaries of the rule state party.'[65]

In Islam violence or force, depending on interpretation, does take place in the private or domestic sphere. Muslim men beat Muslim women. In Judaism violence or force does take place in the private or domestic sphere. Jewish men beat Jewish women and all too often religious authorities fail to acknowledge the unacceptability of such behaviour. Oftentimes faith is represented as the sanctioning force for such behaviours. Nor are women empowered with the right to quit such relationships with dignity and respect by the own free will. Force and violence by men against women and in some cases by women against men is not specific to one faith or one culture but can be found anywhere the world over. In this respect it can be argued that Muslim men are not all violent and nor are they enjoined by their belief system to act in a violent way. Yet, under certain circumstance and according to both Koran and Hadith and current interpretations force (violence) is permissible in regulating the male–female dynamic within the realm of marriage and the domestic sphere. There are some, however, who would associate 'maleness' with such violence. As Vickers has argued, 'it is in the separation of human values into categories of masculine and feminine, as a way of making social and cultural distinctions between men and women, that the roots and the perpetuation of violence are to be found'.[66] In this respect although gender is not a significant barrier in preventing the experience of violence, how that violence is experienced is perceived as a gendered issue. On this ground the stereotypes and patterns emerge in which gender makes a difference – particularly if one reflects on the categories of perpetrator and victim. As I have already related, in the realm of honour crimes, women remain (almost exclusively) the victims of actions perpetrated by men. In other ways, women are victims in male-perpetrated acts of violence.

One dimension where this matters is the explosion of intrastate conflicts in the 1990s and a move from conventional warfare at the interstate level to civil ethno-national conflicts and secession struggles. Such conflicts – where civilians are drawn into war – have resulted in tragedy for women. Thus, women are the most likely victims of violence and warfare in the twenty-first century. It is asserted that 'women are more likely to be killed [along with their children] as civilians than soldiers'; it is they, not the men in uniform who perpetrate such violence, that are the likely victims.[67] In the explosion of violence that has befallen so many Muslim domains it is not merely that most Muslims, as Sardar argues, are victims, but that increasingly the victims of such violence are women. In addition to these particular manifestations of violence that are more prevalent in developing locales, which in turn include Muslim locales, there are gender-religio-cultural biases which need to be factored in here. In the midst of conflict in the former Yugoslavia there is evidence that Bosnian Muslim women were targeted for mass rape as part of Serbian war-strategy, ethnic cleansing and even (controversially) genocide.[68] Here Muslim identity, regarded as a threat by the Serbs, was violated through acts of rape. It is also reported that during the 1971 war in West Pakistan/Bangladesh, 'paramilitary groups, primarily associated with the Jamaat-I-Islami collaborated with the Pakistani army, perpetrating mass killings, plunder and rape. In the course of nine months ... an estimated 30,000 Bengali women were raped'.[69] In the maelstrom of conflict in

Afghanistan, rape, as an act of war, has been perpetrated against women by Muslim men on all sides of the conflict. Additionally, the sanction of violence against women legitimated, regulated and enforced by the Taliban should be considered a major act of state-sanctioned violence and terror enforced according to codes and norms of interpretation of Islamic jurisprudence that have regularised violence and terror against women. In December 2002, a year after the fall of the Taliban, Afghan women remained jailed in Kabul, accused of honour crimes and imprisoned without trial by the Taliban regime and further abandoned by the new political order led by Hamid Karzai.

Muslim states against women?

Before I discuss this issue further, however, it is imperative at this point to reflect on the role of the state and the prevailing legal system in either perpetuating a permissive culture of violence against women or for failing to bring the perpetrators of such alleged violence to justice fairly. First, some Muslim states are, I would contend, responsible for either malignly or benignly sanctioning such behaviours through the legislative process or by failing to implement legislation and orders from the court on such issues. Often the law is deliberately misinterpreted in order to allow men who act in violence against women to literally 'get away with murder'. In Pakistan for example, judicial interpretation of *Shari'a* law has been used to bring to court a woman who reported a rape for the charge of adultery within a Muslim marriage. The story of Zafran Bibi demonstrates the extent to which male violence is interpreted as 'legitimate' by the legal system of a Muslim state. She was sentenced to be stoned to death after convicted of adultery. In 1990 she reported a rape to the local police and was instead charged with adultery and immediately imprisoned. She was tried in a religious court in the town of Kohat in the North-West Frontier Province where she was found 'guilty' of the crime. Despite protestations from her own husband that she had not committed an act of adultery she was put in prison by the courts.[70]

Both traditional and modernist interpretations by male Muslim scholars tackle the gender issue and reinforce the 'rights' of the man and his power over the woman in marriage. The foundation of the married relationship between men and women in Islam is supposed to be a harmonious one, 'Consort with them honourably'; the Koran demands according to the preferential status accorded to the man over the woman. So although respect within the marriage is apparent, the asymmetry of power within the married relationship also needs to be acknowledged, with men ascribed a power over the 'affairs' of women. The 'religious' rights of man are extended to include the use of force/violence against another and codified through law in many Muslim states. In this case the act of violence may be perpetrated within the contract of marriage. The Koran, as I have already noted, permits this use of physical power as a method of control and regulation of women. It is well-documented by authors such as Mernissi or Afshar that women are perceived as the internal enemy.[71] If, as Mernissi and others assert, that male Muslim scholars perceive women as a form of enemy then it appears logical that the enemy must be vanquished and that force is one method to be considered. Force/violence in this context is reflected as a last resort. It is interesting that the *sunna* of hadith scholar Abu Daoud reflects this in the reports and narration regarding marriage where once again the theme of force/violence is addressed:

(Narrated by) Abdullah ibn Abu Dhubab: Iyas ibn Abdullah ibn Abu Dhubab reported the Apostle of Allah (peace_be_upon_him) as saying: Do not beat Allah's handmaidens, but when Umar came to the Apostle of Allah (peace_be_upon_him) and said: Women have become emboldened towards their husbands, he (the Prophet) gave permission to beat them. Then many women came round the family of the Apostle of Allah (peace_be_upon_him) complaining against their husbands. So the Apostle of Allah (peace_be_upon_him) said: Many women have gone round Muhammad's family complaining against their husbands. They are not the best among you. (Book 11, Number 2141)

(Narrated by) Omar ibn al-Khattab: The Prophet (peace_be_upon_him) said: A man will not be asked as to why he beat his wife.[72]

Yusuf Ali: As to those women on whose part ye fear disloyalty and ill-conduct, admonish them (first), (Next), refuse to share their beds, (And last) **beat them** (lightly); but if they return to obedience, seek not against them Means (of annoyance): For Allah is Most High, great (above you all).

Pickthall: As for those from whom ye fear rebellion, admonish them and banish them to beds apart, and **scourge** them. Then if they obey you, seek not a way against them. Lo! Allah is ever High, Exalted, Great.

Shakir: And (as to) those on whose part you fear desertion, admonish them, and leave them alone in the sleeping-places and **beat them**; then if they obey you, do not seek a way against them; surely Allah is High, Great.

Book 11, Number 2142

The translators of these verses and hadith are aware of the power of the words and their import in terms of interpretation. Nevertheless, they all reveal (within semantic degrees) that the act of violence comes after the withdrawal of the husband from the sexual relationship as a means of punishment against women as wives for disobedience. The act of disobedience itself, however, I would argue, needs to be understood in the context of man's power over the woman. The act of disobedience reveals an independence of spirit and autonomy that is not necessarily understood as part of the framework of power relations within a Muslim marriage. This sanction of force within the contract of marriage introduces the norm of force/violence into the heart of a fundamental social and spiritual relationship. For it appears that the right to exercise violence over another in circumstance of disobedience or rebellion is established. Thus one has to ask here whether violence is sanctioned?

Muslim discourse on this topic is rich and varied and has in modern times been part of an attempt by scholars, theologians and legislators to ease the tension that exists between what are interpreted by some men as rights within marriage under *Shari'a* law and the rights claimed by Muslim women in modern societies. Nevertheless, even in theocratic regimes the function/role place of violence admitted and interpreted as part of the faith system is far from resolved. In *Shi'a* discourse, as Afshar highlights, much public debate on this issue has occurred with the theocratic elite in Iran wrestling with competing and contradictory opinions. The very real consequences of such discourse and their effects on the lives and status of ordinary women was reflected in (albeit) limited legislative change in post-revolutionary Iran. In this respect, as Afshar notes, 'in the case of violence women do have some legal redress ... and the acceptance that violence can be separated from obedience and the right of men to beat and imprison their disobedient wives is an important legal and theoretical point for pro-women activists and scholars' in contemporary Iran.[73] In other contexts, however, the matter is far from resolved not just in terms of societal attitudes but with the state and its courts undermining the rights of women and thus ultimately privileging men in sanctioning the use of violence – through rape, beatings, acid attacks, and murder. In Pakistan it is reported that state laws including the *zina* (adultery or sex before marriage) ordinances contained within the *hudood* ordinances 'presuppose a woman's guilt, and thus provides a tool which can be used to intimidate and control women.'[74] Of course culture counts, politics matters and the divination of ancient religious texts and their meaning in modern-day societies all contribute to the context of this debate. Patriarchy shapes the ways in which Islamist discourse is largely fashioned on this topic. This has been the case in Muslim populated secular states where societal forces and the state elite have been challenged by the emerging forces of Islamisation. In these contexts the debate about violence is framed in terms of its use against women. Religious law is interpreted as a means of sanctioning violence as punishment against women who are perceived as wayward (the intimate enemy syndrome again), which was clearly demonstrated in the case of Safiya Husaini from the Muslim-dominated Sokoto province of federal Nigeria. In 2001 Husaini was convicted by a federal court, according to *Shari'a* law, of adultery and sentenced to death by stoning. The State Attorney-General at the time was quoted by the BBC as describing her fate in the following way, 'They will dig a pit, and then they will put the convict in a way that she will not be able to escape, and then she will be stoned.' Husaini herself, in lodging an appeal against the sentence, symbolically highlights how the act of violence and the struggle between secular and Islamist forces in many contemporary societies is being perpetrated on the battlefield of women's bodies. Criminal code in Nigeria's northern Muslim states had been revised as a result of growing Islamist campaigning for greater Islamisation of society and its legal codes. Such alterations have extended to include other acts of violence as punishment for crimes as outlined according to *Shari'a* rather than civil law. The gendered dimension to this debate is apparent in the way in which the Koran is interpreted rather than the verses of the Koran that address this issue. In the Koran the punishment for a proven case of adultery (which is prohibited within the faith) is deemed equal to both the perpetrators, 'And when two of you commit indecency, punish them both.' In many contemporary contexts, only one party is punished by the Muslim legal authorities – the woman. Violence begins the tale of Safiya Husaini, and violence was predicted as the means by which to end it. Husaini alleged she was the victim of a significant act of violence, rape. During that rape she was impregnated and the evidence of the pregnancy was used to demonstrate that an act of adultery (although she was divorced) had been perpetrated in a social and legal setting framed by *Shari'a* law. In the case of Sharifa Husaini, the man (married) Yakubu Abubakar was also accused of adultery and faced the judgement of the same court. He, however, was acquitted following the withdrawal of an earlier confession of the alleged crime. Husaini, on the other hand, was found guilty through the testament of her pregnancy and the birth of her daughter Adama, which resulted from the encounter. Her daughter, Adama, was deemed 'proof' enough for the religious court. The involvement of the federal government in Abuja centred on a legal framework of secular provision further fuelled the tension and debate that surrounded this case. It highlighted the tension between secular forces who consider such judgements inhumane and unjust and the interpretation of certain religious authorities who want to demonstrate that they have the power, authority and control not just over the social realm but the political, legal and often economic ones too.

The first clash of civilisations

It becomes clear that the admittance of violence in the domestic sphere as sanctioned by Islam has consequences for the interface with the public sphere in some modern Muslim societies. This is the case particularly where such societies are already subject to contestation and the symbolic value of the conflict and sanction of violence against women is a manifestation of a wider phenomenon.[75] Of course the division between the public and private realm lies at the heart of the secularisation versus Islamisation discourse in the modern and post-modern context. Qutbian discourse reflects such a dichotomy as a form of 'hideous schizophrenia' manifest in European hands and as a result of European intrusion in the Muslim dimension. In historically reviewing the development of Christianity deviating from religious norms and values and the emergence of the 'White man's' imperial projects, Qutb contends that the development of secular forms of rule result in misery not harmony. What he reveals, long before Huntington's thesis, is a state of affairs which he describes as a 'civilization clash(es) – with the basic nature of humanity [Islam]'.[76] The notion of western civilisation detached from the authority and power of God lies at the heart of Qutb's thesis on this issue and secularism is identified as the chief culprit for humanity's misery. The absence of the 'Divine ideological idea' is identified as the major feature of communist Russia, capitalist America and socialist Sweden, and of course lies at the foundation of these societies accounting for their inadequacies and failures. Qutb proffers the religiously inspired 'social order' as the true alternative and route to harmony 'as ordained by its great Creator', and more specifically the Islamic faith system. Qutb, of course is not alone in drawing these distinctions and his arguments may be viewed as emblematic of significant elements. He reflects not just the radical cohort but also other elements of the modern revivalist movement in terms of its intellectual engagement with the ideologies of the modern age and the manifestation of the modern nation state. For not only do these thinkers dispute the saliency and value of the secularised order to deliver on its perceived promises of happiness for humanity but they seek to stop, halt and replace such social orders not just in terms of the ideological but social form as well. This is problematic, as Tibi has pointed out, the 'Islamists awareness of secularisation is overly polemical and basically based on a misconception of the issue. Islamists do not honour the fact that the process is a by-product of change and related to differentiation within society itself.'[77] The statement above is a significant rebuttal and while the undoubted polemic of the Islamists accounts for much in the semantics of this debate, the notion of misconception is increasingly open to challenge by the variety of Islamist opinion on this topic. There is engagement on a lived and daily basis plus intellectual reflection on the secularisation of social orders as fluid and open to a process of osmosis. The real barrier lies in the political realm where misconception and misunderstanding is not the sole provenance of the Islamist vanguard.

The function of violence, and particularly political violence and terrorism is presently part of this fractured landscape and used to distinguish the fault-line between that which is the sacred and that which is the profane. The sanction of violence within the private realm against those that are most vulnerable and who demand equal respect according to increasingly universalised norms and human rights agenda are subject to the function of physical force as a means of exercising power that is contested in a relationship. This contributes to a very real blurring of the lines in a moral and practical sense.

It is true then that motifs of violence may be found in that which is presently understood as Islamic or Muslim. Violence is identified as part of the Muslim experience in the modern age. Symbols of violence and Muslims and Muslim violence meld together in the western psyche forming fear and articulated as part of a negative construction. In the wake of 11 September 2001 and the suicidal attacks on America carried out by Bin-Laden's devotees many Muslims, particularly those living in the West, reported a rise in anti-Muslim feeling and became targets of hate and harassment. In many quarters the publicly-stated abhorrence by well-known Muslims such as former pop legend Cat Stevens, in which he declared, 'I feel it a duty to make clear that such orchestrated acts of incomprehensible carnage have nothing to do with the beliefs of most Muslims',[78] did little to diminish the sentiment that like the old adage about love and marriage with Muslims and violence 'you can't have one without the other'. The imprint of Islam in the twentieth-first century has been significantly altered by the actions of a tiny fanatical fringe and assertion that they are representative of a wider Muslim attachment to violence as a form of modern power politics. The ambiguity displayed in other quarters of Muslim opinion regarding the ambitions and goals of the US-led war on terrorism which opened its first front in Afghanistan against the Taliban-government and Bin Laden's loose network of al-Qaeda forces has also helped perpetuate a notion of a dividing line between those who abhor terrorism and its consequences and those who appear to endorse it because it is perpetrated by groups, some of whom pursue legitimate concerns who have been denied any other platform, and some of who represent a fanatical fringe common across cultures and historical moments but which have little to do with something that is represented as a communication of faith in the modern age. The red lines within this debate are most starkly drawn when the spotlight is turned on the Israeli occupation of Palestinian territories and the Palestinian violence in response to it. Suicide violence perpetrated by Palestinians against Israeli civilian targets has stirred up a hornet's nest in terms of drawing the red line between terrorism and resistance in the modern era. Yet, if Islam is represented as having 'never been a pacifist creed' and only dimensions of violence are reflected on it, the prophecy becomes self-fulfilling.[79]

4
Sacred Violence

Introduction

> I am the living martyr, by Allah's grace, Mohammed Bakri Farahat, the son of the Battalions of Izz-a-din al-Qassam. I ask almighty God to accept this work of mine. I ask him to join me with my brother martyrs. I ask him to join me with the Prophet – peace and blessings upon him in the highest of paradise.
>
> Transcript of video testament of a Palestinian suicide bomber who on 9 March 2002 blew himself up in a crowded café-bar in West Jerusalem killing 11, and injuring 52

To address the potent issue of violence and its role in any relationship, any society between communities and civilisations and nations as a form of power, context, war, control, 'last resort' of the apparently politically impotent, 'the desperate', and the determined is to address the demons that beset people across time and culture. Many philosophical interventions have been aired and the opposing positions are argued and examined from every angle. Such positions, whether one accepts the discourse of the realists, or those of the idealists matter because they determine and shape responses to violence. Just as importantly, acceptance of a particular discourse shapes views on whether and in what ways violence can be reduced or even eliminated from social interactions on a human level.

To introduce the issue of religion into the discourse on violence adds a further layer of complexity to the analysis and acts as an additional pull on attempts to comprehend and make sense of the impulses that lead to the injury and death of others. The discourse on violence within religious traditions whether they be monotheistic or polytheistic cannot be presented in a uniform fashion. Instead such approaches must be grappled with in their many guises, under many influences that in turn are shaped by culture, context and politico-economic forces. The historic vantage point, for example, that portrays Christianity as a faith system that can be identified as embracing an explicitly pacifist philosophy and demonstrated through the example of Jesus Christ himself is full of import. The examples of the pacifist tradition within the faith can of course be contrasted with the bloody episodes of violence throughout the Christian tradition advocated by its church-based elites, its fundamentalist adherents and princely or political leaders who legitimated their violence in the name of the cross. Indeed, some biblical scholars have highlighted the explicit exhortations to violence and eradication of the other that are in biblical narratives. As Michael Prior noted in relation to the Old Testament, 'the process of taking possession of the Promised Land, a land flowing with milk and honey, required that it flow also with the blood of its indigenous population'.[1] Within the Islamic faith the same kinds of arguments – faith as peaceful or violent – can be made. It can be argued and demonstrated through historical evidence that the fundamental principles of the faith rests on basic concepts of submission and peace. Islam can be represented as a system of religion under which an environment of peace is the status that all adherents aspire to. Yet as with other faiths, paradox is evident in every turn when the concept of violence is factored into the equation.

For when violence is factored into the equation of Islam, many outcomes are perceptible. Some outcomes are determined by the perceived relationship between Islam and violence that is generated as a means of understanding and making sense of Islam and Muslims in other cultures and philosophical traditions. These issues are examined elsewhere in this book. Nevertheless, there is a compelling argument for first of all addressing whether one can argue that Islam is a religion of violence and war as opposed to other religious traditions that appear to embrace more universal pacifistic tendencies. If there is something identifiable as a culture of violence that defines Islam, explains it and shapes it in all its guises, then an examination of Islam that fails to acknowledge this key dimension or thread of the faith system does not go very far in explaining the actions of its adherents.. A culture of violence must necessarily focus on how violence was established as part of Islam. If violence sits at the foundation of the faith, defining it, its prophets and followers, then traditions of violence as codified and practised by its followers becomes explicable. Such a view, embraced by those such as Gellner, has been used to portray violence within and as part of Islam. It is hypothesised as an important dimension of the necessary and needed social-cohesion dimension of the faith system in tribal societies where such forms of social cohesion were already predicated on tough and brutish practices for regulating, managing and resolving conflict.[2] Hence, Muslim society is characterised by antipathy to democracy and pluralism and where violence is regulated by specific interpretation of Islamic legal treaties. This in turn raises the debate about sacred violence to another level. This level features the notion of universalising norms and values in relation to human rights and their abuse and regulation of abuse from a perspective that is recognised in the subaltern realm as having very little to do with an attempt to homogenise or synthesise that is cognisant of pattern outside the western norms and steering of the debate.

If, however, violence is understood as a cultural dimension of the development of Muslim societies and civilisation, then this is different from those who argue that there is a dimension to Islam that is predicated on a culture of violence. This alternative dimension recognises that sometimes there is a striking interface between adherents of a religious faith, their leaders and violence. Such an approach could be said to reflect a perspective that is not founded on the assumption that Muslims are defined as experiencing some primordial or predestined relationship with violence. This perspective does not work from the assumption that violence is innate to Islam or that when combined with the political it puts it on a crash course with other systems or civilisations.

The notion of sacred violence as an Islamic phenomenon thus needs to be examined with reference to specific issues of sacrifice (of the self or by others), vengeance, redemption and feud. It will be argued that what is revealed in terms of the sacred aspect of violence is that Islam is not necessarily unique in this respect, but in fact what others offer as evidence of Islam's specific sacred dimensions are present not only in other faiths but in the secular context as well. Such a proposition may indeed go some way in emptying the sacred dimension out of certain violent acts undertaken by Muslims that are nevertheless labelled by others as evidence of Islam's dangerous and lethal character. This does not mean that I am arguing that sacred dimensions of violence within Islam are absent, but rather that the sacredness of violence in opposition or as part of modern-day conflicts has a broader context. In other words I pose the conundrum: How often are the modern-day conflicts which embrace Muslims purely about religious ends, and how often are they a combination of other myths and motifs that have more to do with nationalism (and its fuzzy boundaries with religion), economic inequality, the absence of meaningful political participation and so on?

I am, therefore, addressing a particular dimension of violence that has appeared to dominate the Muslim realm in the latter twentieth and early twenty-first century. It has been argued that 'Suiciders', 'Islamohomiciders', 'martyr-seekers', 'self-immolators' and 'mujahideen' have added a new and more lethal dimension to Muslim politics and terrorism underscoring a fundamental threat to those identified as the enemy in Islamist circles. As earlier chapters in the book have demonstrated, although sacred violence has a historical place in the Muslim vista, such episodes as either a form of defensive warfare or conflict were limited in scope and impact and certainly did not, as others have contended, define the faith or colour it in a monochrome fashion.

Sacred sword

When Muslim polities are drawn into conflict or engage in conflict, what is the function of combat in such contexts? In the modern killing fields of interstate and intrastate conflict, religious identity matters. War does become part of the religious experience in Muslim polities that are forged out of conflict, such as in Sudan and Somalia or where conflict – irrespective of its roots and nature – are brought to the door of Muslim polities that demand a response if the community is to be defended. In this respect, the sacred dimension of violence is forged and subject to new interpretation alongside the modern-day demand for nation-states to defend themselves and their territorial integrity. While historical record may play an important part in generating the religious myths that the political and military elite deem important to creating national consensus, they are not the reason for war or combat at either an inter or intrastate level. One example that illustrates this is the war that engulfed the Islamic Republic of Iran from 1980–89. The relatively new Islamic republic found itself drawn into territorial self-preservation against its aggressive Iraqi neighbour. The *Shi'a* character of the state, it was alleged, propelled it to a more violent and lethal strategies. As Keddie and Monian note,

> today it is widely believed that *Shi'ites* are more inclined to violence than non-*Shi'ites*. This greater propensity to violence and death is supposedly the result of a *Shi'ite* martyr complex ... However, ... Husayn's martyrdom was not, until the late 1970s, generally taken as a model for rebellion or assassinations but rather as an occasion to ask for intervention with God.[3]

Keddie and Monian demonstrate that the perception of Muslim character and behaviour is subject to the ascription of values and relationships that are not necessarily intrinsic to a particular Muslim experience. Opponents of this view point to the Koran as a significant source of the violence and faith matrix. The command to violence is interpreted in the following:

> So when the sacred months have passed away, then slay the idolaters wherever you find them, and take them captives and besiege them and lie in wait for them in every ambush. (Sura 9:5)

> The punishment of those who wage war against Allah and His apostle and strive to make mischief in the land is only this, that they should be murdered or crucified or their hands and their feet should be cut off on opposite sides or they should be imprisoned. (Sura 5:33)

> And let not those who disbelieve think that they shall come in first; surely they will not escape. And prepare against them what force you can and

horses tied at the frontier, to frighten thereby the enemy of Allah and your enemy and others besides them, whom you do not know (but) Allah knows them; and whatever thing you will spend in Allah's way, it will be paid back to you fully and you shall not be dealt with unjustly. (Sura 8:59–60)

It is the adherence, either in state form or in non-state movements and organisations, to a religious doctrine that commands violence, and that labels Islam as violent. As Joffe asserts,

many of the movements are indeed violent and they're violent first of all because they believe that there's no other way in which their arguments can be heard. Secondly that the movements themselves have an ideology on occasion, although this isn't universal that requires a violent response to confrontation from a world that they do not accept as being legitimate.

Religious doctrine is seen as key to the explanation for violence:

Behind all this is a particular view of the political and social order today that is rooted in a religious vision. That religious vision is exclusive and calls for violent confrontation to correct what are seen to be fundamental errors in the organisation of human society because it's not organised along what these groups would consider to be proper Islamic lines.[4]

Joffe admits that violence is not an exclusive part of the contract for all Muslims. Nevertheless, his views are reflected in growing numbers who also believe that Islam is representative of violence. Polls show an increase in numbers in the United States of America that believe Islam is violent.[5] In state and non-state form, the sacred sword of Islam appears to dangle over the heads of the non-Muslim world.

A multitude of martyrs

One means of analysis of this issue is to reflect in some depth of the Iran–Iraq war from the standpoint of viewing it as a religious-political struggle.[6] Although this was a thoroughly modern interstate war for reasons of national interest and regional hegemony in which ideology, ethnic rivalries and religious fervour played their part. The sacrifice on religio-nationalist grounds of some estimated 600,000 Iranians was significant in terms of embodying the theocratic foundation of the Islamic Republic in the wake of the overthrow of the Shah in 1979. One unintended consequence of the revolution of 1979 had been the purging of the officer class from Iran's armed forces leaving the country ill-equipped to meet the threat posed by Saddam Hussein's Iraqi forces. Nevertheless, the ability of the leadership of the

Republic – particularly Ayatollah Khomeini with his much-remarked 'martyr complex' to marshal ordinary Iranians to the demands of war as a religious national imperative proved powerful. The symbols of Iranian forces in the war were deeply religious reflecting the ability of the political elite to infuse their endeavour with the notion of martyrdom and sacrifice. In this respect ancient myths of faith and sacrifice were resurrected in an epic modern war saga. During the war many of the symbols of ancient religious and epic Arab and Persian battles were employed in the propaganda efforts of both sides.

The war itself, however, was a very modern phenomenon – it took place in the context of an international stage beset with Cold War rivalries, the Arab–Israeli conflict and the economic dimensions of oil. While neither party to the conflict had a nuclear capability, both Iraq and Iran deployed lethal chemical weapons against each other and caused thousands of deaths and casualties. The war according to most estimates cost US$ 200 billion directly and another $1000 billion indirectly. By the end of the war each side had more than 1.3 million under arms; one half of Iraqis and one-sixth of Iranians of military age. Both sides stretched the definition of 'military age' using youngsters barely in their teens as conscripts who became martyr fodder. In this respect the escapade in which so many were sacrificed was legitimated by the religious ruling elite in Tehran as part of the struggle to export the theocratic ideal that the country represented in the post-revolutionary era. Nevertheless, Iranian-Iraqi relations were founded on a historical mutual antagonism that was compounded by rival ambitions for political and economic hegemony in the region. The Iranians, despite the territorial dimensions of the dispute (particularly as they related to the important Shatt al Arab waterway – from the confluence of the Tigris and Euphrates to the Gulf) were on an ideological collision course with secular nationalist Ba'thist Iraq. As one official version of the war illustrates,

> Islamic Iran was alone in its defence against the global infidel front and the small and big satans, and received help from only one but the Merciful God ... Today, irrefutable documents are now available from history which show that this war broke out due to the desire of the arrogant, reactionaries, and Zionism to defeat or at least weaken the Islamic Revolution of Iran.[7]

The act of aggression was interpreted and used to rally domestic support in Iran as a full-assault on Islam and this had a powerful impact. I would contend that Saddam Hussein himself may have drawn some lessons from the value attached to Islam and its potency as a rallying point in national crisis with his somewhat crude attempt as formulating Islamic dimensions to his invasion and occupation of Kuwait in 1990.[8]

The ousting of the Shah more or less coincided with the emergence of Saddam Hussein as President of Iraq and chairman of the ruling Ba'ath party's Revolutionary Command Council (RCC). Relations between Saddam's Iraq and Khomeini's Iran deteriorated rapidly. The Iraqi *Sunni* leadership of a predominantly secular state was concerned that the appeal of revolutionary Iran might provoke opposition amongst Iraq's *Shi'a* majority who are estimated at 55 per cent of the population. The Iraqi *Shi'a*, since the formation of the modern state, were in some respects a politically margin-alised majority. When the British established modern Iraq in the 1920s they relied on many of the old political-social alliances, formed under the Ottomans that contributed to a privileging of the *Sunni* upper classes. In addition elements, though not all, of the *Shi'a* clerical elite and ruling tribes, and merchant classes opposed the establishment of a secular nation state under foreign influence. There was at a governmental level ample evidence of long-standing grievances within the community of aggressive co-religionists advocating resistance to *Sunni* oppression throughout the region. Iraq was the birthplace of *Shi'ism*, the site of some of its most important shrines and religious seminaries, the new *Shi'a* theocratic elite in Tehran would be concerned to preserve their influence in such places in Iraq.

The war, launched as a result of Iraqi invasion on 22 September 1980, was understood and legitimated in terms of resistance and counter-offensive from an Iranian dimension in religious terms. What is interesting is that this advocacy of counter-aggression ran counter to the earlier *Shi'a* traditions of 'redemptive suffering'. Yet in terms of the doctrine of jihad as a defensive doctrine the Iranian response was perceived from within as justifiable. Put more plainly the Iranians didn't look for a fight, but in terms of the nascent theocratic state that was being built, the Iraqi invasion and resistance to it could be understood in modern theocratic terms as demanding defensive action (jihad) to protect its sovereignty. Despite considerable early territorial gains in the south east of Iran by Iraqi forces, Iranian resistance ensured that the war soon stopped the Iraqi advance. By the Spring of 1982, an Iranian counter offensive regained most of the territory occupied by Iraqi troops including the recapture of the city of Khorramshah. Both sides subsequently became deadlocked into a war of attrition. Saddam Hussein under-estimated Khomeini's ability to unite and inspire his people to resist and defeat Iraqi aggression: motivating his troops with a uniquely religious fervour. As the war progressed there were many eyewitness accounts of the often 'suicidal' Iranian soldiers apparently eager to die in battle in human wave attacks. As the war progressed the Iranian state system ensured that popular culture – through the medium of the media and so on – reinforced the Islamic dimen-sion of the war particularly as it related to 'cultures' of martyrdom and sacri-fice with a specific *Shi'a* hue.

The Islamic import of sacrifice went some way to defining society during this period and remains a legacy of this devastating conflict. With figures for martyrdom running into hundreds of thousands, this form of self-sacrifice became a means by which a poorly equipped and ill-prepared theocracy beat back a western-backed and relatively well-equipped Iraqi aggressor. The motif of martyrdom became the central theme of the war propaganda and propagation effort in Iran. While it is true that for a great number of ordinary Iranians the war and defence of the country from an invading nation was primarily interpreted in terms of national defence of a homeland, it is also true that through the employment of the martyr motif the Iranian state was able to persuade its citizens to make otherwise unthinkable sacrifices including the use of very young 'soldiers' for mine clearance in the clear knowledge that they would lose their lives to clear the field for other combatants. The promise of martyrdom was symbolically more compelling than the mere defence of nation and the clerical elite exploited this. Down at the battle-front narratives, songs, stories and images were purposefully employed on the eve of many battles and military skirmishes against the Iraqis to encourage the martyrs to step bravely into the bloody arena of battle. Like sheep to an Eid al-Adha slaughter their actions were sacrilised by the theocratic leadership of the revolutionary state. The red and green banners, the exhortations to follow in the footsteps of the Mahdi, the united front against the despicable Iraqi enemy in the name of Islam, as well as the nation, gave impetus that would otherwise have been missing from the Iranian defence.[9]

The prospect of an Iranian victory against Iraq on the stability of the region was keenly felt in a variety of Western capitals. Any 'export' of what was perceived as a subversive form of aggressive Islamic fundamentalism not only had potential to inflame the *Shi'a* populations of Iraq and other Gulf countries such as Saudi Arabia, but also encourage Islamic communities in nearby regions of the Soviet empire. The Soviet Union accordingly became, once again, the principal arms supplier to Iraq. European states such as France and Britain also benefited from satisfying Iraqi arms demands as they attempted to shore Iraq up against the Islamic threat posed by post-revolutionary Iran.

Iran experienced considerable problems both militarily and diplomatically. The lack of military capacity – in the air, sea or in terms of modern armour prevented a successful frontal assault towards central Iraq. The ability of the leadership to stir up Iraq's Kurdish population against Saddam Hussein was initially inhibited by fear of repercussions from its own Kurdish community stirred in turn by the Iraqis. Iran concentrated its war effort on its southern border area where the military and political leadership hoped – vainly as it happened – that fellow *Shi'a* in Iraq would join the military campaign to capture Faro. Thus the establishment of and recruitment to 'martyr battalions' became a crucial and defining feature of Iranian fighting forces. The rites of mourning associated with such deaths only deepened the traditions of martyrdom as cultural representation in modern-day Iran. The historical spectacle of theatre played out in the Iranian tradition of *Ta'ziyeh* was essentially made real on the battlefields, and behind this force lay the legitimating function offered by Iran's clerical establishment translated into the hegemonic ideology of the revolutionary state. As Beeman highlights,

'Participants and spectators do not view *ta'ziyeh* as theatre, but rather as part of ritual mourning ... The performance may be preceded or followed by communal mourning ceremonies, consisting of processions, religious chanting, and self-flagellation. Often persons leave a bequest in their wills to contribute financially to the annual support of these rituals.'[10] Old rituals of performance were re-enacted and made modern by war with Iran's neighbour. The religious symbolism was entrenched deep into popular culture through a variety of vehicles. The theocratic establishment at the heart of the revolutionary structure of Iran encouraged a fundamentalist approach to war – changing its character in the modern context. In this context the martyr-seekers were the battalions of God prepared by the clerical establishment to engage in a defensive jihad against Iraq. Iraq – along with its Western backers – was the enemy of Islam and, therefore, Iran. Hundreds of thousands of Iran's poorest were placed under arms in the name of Islam.

Such sacrifice was positively reinforced by the rituals of death and mourning which had already characterised the narrative of revolution and identity under the Islamic republic. Additionally the status of *shahid* (martyr) was reinforced socially in the elevated status accorded to surviving family members and the financial assistance distributed by the state. Yet, as the cemeteries filled with thousands of the martyrs graves the rapacious war machine demanded only more sacrifice in the name of Islam. Behesht-e-Zahra cemetery in south Teheran, where the mausoleum to Ayatollah Khomeini was constructed is also the site where over 27,000 martyrs of the war are buried. The cemetery symbolises the essence and outcome of martyrdom in the modern Iranian context. In row upon row, the graves of those who were sacrificed in the name of Islam are situated. The state even maintains a museum at the graveyard dedicated to martyrdom. Martyrdom has shaped the cultural landscape of the country. Reminders of sacrifice were part of the industry of state. The War Propagation Department not only ensured that popular media, printing presses, publications, music, literatures and arts promoted martyrdom but even public architecture projects – including sculpture – would be harnessed to this end. Yet, in present day Iran a new generation that didn't have to sacrifice itself in the name of Islam on the battlefields of Khorammshah are re-appropriating the symbols and rhetoric of sacrifice to urge for reform and to move away from the hardline clericial establishment that urged their predecessors a generation ago to martyrdom against Iraq.[11]

By 1988 the Iraqis declared themselves the victor in the contest against Iran. Certainly they had had the best of the last few months of fighting – liberating all their territory and occupying parts of Iran. But in truth this devastating war, the greatest interstate conflict in the second half of the twentieth century, ended with neither side a true victor. Most of the so-called victories were dwarfed by the larger consequences of engaging in conflict. In terms of casualties, damage (to 50 large towns or cities) and bleeding of resources both countries were the losers. Said Aburish called it 'An Aimless War', yet in reality it was more a case of the aims being pointless when measured by the sheer human cost of this conflict.[12] The longevity of the conflict was primarily down to the determination and stubbornness of the two main protagonists – Saddam Hussein and Ayatollah Khomeini. Neither was prepared to give way and both managed to gain and retain sufficient control to ensure that they got their way. Despite the evident futility of the war – especially as it appeared to foreign observers – the position of neither leader was seriously threatened by the indecisive outcome of the conflict. Indeed for some years the war against old enemies was popular enough in both countries. Small successes could be presented domestically as major national triumphs. The ebb and flow of contest gave both nations hope of ultimate victory from time to time. But one should also question the extent to which it also suited both regimes to have an external enemy to distract the populous from internal issues of discontent. In addition, as the war dragged on there is a suspicion that both leaderships may have hesitated at calling an end to the war when so much effort and bloodshed had achieved so little. As the casualties mounted very few families in either country were left personally untouched by the carnage of war.

Throughout the war both regimes were playing for big stakes. Each saw the other as a formidable obstacle to their ambitions. Khomeini remained intent on the export of his revolutionary ideals via co-religionists further down the Gulf and in Lebanon. Saddam's desire for his regional hegemony to be recognised and his position in the wider Arab world to be appreciated drove him on. Both leaders glimpsed fleeting opportunities of victory; Iran in the land battle, Saddam via the air war. This helped to keep them going. Saddam also felt that the apparent support of the international community with both Superpowers more hostile to Iran might in the end be decisive. Ultimately, as stalemate set in, both leaderships recognised that the chances of decisive victory were illusory and that there were limits, even in autocracies, to what could be expected of exhausted and demoralised armed forces. Moreover, both economies were badly damaged by nearly ten years of conflict. Although Saddam may have been tempted to carry on when his army started to get the better of the land war in the dying months of the war he probably was reluctant to push his troops much further. So in the end grim determination and the mutual personal hatred, which motivated both leaders was just not enough for one to see off the other. Ultimately hundreds and thousands were 'sacrificed' and martyred by both parties to the war. In some respects both leaderships were guilty of exhibiting a martyrdom complex that was ruthlessly exploited through their almost exclusive control of the state. To this extent a nation blighted by martyrdom was significant to defining the national, social and political character of both countries in the wake of the war. In this way religion suffused politics, society and culture to bring new meaning to the interface between faith and polity.

The recent secessionist conflicts in Chechnya and Jammu and Kashmir also go some way in illustrating how the martyrdom motif has been employed for religo-political motives. In Kashmir the alleged involvement of other influential Islamist forces has been considered significant in the establishment and training of 'suicide' squads in the campaign against India.[13] By dint of association through secessionist demands, Islamists have embraced suicide (martyrdom seeking) as yet another tactic in their campaigns. In Chechnya the appearance of suicide squads among Islamic rebels has been fuelled as a result of an increasingly bitter contest with the Russian authorities. Islamist involvement in the Chechen campaign against Russia is a relatively recent development in this historic dispute and adds but one dimension to the very modern multi-faceted ethnic secessionist conflict. Yet there is little doubt that this Muslim ethnic minority has been increasingly influenced by the orthodoxies of radical Islam which espouses martyrdom as an important dimension of asserting the Islamic agenda. In the case of both Kashmir and Chechnya, however, the Islamist dimension has emerged from resistance by central state authorities to secessionist demands, which are also coupled or seriously affected and altered by the involvement of external actors. Hence secessionist conflict is subject to an Islamisation which is reflected not only in the way in which demands for independence and self-determination are articulated but also in the ways in which such demands are achieved. The outcome of this process was tellingly played out in the attack on Beslan School in September 2004 where hundreds of children became victims of Chechen 'suicide squads' and 'black widows'.[14] One is also compelled to ask whether the Muslim perceived failure of the international community to give a fair hearing and protection to such secessionist communities and their demands creates a breeding ground for the fanatical forces that make the 'suicide squads' a conceivable outcome of brutal acts of war and suppression? I would argue that in some respects new wave terrorism – which features acts of suicide bombing – are explicable by a closer examination of modern post-Cold War ethno-national disputes and that the explanation does not lie solely within the realm of Islam.

Sacrifice and suicide

> If sacrifice is made in the name of Allah then life and death are the same
>
> Graffiti, Gaza city, September 2002

> Each feat of arms hailed and celebrated by the tribe in fact obligates him to aim higher ... realising the supreme exploit, he thereby obtains absolute glory, death.
>
> Clastres, P., 1980, pp. 232 and 237

I love life ... But if I have to sacrifice myself so Palestine can be free
and the people can return to their land, I will do that, without fear.

Hamed, aged 15 years, Palestinian refugee

The term sacrifice is so familiar to western modern-day discourse. Film stars
acknowledge in award acceptance speeches the sacrifices made for them by
others in the endeavour to complete an artistic project. The notion of a valued thing or commodity – time – for example, that which is given up or
offered for the sake of an activity, task, action or endeavour that is considered more important or in order to achieve something else, is how sacrifice
is defined in modern discourses. Those, like actors or athletes, who speak of
the act of sacrifice, tend to do so in contexts of performance in an arena that
is constructed as an artificial context or something that is mimetic of a real
experience. The sacrificial function of modern-day life is individualised in
terms of a personal mobilisation over issues, in the West, that relate to our
place in consumerist societies where sacrifice is almost inextricably linked
to the notion of giving into temptation. That temptation may be in the
form of food, fitness, fashion, drugs, alcohol, and sex but it is on the scale of
personal battles and individual conscience in which the notion of actual
sacrifice (by others or the self) is relative to the bewildering array of con-
sumer-based choices and temptations that are set before us through the daily
presence of media-based advertising. Sacrifice, and in particular, self-sacrifice
is not part of a set of society-based values or norms which reflects a community or communities brought together for some kind of task that is inclusive
of the concept at a local, regional or national level. Instead we are urged
in the opposite direction – 'Go on, indulge yourself ... Help yourself to a
treat' ... 'Its time to treat yourself' ... 'You can't resist it' ... are the declara-
tive statements forming the foundation of advertising exhortations for
everything from cars to chocolate muffins.[15]

Sacrifice in this context is far removed from its original form. In its original
form the term was understood in a religious dimension. The religious dimension of sacrifice which implied the slaughter of a victim or the offering of
something else of value to win God's favour is increasingly laid by the
wayside in the modern secular societies. In this respect sacrifice has lost its
meaning. The function of sacrifice as a religious act, an act of faith, worship
and, perhaps, appeasement is thoroughly diluted. The relative importance of
the victim, whether sacrificed by others or in sacrificing him or herself, is
weakened in the secularised dimension of the concept. Yet without the victim (human or otherwise) the notion of sacrifice in the religious domain is
substantively weakened. The victims of sacrifice in the secularised context
are, however, often self-defined and self-selected. Such acts of sacrifice do
not connect with the necessary dimension of violence that authors such as
Girard believe to be so important.[16] In the western context, sacrifice is
generally linked to the religious by the mass media through the notion of

Goths, Vampires and Occult worship as part of the cultic fringe. It is rarely represented as part of the mainstream theological culture of monotheistic faiths in the West. Sacrifice appears to enter the popular imagination through cultic images drawn from horror movies and TV programmes. The debate that takes place among scholars such as James G Williams about the intimate link between the sacred and violence within Christian texts is also largely overlooked or ignored as a result of the new linkage between sacrifice and popular consumption.[17]

I would argue, therefore, that the notion of sacrifice is quite superficial in terms of a popular western understanding. It gains meaning in secular contexts only to those that define it in the narrow confines of art, fashion, diet, sport, theatre, film, consumer-led desire, work and family life. The demand for sacrifice will stand out during times of national political crisis only. Even in that particular arena ambiguity is demonstrated in terms of a fully sanctioned and society-wide embrace of a demand for others to face the possibility of 'sacrifice' in defence of values and principles considered constituent elements of a modern liberal-democracies and other Western societies. The prospect of consensus on the demand for sacrifice in the prosecution of such norms and values in territories external to the sovereignty of such modern liberal-democratic states is even more difficult to generate and maintain.

The popular ambivalence in secular cultures towards the concept of 'sacrifice' was demonstrated in the national debate that was generated surrounding the decision of the British Prime Minister in the Spring of 2002 to send 1700 British troops to Afghanistan. The troops were to be despatched in support of the US-led global war on terrorism to engage in combat against hostile elements in the Afghan theatre. The decision to despatch the troops to a foreign territory on which no British sovereign rights were threatened was all the more significant because British troops were being sent out for war not peace-keeping. An Op-Ed in a major circulation British tabloid communicates the 'sacrificial' dimension of the decision: 'We're Bush's Cannon Fodder,' declared the headline. Such sentiments were demonstrative of press and public opinion, particularly as it related to the further prospect of Britain involving itself in a war on Saddam Hussein of Iraq. The sacrificial facet of the decision was all-too-apparent in the statement of the British Defence Minister to the House of Commons when he declared 'These troops are being deployed to Afghanistan to take part in war-fighting operations. We will be asking them to risk their lives.'[18] Indeed the remark that British Marine's would be 'asked' by the state to risk their lives is, in this context, misleading. The troops were knowingly being sent into war in the wake of a degree of acknowledged failure by US troops and their local Afghan allies to bomb and destroy, through related military operations, the remaining elements of al-Qaeda and the Taliban. In Britain a nation's armed forces are thus composed of personnel who are willing to be sacrificed in the name of the Queen, sovereignty and the political values of that state. The unease and reluctance of many of the nation's politicians stemmed from the notion of sacrifice that the despatch of the 1700 implied as opposed to those already stationed in Afghanistan for time-limited peace-keeping purposes only. In one respect this reflects the changing character of war in the modern era and an increasing wariness regarding the prospect of committing troops to combat in conflicts not of one's own making.

Throughout the 1990s and into the twenty-first century the apparent reluctance, by Western governments, to 'sacrifice' their troops in what appeared to be the ceaselessly erupting conflicts in domains such as Liberia, Rwanda, Bosnia, Somalia and Kosovo demonstrated the awareness that sacrifice symbolised by the return of soldiers in body-bags or coffins matters much to domestic opinion and the electorate. The notion of national sacrifice had altered and been contained in public discourse. This secularised notion of political sacrifice, however, was altered by two dimensions in the Afghanistan context, both with strong and historic resonance. In their war on terror the United States of America and its allies despatched troops from modern secular states to engage with an enemy motivated by political and other, specifically religious factors as well. This is the dimension to the war that creates a new dimension to conflict. The modern force of a sovereign secular state is sent into combat against the religious cadres of a theocracy and a loose network of *mujahideen* motivated by a fundamentalist and specifically inspired agenda of a loosely-titled clerical type known as Sheikh Usama Bin-Laden.

The Taliban epoch of 1994–2001, forged on the heels of the Afghan jihad and ethnic-contest between rival constituencies in the wake of routing the Soviets, had established something different in terms of a combat-ready army motivated by strict religious interpretation.[19] Taliban leader Mullah Omar had already waged many a battle against his internal enemies on ethnic as well as religious grounds. Pashtun-Tajik-Uzbek entanglements demonstrated that a particular Islamist discourse forged in the *madrassas* of Pakistan and elsewhere, exported across the border, could contribute to a critical mass of some 30,000 *talibs* successfully facing down their Tajik and Uzbek opponents. Their combat against their internal enemies was sanctioned by the Afghan Mullahs. Their strategy was to ensure a progressive drive to a monopoly of force, including the disarmament of its opponents. The Taliban's military motives could not be compared to its western counterparts. Such an attempt would be like comparing apples with pears; they are both fruits but there the difference ends. In this respect the notion of sacrifice by the *talib-mujahideen* had at its foundation a theocratic dimension and inspiration that is very different from that of the notion of sacrifice articulated in the context of sending British Marines into combat in Afghanistan.

It is important, however, to recognise that such acts of sacrifice are recognised as demanding religious sanction either through a theological notion of just war or in terms of the religious legitimacy lent to such acts through the spiritual support and sanction of army chaplains. Sacrifice is recognised as a secondary religious function as part of the foreign and strategic policy of a secular nation state. This dimension of combat should not be ignored or underrated but it can not be paralleled with ease to the Taliban phenomenon. For the Taliban and other Jihad-motivated groups in Chechnya or other former Soviet Muslim republics, the sanction of violence through jihad establishes a certain *raison d'etre* to the modern phenomenon. Religious leaders or figures urge followers to acts of sacrifice as the fundamental tenet and dimension of expressing Muslim identity. In this sense sacrifice, when coupled to violence, does begin to define these elements and is a core legitimator of Muslim authority and power.

Other parallel examples of sacrifice within the Muslim context are to be discovered in a variety of locales – as a means of legitimating the state and its battle-cry against an enemy or as a means of opposing rule or state sovereignty that is regarded as illegitimate and unmovable without combat. This is not, however, the same as asserting, as Anspach does, that 'violence channelled outward against the infidels appears to be a ritual requirement in Islam ... internal violence seems to accompany it in ritual or quasi-ritual fashion.'[20] This is an interesting assertion and may be beneficial in re-thinking or creating, for example, new interpretations of populist *Shi'a* rites associated with commemorating the martyrdom of Imam Hussein with acts of self-violence. The assertion, however, draws a distinction to Islam in relation to the embrace of violence, and, therefore, sacrifice as fundamental or, 'obligatory' compared to other faith systems where the notion of a fixed and permanent relationship to and with violence is, according to Anspach and others, less apparent. As the example of the Taliban illustrates, violence becomes a defining feature not because of Islam itself but also due to the geo-political context which can engulf Muslims in the modern era. Afghanistan has been subject to successive attempts by foreign powers to control and subdue its population. Afghanistan's citizens, irrespective of their ethnic or religious identity, have always resisted such attempts. In this context Islam and Muslim dimensions of defence and legitimacy have served as a facet of resistance. Such motifs, however, are not always called directly into play in arenas of war or conflict where Muslims dwell or resist; military action or aggression is demanded of them. One under-remarked dimension of the Allied war against Iraq in the Spring of 2003 was the apparent restraint demonstrated by the *Shi'a* al-Badr Battalions that were not deployed into the arena of conflict in sacrifice of human life in a jihad either against the Ba'thist regime of Saddam Hussein or the Western forces who waged war on Iraq. The much-feared religious dimension of the conflict failed largely to manifest itself. It could be contended that in this context, *Shi'a* religious and political forces acted as a moderating and restraining power on a populous that had suffered grievously under Saddam Hussein's rule. Following the 1991 *Shi'a* uprising in the south of Iraq, Saddam Hussein's regime had executed thousands of *Shi'a* and many more were imprisoned or 'disappeared'. Nevertheless, the Iranian-based *Shi'a* Supreme Assembly of the Islamic Revolution of Iraq (SAIRI), led by Ayatollah Mohammad Baqer al-Hakim with an estimated 15,000–25,000 under arms did not Islamise the conflict by engaging their troops in Iraq. Moreover when the American-sponsored Interim Governing Council of Iraq was established in July 2003, a senior leader of SAIRI, Abdel Aziz al-Hakim was declared a member of the rotating presidential pool. One of the most well-organised and significant *Shi'a* organisations in Iraq, now appeared to be throwing its considerable political weight behind a new political order perceived by elements as pro-American. Ayatollah Mohammed Bakr al-Hakim had spent more than a decade in exile after having fled Ba'thist ruled Iraq and established a religious movement with an agenda of Islamic governance for Iraq. In this respect, an accommodation between theocratic aspirations and real politick appears to have been struck without conflict or bloodshed. Religious weight was brought to bear within the political process emerging in Iraq and not at its violent fringes. This approach is not without its opposition within *Shi'a* ranks, but nevertheless it highlights the flaws in the myth that within *Shi'a* Islam in particular the 'martyr complex' will go out and violence will follow.

The Girardian perspective

In the modern age, then, one is compelled to ask: is sacrifice part of the obligation of Islam and violence in the contests that Muslims find themselves engaged in? What forms of sacrifice prevail and in what way is such sacrifice imbued with religious (or sacred) rather than other traits? In such contexts, are we to accept that sacrifice is about the Girardian perspective on the regulation of religious community in terms of preventing conflict from within destroying the community? Here the victim serves as a scapegoat for the violence that might otherwise threaten to pull down the community into chaos and destruction. As Girard argues, 'the function of sacrifice is to quell violence within the community and to prevent conflicts from erupting'. This is a characteristic of societies that he recognises as 'imbued' with religion and an important part of the regulatory mechanisms of such communities.[21] Such societies are regarded as 'primitive' and 'different from our own [in the West]'; 'for us the circle has been broken.'[22] It is difficult to reconcile such views with the development and modern characteristics of the many Muslim polities that exist across the globe. In such polities there is sometimes a pull between that which is considered to be 'primitive' and therefore mostly un-Islamic and Islam as a system of belief that is lived on a daily basis by millions of people as a modern, sophisticated and dynamic phenomenon. The point here is that that which is understood or regarded as primitive is not Muslim or Islamic but outside the rites and rituals of Muslim communities and polities.

The additional dimension introduced by Girard to this debate, however, is his contention that rites and rituals of violence have a beneficial consequence in society by providing an alternative focus and regulatory function for violent behaviour that would otherwise push such societies into frightening and destructive chaos. Violence – of the sacred type – becomes, from this perspective, a positive mechanism for society. Yet one has to question to what extent Girard's theory is truly helpful in explaining the so-called phenomenon of religious violence that according to a variety of authors defines and grips a number of diverse societies in Africa, Asia and Europe. For if the purpose is to define Christianity in contrast to Islam – one freed from the cycle of violence and the other tied to it – then the purpose of such work is apparent. This, contends Scruton, is what Girard seeks to argue. Yet, there is little to divine from such trite interpretations in terms of making explicable the so-called contrast between a pacifist and violent concept of faith systems.[23] While it may to true that within the parameters of the civil conflict in Lebanon religion has played a part in the explanation for conflict and violence, this is because such a conflict is about the contest of identity. Such an explanation, however, ignores the more pertinent dimensions of modern-day conflicts that centre on inequalities of power and wealth perpetuated by a variety of local, regional and global factors as well. If Girard's argument is to remain credible then perhaps it is better to assert that it is more appropriate to reflect such discourse as it relates to modern-day cults and violence which I addressed in Chapter 3. John Hall addresses this dimension of sacred violence in relation to the Girardian perspective but dismisses its usefulness in explaining the religious dimension of contemporary conflicts and manifestations of violence.[24] The issue here, however, is not so much the original thesis offered up by Girard in the 1960s but the subsequent discourse of interpretation and application of his approach to the manifestation of mainstream conflicts in the modern age. These interpretations put an emphasis on making violence intrinsic to religion – particularly Islam – and is utilised to bolster the supposition that this is what marks Islam out from other religious traditions. The extent to which this works is limited. Re-sacrilizing violence in the context of the modern era has, I would contend, much more to do with socio-economic and political struggles and fundamentalist revivalism, more generally than some ancient mimetic impulse to sacrifice, that Islam, unlike Christianity, seems unable to break free from.

Martyrdom

The Rose Tree

O words are lightly spoken
Said Pearse to Connolly
Maybe a breath of politic words
Has withered our Rose Tree

or maybe but a wind that blows
Across the bitter sea

It needs to be but watered
James Connolly replied
To make the green come out again
And spread from every side
And shake the blossom from the bud
To be the gardens pride

But where can we draw water
Said Pearse to Connolly
When all the wells are parched away?
O plain as plain can be
There's nothing but our own red blood
Can make a right Rose Tree
WB Yeats 7 April 1917[25]

Source: http://www.sobh.org/Events/Iran-Norooz/Iran-Norooz-Card4.htm

'And expend in the way of God;
and cast not yourselves by your own hands
into destruction, but be good-doers; God
loves the good-doers'
Sura 2:190

Martyrs are the burning candles of human beings
Ayatollah Khomeini

Martyrdom seekers are a glimpse of hope on the road to victory and
liberation
Graffiti Gaza Strip 2002

Suicide as an act of intentionally ending one's life is still considered to be a
major modern-day taboo in most cultures. Suicide is also considered to be
a transgression of religious edict in most major faith systems including
Christianity, Islam and Judaism. When in October 1999 an Egyptian-
piloted airliner crashed off the coast of the United States of America, it was
initially concluded that a terrorist act had been perpetrated. Yet such speculation ended when a counter-explanation emerged that pilot Gamel
al-Batouti had taken control of the planes controls and in an act of suicide
ended his life and those of 217 passengers on board. Al-Batouti's family
denied the conclusions of the crash investigators disbelieving the suicide
theory. In 1997 INXS pop star Michael Hutchence committed suicide in the
early hours of the morning in his hotel room by hanging himself. This
taboo-breaking act was vehemently denied by his then-partner and mother
of his child Paula Yates. Suicide creates disbelief and a sense of rejection
among those left behind. It is regarded as demeaning the sacredness
attached to all human life. Suicide is also about violence as a disruption to
life. The decision to engage in a campaign or act of suicide bombing is a relatively recent and modern phenomenon of the changing character of war.
Acts of suicide or martyrdom for political and religious reasons do, however, have ancient historic resonance. The poignant example of the Jewish
Zealots of Masada who killed themselves rather than submit to the power
of the Roman occupying authorities as related by Josephus is powerful. Its
relevance, however, is made all the more compelling as a national myth at
the heart of the modern Israeli state. Today Masada is employed by the
Israeli state as a symbol of Israeli freedom and independence. Indeed, in
mimetic appreciation of the ancient Zealots, modern-day recruits to the
Israel Defence Forces (Armoured Unit) swear their oath of allegiance to the
state in a ceremony on the summit of Masada. Their defiant cry is: 'Masada
will never fall again.'

Suicide bombing, where the intent is to end life for political reasons,
however, somehow has begun to undermine the taboo. The prohibition –
where life is regarded as sacred – is, in some way, damaged by the linkage
to the political. Yet suicide attacks, as the example above demonstrates,
are part of conflict as both an ancient and modern phenomenon. As I
highlighted in an earlier section of this chapter, one of the defining features of the Iran–Iraq war of 1980–89 was the martyrdom of Iranians as
they defended their state. Yet, the point here is that if suicide bombing is

part of the act of war or conversely insurgency or resistance, is it an acceptable one?

Suicide bombing became a feature of Second World War when Japanese bombers deliberately targeted their planes at US targets. Here the important distinction to draw out in relation to the debate is that the suicide (Kamikaze) action took place within the arena of war with one military force facing off against another military force and target. Such suicide attacks were not intended for civilian targets. Of course, state forces on either side of the war were not so circumspect about civilian life when they dropped bombs on cities like Coventry, Hiroshima and Nagasaki, Dresden and other German cities, and perpetrated such atrocities as the Nazi holocaust against the Jews and others, or organised the Nanjing massacres as the Japanese did.[26]

The other Asian example of suicide for political means is located within Sri Lanka and the Tamil secessionist movement. The Tamil martyrs in addition to orchestrating attacks on military targets also targeted civilians with, for example, nearly 100 getting killed by a suicide attack on the Central Bank in Colombo in 1996.

These attacks are driven by a variety of motives and not just the despair behind major modern political conflicts in vulnerable developing societies. To ascribe the motives behind such attacks as rooted in millennial and apocalyptic zeal and hence put them beyond traditional, political and mediated solutions is deeply problematic and echoes Hall's concerns. Part of this, of course, returns us to the age old problem of meeting and addressing the grievances of those raised through the violence of terrorism. For there is a growing consensus that suicide attacks as a dimension of terrorism – particularly against civilian targets – cancel the legitimate motives of the perpetrators and their leaders. Sucide attacks against civilian targets become evil acts of mindless terrorism.

The suicide bomber is not experiencing a trauma or psychotic crisis where life loses its meaning, but instead identifies him or herself with the destruction of their life and that of the enemy as well. The intent of the suicide bomber is in taking one's life to take others with them, rather than the destruction of the building or installation. The objective of the act is the enemy and its destruction, yet the paradox is the extent of the internal destruction to the perpetrators own society as well.

Context matters. In the past such acts were carried out by faithful adherents with political grievances in a bid to end what they perceived as injustice, tyranny, and servitude. They were rare examples of violence against the odds by so-called believers and strugglers. As I have noted, in the late twentieth century, the suicide or martyr phenomenon and its political dimension made a re-appearance in a variety of contexts including Northern Ireland, Lebanon, Turkey, Tanzania, Sri Lanka, Iran, Israel, India, Panama, Algeria, and Pakistan. By this point, the phenomenon could be associated with the typology of ethno-national conflict and additionally the transnational dimensions of radical Islamism. Nevertheless, the modern phenomenon should not be perceived solely as another dimension of the fundamentalist wave and its clash with the post-modern secular order, for to do so would be to ignore secular-nationalist groups who have embraced the tactic as part of their armed strategies. The acceptance of such facts complicates the explanation and demands a significantly more nuanced approach even when looking at the Islamic dimension of such violence.

Among those who have embraced suicide for political reasons are the al-Aqsa martyrs brigade, al-Qaeda, PIRA (Provisional IRA), Hamas, Palestinian Islamic Jihad- Shiqaqi faction, Hizbullah, various insurgent groups based in Iraq, the Tamil Tigers, the PKK – Kurdish Workers Party, Barbar Khalsa International (BKI), the Syrian Nationalist Party and Amal. These 'suicide terrorists', as they are referred to, have used their own bodies as weapons in a political struggle against both, the state and its armed forces as well as the civilian populations of such states. Suicide – martyrdom – has become the weapon of intention among hunger strikers and bombers.

The al-Qaeda movement headed by Usama Bin Laden had suicide operations as part of its signature against Western targets. Transnational in reach, al-Qaeda reflected the disparate nature of its leadership base and the Arab *Mujahideen* phenomenon first apparent in the modern warfare of Afghanistan, then Bosnia and a variety of other conflict contexts. Bin Laden's extreme rhetoric of anti-westernism inspired acts of violence against American targets in Africa, the Muslim world and the United States of America itself. In a significant departure al-Qaeda used suicide to bring a war to America on its own soil and this had a fundamental effect on the American psyche. From Afghanistan Bin Laden and his closest associates turned so-called martyrdom operations into an offensive act of war against both American military and civilian targets. American security planners appear to have failed to recognise the different tenor to the fundamentalist manifestation that marked al-Qaeda out from other radical Islamist movements. The 1998 suicide-embassy bombings in Kenya and Tanzania while assessed as a significant threat to American interests in some ways were not necessarily understood by US policy-makers in terms of the import, as its related to the transnational dimension of al-Qaeda's ideological base and the projected martyrdom as something different altogether. They were indicative of a new reach in Bin Laden's war against the United States of America. For in framing his enemy, Bin Laden indicted the United States of America as responsible for the major conflicts, 'atrocities' and massacres that characterised the globe through the series of ethnic and national conflicts that beset Tajikistan, Kashmir, Somalia, Chechnya, Bosnia, Eritrea, Burma, Assam, the Philippines, and Ogadin in the uni-polar order that the United States of America became straddled in the wake of its Cold War victory. The American presence in Saudi Arabia, the holy of holies, only served to further antagonise and confirm Bin Laden's viewpoint. Bin Laden believed that the Muslim victims of the 'Zionist-Crusader alliance' were to be found in the wealthiest state of the Middle East: in uniform, civilians, old, young, rich, poor, educated and uneducated, merchants and clerics. Bin Laden, inspired by Ibn Taymmiyah, urged unity among Muslims in a confrontation with the '*kufr*' of the Muslim world and beyond. In this increasingly de-humanised understanding of contemporary global relations, views were extreme and turned on the premise that Bin Laden and his followers dwelt in a Qutbian described state of righteousness in the face of the *jahilli* reality of transnational proportions.

Jihad as conceptualised and interpreted by Bin Laden and his supporters did mean that the war would be taken across the borders of West Asia and the Middle East into the heartland of the 'Great Satan' (United States of America) with its symbols the main targets. The means of suicide or self-martyrdom implied a formidable threat to those within Bin Laden's sights, as new fronts in this particular episode of conflict between radical *jihadi* Islamist elements and the West were opened up. Bin Laden was playing a long-game, in this respect, in common with others in the radical Islamist spectrum. Bin Laden believed that time was on his side and that Islam would inevitably rise again with a concurrent collapse of the 'artificial' Zionist entity and the US-led Crusader alliance. Suicide bombers would turn out to be a powerful element in Bin Laden's arsenal against the West. The deployment of suicide bombers by al-Qaeda altered the dimensions of Bin Laden's conflict with the West.

Sacrifice and self-sacrifice are a recognisable phenomenon and depressingly so. The religious dimension of such acts, however, is open to interpretation and is difficult to draw out in a single strand from the intricate fabric that is modern-day conflict – particularly of the intrastate or ethno-national variety. Thus, at first glance it may be argued that the reason why the Palestinian–Israeli conflict is different from the conflict in Northern Ireland or Rwanda is because of its religious dimension with respect to suicide bombing. Indeed, some analysts would say that such conflicts in a comparative dimension have much in common – such as being colonial in origin, affected by settler communities, issues relating to internationalisation and economic and class factors – but that in religious terms there would be very little room or common ground of comparative value. One significant phenomenon that many would argue now marks the Palestinian–Israeli context out, therefore, is that of suicide bombing.

The Palestinian suiciders

Suicide or self-annihilation may indeed be regarded as the ultimate sacrifice. In the Palestinian–Israeli context, however, it is a relatively recent phenomenon and not something that hitherto had defined or marked out the religious dimensions of this conflict between Palestinian and Israelis, Jews, Christians and Muslims. It is, however, currently understood as very much a Palestinian-Muslim phenomenon, a religiously sanctioned weapon that had previously been manifest only in the context of *Shi'a* Lebanese attacks in the early 1980s on Israeli, US and French targets in Lebanon. During the first 18 months of the second Palestinian uprising (September 2000–March 2002) over 60 Palestinian suicide bombers killed over 120 Israeli civilians in suicide attacks on discos, cafes, pizza restaurants, bus-stops, shopping malls and streets, throughout Israel. Sucide attacks carried out by Palestinians against Israeli targets had, by 2005, caused more than one thousand deaths. For many Palestinians the conflict with Israel is now understood through a primary lens of Islamism. Hence the explanation in terms of ascribing the conflict as 'a civilizational conflict' waged between, on the one hand Islamic civilisation with its divinely inspired laws and mission to create on this earth the society of justice and freedom which has been ordained by Allah; and on the other hand, Western civilisation with its materialistic culture, worship of ethnicity and the state, and denial of God's supremacy.

This weapon of war has become increasingly recognised and even valued in the Palestinian context, irrespective of religious motivation, as part of the national strategy of Palestinian resistance. Evidence of this inclination on the part of the Palestinian population is demonstrated in opinion polls that record the fact that a significant number of those polled – included a majority in the Gaza Strip – strongly supported suicide bombing operations. In addition, more people supported than opposed the attacks on Israeli civilians, betraying an attachment rather than any kind of ambiguity towards such acts:

And what way is your feeling about suicide bombing operations against Israeli civilians in Israel? Do you strongly support, somewhat support, somewhat appose, or strongly oppose suicide bombings against Israeli civilians?

	Total n = 1200	West Bank n = 760	Gaza Strip n = 440
Strongly support	54.4	49.6	62.7
Somewhat support	19.3	17.9	21.8
Somewhat appose	10.1	10.0	10.2
Strongly appose	5.8	7.8	2.3
Don't know	7.1	10.3	1.6
No answer	3.3	4.4	1.4

Source: JMCC, April 2001.

What is your feeling towards suicide bombing operations against Israeli civilians, do you support it or oppose it?

	Total n = 1201	West Bank n = 761	Gaza Strip n = 440
Strongly support	43.5	39.0	51.4
Somewhat support	20.58	18.9	23.2
Strongly oppose	10.5	12.5	7.0
Somewhat oppose	15.5	15.8	15.0
I don't know	7.5	10.2	2.7
No answer	2.5	3.6	0.7

Source: JMCC, December 2001.

Popular support for this tactic, however, has waned throughout the second Intifada, particularly following events such as the Israeli retaliations and other collective punishments against Palestinians in the wake of suicide attacks.[27]

Suicide bombers initially emerged as a weapon of the Islamists; the bombers engaging in an act of calculated vengeance for the massacre of Palestinian worshippers in the Ibrahimyia mosque in Hebron by a right-wing American settler in February 1994. The religious dimension of the revenge act could not have been stronger. First, although Hamas and Islamic Jihad had engaged in attacks and operations against Israeli (military and settler) targets before this point, they had not undertaken any suicide attacks since their foundation in 1988. In this respect self-martyrdom rather than preparedness for martyrdom in the course of defensive jihad was never a fundamentally religicised component of Hamas. In the case of Islamic Jihad, although the vanguardist nature of the *mujahideen* endeavour did characterise the organisation and its ideological impulses, this did not include self-martyrdom or suicide. In the Hamas covenant, the charter of the organisation, however, it is stated that, 'there is no solution to the Palestinian problem except through struggle (jihad) ... The Islamic Resistance Movement [Hamas] is a link in the chain of Jihad against the Zionist occupation'.[28] How this stricture is interpreted is important. Questioned about the concept of jihad and Hamas in the late 1980s one leader declared, 'This is about our right to self-defence and resistance against those who are illegally occupying our land and murdering our families ... Allah commands us and our conscience demands us to defend ourselves from such illegality.'[29] Tactics for self-defence and resistance, however, would come to mean everything.

The Hebron massacre signalled the crossing of a Rubicon for Palestinian Islamists and the religious motive behind the act of revenge was symbolically linked to the traditional 40-day Muslim period of mourning for the victims. Then, for the first time Palestinian bombers with explosives strapped to their own bodies travelled to the Israeli towns of Hadera and

Afula and exploded themselves, killing 12 Israeli civilians. The communiqué issued in the wake of the Hadera bomb illustrated the extent to which sacrifice, self-sacrifice and revenge were intricately tied to a religious interpretation of an act of war in a conflict that had engulfed Palestinians and Israeli for the best part of a century: 'Compelled by its loyalty to the spilt blood of Hebron's recent martyrs, the Qassam brigades decided to avenge this blood ... it has always been Hamas policy to attempt to direct military operations against Zionist military targets ... The Qassam brigades have always tried to avert civilian casualties ... But the outrageous criminal actions of the Zionists against Palestinians ... forced the Qassam Brigades to treat the Zionists in the same manner. Treating like with like is a universal principle'.[30] Hamas had marked itself out from its co-religionists in Lebanon as well, for the Lebanese suicide bombers (mujahideen) whether drawn from Hizb Allah or Amal had only perpetrated acts of self-martyrdom against primarily military targets (although this it not to say that civilians did not perish in the attacks). Hamas, and Islamic Jihad, however, appeared to sanction a form of jihad against civilians, or to put it more bluntly, against women and children.

How could this be justified? Which Muslim clerics had sanctioned such acts as a revenge for the death of Palestinian civilians? Who had interpreted *Shari'a* law to permit and glorify these acts of violence? Much of the answer to this lies in the general political environment that now defines the Palestinian–Israeli arena. This environment is dynamic and subject to prevailing forces; the suicide phenomenon, likewise, is not static but has become part of the landscape of conflict, admissible evidence of how brutalised and de-humanised the conflict has become – on both sides. The perspective held by the Islamist leadership on this issue demonstrates the extent to which revenge acts as a motive in orchestrating a religio-political agenda in a theatre of low-intensity conflict with Israel. Hamas leader Ismail Haniyeh remarks that so long as Israel is perceived as committing 'aggression' against the Palestinians, 'we are left with no choice but to defend ourselves even with these martyrdom attacks. But at the same time we have no intention of harming civilians and we didn't initiate this process ... they [Israel] started it with Hebron and they've continued to Jenin and Gaza last month. Which people who were subjected to this would not defend themselves?'[31] I have argued with such leaders that there is no Islamic sanction for killing civilians – even in battle. I have attempted to employ the positions of such Muslim scholars as al-Marwardi who ruled such attacks as impermissible. Revenge against brutal Israel is always cited as the counter-argument. Islamic Jihad leader Sheikh Shammi asserted in the context of this discourse that, 'We are left with no choice but to answer Israel with martyrdom operations to let them feel our bitterness ... And with all of this we offered to stop killing civilians if the Israelis stop targeting our civilians and destroying our homes and trees but they refused ... Now there are no martyrdom attacks but their tanks still kill our people sleeping in their houses, and our children in Toubas ... their soldiers killed the workers ... this is all against Palestinian civilians ... and why don't we hear loud voices saying they are criminals against humanity? How come he [Israel] can claim self-defence but we can't? That's what makes us get a grudge against the Americans and the West. Even when we attack their army we still get Bush on television calling us criminals and terrorists ... The Koran tells us we can return the same hurt to the enemy that they hurt us with but also that a punishment should not be excessive ... These rules are a source to the *mujahideen* brothers to react against the crimes of the occupiers ... they are not allowed to initiate the aggression but they may react using the same methods'.[32] As Hafez contends, such actions are justified in terms of the mechanism of advantageous comparison, 'The purveyors of violence justify their actions by framing theirs as "minor" transgressions compared to the cruelties inflicted on them by the enemy.'[33] The point of such arguments is not that they fail to convince a member of the Western audience such as myself of any moral or ethical clout but that such arguments and justification resonates in many Palestinian quarters so strongly that martyr-seekers become the acceptable face of national and Islamic resistance.

The Palestinian religious establishment has actively avoided issuing a definitive position or sanction to suicide operations carried out by Palestinians against Israeli targets. Palestinian Grand Mufti Sheikh Ekrima Sabri has been accused, by Israeli right-wingers and settlers of sanctioning such attacks but in public he has been quoted only as saying that: 'The person who sacrifices his life as a Muslim will know if God accepts it and whether it's for the right reason ... God in the end will judge him and whether he did that for a good purpose or not. We cannot judge. The measure is whether the person is doing that for his own purposes, or for Islam.'[34] Such ambiguity has been interpreted as sanction but in reality it is nothing more than a meaningful indication of the problem that many have with the motive rather than the method behind such attacks. The motive for the attacks is political not religious and the strategic importance of such actions as part of a wider arena of conflict is also relevant. This ascribes a far more prosaic character to something that has been imbued in the popular imagination with more powerful meaning. Other influential Muslim scholars have been unambiguous in their support for Palestinian suicide attacks, even when against Israeli civilian targets. Sheikh Yusef al-Qaradawi who is one of the most significant *Sunni* scholars in the modern era has declared, 'I consider this type of martyrdom operation [attacks on Israeli civilians] as indication of justice of Allah almighty. Allah is just. Through his infinite wisdom he has given the weak what the strong do not possess and that is the ability to turn their bodies into bombs like the Palestinians do'.[35] The spiritual leadership of Hamas moreover has clearly provided religious sanction to such attacks. They have decided that the stricture of jihad against Israel includes creating civilian victims as a result of military and strategic action.

By 2002 suicide bombing was almost endemic to the Palestinian–Israeli arena. Yet, in the words of eminent Palestinian psychiatrist Eyad Sarrajj the only wonder was, given the conditions, he believed Palestinians were subject to by Israel's occupation; it was not more widespread.[36] Such views were reflected in the sentiments of the wife of the British Prime Minister, Cherie Blair, when she controversially declared that 'As long as young people feel they've got no hope but to blow themselves up we are never going to make progress.' Suicide bombing was no longer a phenomenon that could be laid solely at the door of Palestinian Islamists in their campaigns of sustained attacks against the Israeli population. From 1994 to September 2000, suicide bombing had been fully integrated into the consciousness of most Palestinians as part of the mechanism of struggle against Israel. Where in the past public opinion had demonstrated a notion of ambiguity in its attitude towards suicide bombing with the costs being perceived as outweighing any political benefits, it became increasingly apparent in the wake of the Oslo collapse that suicide bombing was another way of war. The leadership of Hamas and Islamic Jihad pursued their strategy. In 2002 Hamas leader Sheikh Yassin, responding to Saudi pressure for an end to suicide bombings, argued, 'Our only initiative against the enemy is resistance, until we liberate our homeland ... The Palestinians have the right to use all their weapons against this enemy, including the martyr [suicide] death attacks. If we are asked to stop these operations, Israel must be forced to first stop its occupation of Palestinian lands. If the Israeli enemy wants to decide for me how to handle opposition against him that would no longer qualify as opposition.'[37]

Yet it was a way of waging war with Israel that was also re-shaping the moral climate of Palestinian society. As Hammami and Budeiri asserted, 'the fortitude and determination exhibited by the militants, who are ready to sacrifice their lives on behalf of the rest, risk transforming Palestinian society into one in which only people with a political role are those willing to die or to kill while they die ... Is it possible that there is no other way to utilize those willing to undertake the ultimate sacrifice ... in any other way than to send them to their death?'[38] Suicide bombers were becoming popularised and revered figures. Video testimonies known as 'living wills' of suicide bombers were widely disseminated throughout the West Bank and Gaza Strip. Foreign journalists made a speciality of seeking out Palestinian families who were either bereaved or knew of a bereaved friend, relative or colleague who were ready to attest to their own willingness to sacrifice either themselves or their children. The notion that children as young as four were uttering statements attesting to their own desire for annihilation – that thousands of young people stood ready to undertake the kinds of acts of violence that suicide bombings wreaked on Israeli civilians was beginning to define the Palestinian people. Increasingly media representation focussed on this new dimension of Palestinian identity. For much of the Israeli media, this identity was not new but the old image of the Palestinians as terrorists just re-packaged. They seized on statements issued not only by the leadership of Hamas and Islamic Jihad, but Palestinian Authority President Yasser Arafat as evidence that the Palestinians had reverted to 'terrorist-type'. Indeed, by the Spring of 2002 the defining image of the second Intifada of the child-victim Mohammed Durrah who had been shot dead by Israeli soldiers as he cowered defenceless in his father's arms had been replaced with the posters of suicide-bombers. In shops, homes, public spaces, mosques and offices the visual jumble of victim and victimiser, all young, all posed against a backdrop of the holy sites of Muslim Jerusalem, all fixed and frozen immortalised on paper, betrayed the obvious grip of self-annihilation on Palestinian consciousness. As one young teenage girl from Bethlehem was quoted as remarking, 'We want heroes, just like other countries have heroes. But our heroes are not soccer players or movie stars any more. I'm just one of the girls who'd like to carry out the same act as Mohammed [a suicide bomber].' Such statements were all the more ironic when contrasted against the Uprising of 1987–93 when the perpetuation of life as part of the demographic struggle against Israel was given an added political potency through the society-wide phenomenon of early marriage and increased birth. While martyrdom was demonstrated as an act of resistance by Palestinians the intent was never to engage in a form of auto ethnic-cleansing that would contribute to the literal depopulation of Palestine by the Palestinians themselves. Indeed consciousness around this issue betrayed an awareness that the new generation must be perpetuated before sacrifice could be countenanced.

Significant elements of the Palestinian political elite played their part in generating this death-wish to a cultural norm that transcended class, gender, age, family attachments and spiritual transcendentalism. Sometimes the link between the theological dimension and the demands of modern-day conflict are inextricable. Sheikh Ahmed Yassin's statement on the eve of Eid al-Adha (The Muslim festival commemorating Abraham's sacrifice) outlined the demands of jihad: 'Jihad may be a bad word in the West, but we understand it as a moral duty against oppression, injustice and all forms of inequity ... Sons of Islam everywhere, the Jihad is a duty to establish justice and equality on earth and to liberate your countries and yourselves from America's domination and its Zionist allies; it is your battle – either victory or martyrdom,' he declared. This statement is inspirational enough for the young who gathered in Gaza's mosques to read it as a sanction to self-destruction. Indeed, in the statements issued by the martyrs before embarking on their suicide missions the imprint of sanction is all-too-apparent. Those who committed themselves to self-martyrdom were, however, sacrificed by others, the 'community' and prepared with the knowledge that there is some kind of reward – a non-death – in the transcendental sense that is creamed from the Koran in verses such as, 'Count not those who were slain in God's way as dead, but rather living with their Lord, by Him provided' (Sura 3:160). For the suicide bombers of Palestinian Islamist brigades such rewards were voiced in the process of preparation for death. Such acts were not countenanced as suicide (which is forbidden in Islam) but rather an act of martyrdom against an enemy. Religious sanction, however, does not entirely explain why the phenomenon has become so widespread, so acceptable. Its acceptability is explicable by other political factors including a nationalist interpretation of sacrifice for independence that translates into a society-wide conviction that each offers itself to the battle knowing that death is part of the equation.

Of course the sacrifice is also reactive. Hamas leaders tell us that suicide missions are a response to the brutalising and de-humanised vision of Palestinians that is perpetrated in the Israeli body politic. Furthermore, they argue that the Intifada generation, those born during the late 1980s and who came of age during this period, experienced both the exhilaration of changing the status quo with Israel and the descent again into an seemly bottomless spiral down of violence expressed through the arm of the Israeli state leading many to seek their own deaths, taking Israelis with them, rather than letting Israel remove the potentiality of their very presence. Control over death is wrested from the enemy and the death of the enemy is part of the equation.

By 2002 suicide bombing had claimed its first women perpetrators. The first was a young paramedic called Wafa Idris, whose act of self-annihilation culminated in the death of an elderly man. She had undertaken her act on behalf of the al-Aqsa Martyrs Brigades – a wing of the nationalist Fatah movement. In the wake of her death al-Aqsa Martyrs Brigades issued a leaflet stating Idris carried out the bombing in response to Israeli military actions, including the virtual house arrest in Ramallah of PA President Yasser Arafat. The Al-Aqsa Martyr Brigades – formed as a paramilitary arm of Fatah's Tanzim have, since 2002, resorted to suicide bombing along with other forms of attack on Israel. While not explicitly linked to the Hamas military arm known as the Izzi-a-din al-Qassam brigades, the al-Aqsa Martyr Brigade cells are know to maintain close contact with Hamas and other rejectionists of the Oslo process including lefitist PFLP (Popular Front for the Liberation of Palestine) elements. Strategic cooperation between Fatah's military wing and the other organisations is manifest in the harmonised rhetoric and eulogising of suicide attacks as well as growing evidence of shared technical expertise and equipment.

Another paradoxical layer is then added to the suicide phenomenon. For not only are the theocratic rules of engagement stretched to breaking point but the religious import of such acts is diminished. The mourning family members of Wafa Idris are left with the consolation that here was an individual who sacrificed herself for the concept of a nation, a nation under siege, a nation encircled and threatened. She may have wanted to die a 'martyr' and she was prepared and included in a sacrifice by others who were willing to employ her for the purposes of war for a nation. This was not the first time that women had become suicide bombers in the Middle East. In Lebanon in the mid-1980s Muslim women, including *Shi'as* had been employed in suicide missions by pro-Syrian elements. Hizb Allah clerics in Lebanon, however, made explicit their prohibition of such acts. In Islam women, are permitted to engage in the jihad, and the Hamas covenant states that, 'if an enemy invades Muslim territories then jihad and fighting the enemy becomes an individual duty on every Muslim. A woman may go and fight without her husband's permission'.[39] In the wake of the missions undertaken by Wafa Idris, Hamas founder Sheikh Yassin declared, however, that women were not required to undertake such acts.

Women and conflict

The import of such acts lies not just in terms of strategically undermining or outwitting the enemy but the debates about women and conflict more generally and the gendered dimensions therein. Further dimensions of this issue were apparent in the suicide attack undertaken by a 18-year old women from a West Bank refugee camp in March 2001. The bomber, Ayat Akhras detonated herself in a West Jerusalem supermarket on a busy Friday lunchtime. Her only victim was a similarly aged teenage girl called Rachel Levy. Akhras was another bomber member of the al-Aqsa Martyrs brigades willing to defy fundamental gender taboos about combat and conflict. Born in Dheisheh refugee camp near Bethlehem she was young, gifted, engaged and planning a university career. She was not a member of any Islamist movement or supporter of the Islamist tendency. Her 'living will' videotape showed her draped in the Palestinian kefiyyeh dedicating herself to the liberation of Palestine. Her suicide mission was motivated by conditions of war and conflict rather than religious factors. Indeed Akhras was no modern-day Joan of Arc sacrificed and sacrificing for her religious beliefs. Her motives were more prosaic and born out of the cusp of conflict that had dominated her life from birth in a refugee camp to death by self-annihilation in an Israeli supermarket. Violence appeared to dominate the life of Akhras. Press commentary at the time of the attack highlighted that the mission was part of a spiral of violence against Israelis that left over 120 dead in one month. In turn this took place as Israeli troops re-occupied Ramallah and made Palestinian leader Yasser Arafat a prisoner in his own domain. Her motive appeared to be 'nothing more or less' than a protest against Arafat's humiliation, a way of still hurting the enemy as the enemy tried to hurt the Palestinians back. Akhras was only atypical of those who had gone before her because of her gender. Her status as a dispossessed refugee did not mark her out, her youth did not mark her out, her experience of a conflict with a foreign occupier did not mark her out, her poverty did not mark her out, her political beliefs did not mark her out, her brutalised experiences did not mark her out. She was as typical as any

other in this spiral of conflict where fundamental values respecting the right
to life, especially by civilians, rather than military combatants have become
routinely abused, ignored and trampled on by both sides to the conflict.

Yet there were aspects of the attacks by the female suicide-bombers that
confounded. The perpetration of an act of violence by women in the
Palestinian–Israeli conflict, particularly as frontline combatants, provoked a
reflection on the way in which one assessed the reasons for violence as traditionally associated with male perpetrators in conflict. It is known that men
make war and enjoin each other to violence 'for many reasons – for money,
honour, patriotism or brotherhood, in self-defence, for liberation, to liberate
others', yet do such patriarchal factors explain the admittance of Palestinian
women to the gladiatorial arena of the twenty-first century?[40] The evidence
to date would suggest that the presence of Palestinian women as combatants
in conflict against Israel is not about a sea-change in the Palestinian national
struggle as its male leadership re-assesses its patriarchal attitudes and
attempts a strategy that promotes gender equality in parallel to the liberation struggle. Gender mattered in this context only because it had been
'used' and 'abused' by men. Such a perspective may support an argument
that men have turned Palestinian women into suicide bombers as part of a
war strategy and the women who are sacrificed have not necessarily
advanced the cause of equality or even liberation. The male still dominates
in this militarised landscape – on both sides of the conflict and even its inter-
nationalised fringes – their rationality, their strategy, their tactics remain
unchallenged. This perspective or argument, however, is not the same as
that made by Dworkin who used the story of women suicide bombers to
engage in a polemic against Palestinian society as epitomised as a nation of
male sexual abusers. This argument fails to engage with the discourse on the
right of resistance and the foundations of the legitimacy to resistance in conflict contexts where the usual international rules and norms are flouted and
defied by the occupier and oppressor.[41]

The self-martyrdom by Palestinian women, against mostly Israeli civilians,
did not alter the nature of this terrorist phenomenon. It only altered the terrorist phenomenon in terms of security strategy, counter-insurgency and
policy-making. In reality the preparedness of thousands of Palestinian men
or women to sacrifice themselves through suicide against Israeli targets was
only meaningful in terms of the wider issues of the war. In this respect, time
dwelt on identifying the 'typical suicide bomber' detracted from the real reasons of why the Palestinian–Israeli conflict had taken such a turn. Turning
young women into suicide bombers, however, is deeply symbolic in the
arena of war and conflict. In all too many nationalist struggles women
are utilised as symbols of nation; their status as wombs of the nation assume
incredible significance in ethno-national conflicts that pitch opposing nations
in demographic battles. High proliferating birth rates among Palestinians
had traditionally been recognised as a 'weapon' in the conflict with Israel.

Issues relating to the experience of women also play their part in defining the nation, its credentials and aspirations. In war women are part of the conflict. Women are perceived as in need of sacred protection and no more so in the Israeli–Palestinian arena where women, on both sides of the conflict, are viewed as the biological locus of identity and the nation. Thus the sacrifice of women in such conflicts can be read in a number of ways. In one respect the admittance of Palestinian women to this particular arena of conflict defies conventional thinking as they relate to war and gender. In this context woman as martyr seekers are the antithesis of normative theorising that persists about women as peacemakers. The sensationalism attached to this particular image of women as warriors is explicable in terms of their combat-readiness and participation. Even in the most 'liberal' armed forces of the developed world, which employ women as visible elements, they are still kept away from the field of combat and from the firing line. Israeli women serve in the nation's armed forces but not on the frontline in a combat role; Palestinian women have struggled to play their equal part in the liberation from Israeli occupation but have been largely excluded by traditional patriarchal attitudes across the political spectrum. In modern nation states like Israel and the United States of America the notion that all citizens are equal and equally defend the nation in its armed forces is symbolically reflected in the presence of women – and in Israel's case the relative absence of its Arab citizens from its ranks. Palestinian women suicide bombers perpetuate a psychological advantage over their Israeli adversaries who have traditionally denied combat roles to conscripted Israeli women and illustrate a perverse paradox about conflict, gender and equality as it is truly experienced. The 'hidden' nature of women in conflict is destroyed by these very public demonstrations of destruction. What does all of this tell us? In truth it reveals 'much more than just the fact that women bear no essential relationship to peace and non-violence. It also shows that different contexts [including the Palestinian–Israeli arena] produce different gender constructions.'[42]

Islamists in Hamas, however, while provisionally prohibiting the participation of women in combat refer to women as 'the maker of men and her role in guiding and educating the generations is a major role ... caring for the home and preparing ... [her children] ... for their contribution to the jihad that awaits them ... ' emphasising the symbolic function of women in the conflict.[43] In this respect the knowing sacrifice of women in suicide missions can be viewed either as a sign of weakness or strength. For if women are the locus of the nation then their sacrifice (by others – males specifically) betrays an impotency in the macho battle between men and a sub-conscious cancelling out of the nation that struggles to be recognised as possessing rights to self-determination and independence. There is evidence that Islamists have moved from such rigidly held positions. The leadership of movements like Hamas and Hizbullah have indicated an additional perspective on this issue. Hizbullah MP Mohammed Fnaysh has acknowledged that women have an important part to play in resistance efforts, 'nothing prevents the participation of women ... in facing the occupier and the justification ethically of men and women to resist in the same'.[44] The female suicide bombers are also symbolic of the modern-day phenomenon of conflict where the traditional rules of the game are ignored, where the casualties of conflict are found in cafes and shops not battlefields and borderlands. Female suicide bombers indicate the subtle changes to modern-day conflict in the post-Cold War era where war is everyone's affair and the frontline straddles the streets of town and cities and where ordinary combat preparedness does not give one the military advantage. The female suicide bombers are further evidence of the nature of ethno-national emergencies where everyone is considered to be a combatant irrespective of age, gender, location or class.[45] In this respect the convention of the uniform means little, for all too often the political leaders engaged in such conflicts are barely out of uniform or the nation wears the uniform and the civilianising of war becomes commonplace. In this context nations find themselves as one in war with the other. Everyone is a combatant; everyone has the potential to fight their own war of independence from the other.

In this context the semantics of terrorism and force pale in significance to the actuality of the conflict as lived. Terror, the experience of extreme fear, is not visited upon a group of victims in the night like the legendary horror associated with the ghoulish gambols of Dracula; everyone experiences the insecurity and the extreme fear. Terrorism – the use of 'violence and intimidation, especially for political purposes' – is not in the monopolistic grip of one party over the other. Sacrifice and suicide become blurred and lost in the carnage of lost human lives. The political dimension of such acts betrays the secularised arena in which modern-day conflict takes place. In this arena the religious message of liberation must compete alongside the more secularised call of others for the same goal. Yet in the propaganda battles that wage between Islamists and nationalists, Palestinians and Israelis, the sanction of suicide as martyrdom is legitimated and the boundaries of religious interpretation stretched further than ever before.

The 9/11 Bombers

> The brothers, who conducted the operation, all they knew was that they have a martyrdom operation and we asked each of them to go to America but they didn't know anything about the operation, not even one letter. But they were trained and we did not reveal the operation to them until they are there and just before they boarded the planes.
>
> Transcript of Usama Bin Laden videotape released
> by the US government, 13 December 2001

In the wake of the attacks on America on 11 September 2001 perpetrated by 19 Muslim suicide bombers and as governments, pundits, academics and ordinary individuals sought to make sense of an act of violence so intense that it undermined the sense of security of much of the western hemisphere, millions of column inches were dedicated to exploring the lives of the bombers. The 'facts' about the bombers emerged in a piecemeal fashion. In the days, weeks and months that followed, a form of consensus emerged about who the suicide bombers were, and what had motivated them.

They were declared as having killed in the name of God, in the name of Islam, that they should be understood as they perceived themselves: *mujahideen* despatched by their 'religious' leader. There was consensus that these bombers who had willingly annihilated themselves had been despatched on a sacred mission and that their violence was motivated by holy obligations to the leader of al-Qaida and his interpretations of Islam.

In other respects, however, the bombers confounded the experts. The emerging profile of the men who perpetrated the attacks bemused the experts and was subsequently deployed in defence of the failure of the intelligences services to prevent the devastation. These bombers were described and understood as adherents of a radical extremist Islamist movement, but it soon became clear that they did not fit the profile of the other radical extremist suicide bombers that the intelligence communities of Israel and the United States of America in particular had spent years so carefully constructing. The profiles had proved ineffective. The 11 September bombers did not appear to have much in common with the psychological profiles of bombings associated with the Tamil Tigers and Kamikaze Pilots of Japan's air forces in the Second World War or the imprisoned Muslim militants languishing in Israel's jails as a result of conflicts with the Palestinians and in Lebanon. These bombers were not and did not epitomise the dispossession, poverty, lack of education, marginality, commonly associated with the stereotype of radical Islamism and its 'suicidal' or martyrdom elements. And while it first appeared that the attacks did appear to epitomise the common myth that Islam was a faith system that encouraged violence, there was much more to this particular act than that which initially met the horrified and transfixed eye.

The 19 men who undertook a death mission that wrought havoc on the United States of America engaged in an act of terrorism that was condemned by the Muslim clerical establishment. The deliberate targeting of civilians was considered unjustified and the act was condemned, even within certain radical Islamist ranks, across the Muslim world. In Egypt, for example, the Islamic religious establishment as well as opposition elements were united in their condemnation of the attack as an act of terror against civilian elements. Additionally they refused to condone such an assault as legitimate according to Islamic jurisprudence. A publicly issued statement remarked that: 'All Muslims ought to be united against all those who terrorise the innocents, and those who permit the killing of non-combatants without a justifiable reason. Islam has declared the spilling of blood and the destruction of property as absolute prohibitions until the Day of Judgment.'[46] In this respect the 'representative' nature of the violence and terrorism carried out on that fateful day are undermined from the response within the Muslim domain.

As my earlier discussions in this text have demonstrated, there is a dimension to the debate about terrorism and political violence that reflects on the representative dimension of such acts. It becomes increasingly apparent that there is little ambiguity within the Muslim domain that such an assault – despite the claims of the attackers and their leader – was considered unrepresentative of Islam or the legitimate grievances of Muslims in locales experiencing major upheavals and conflicts. What Bin Laden had managed to assemble around him were a cohort of Muslims who subscribed to his specific vision of the world which was shaped in turn by his own experiences – in Saudi Arabia, Afghanistan and Sudan –, his wealth and his myopic vision of the world. Like the cultic followers of David Koresh Bin Laden's recruits to al-Qaeda should be understood as a fringe manifestation of the modern era.

Here of course though the motive and the method demand address, Bin Laden's motive owes much to the radical and fundamentalist discourses of Ibn Taymiyyah and Sayyid Qutb. Such discourse is also deeply and fundamentally anti-American and anti-Western rather than being based on other motives which may be commonly found among other radical Islamist movements in the contemporary era. 'Islam's battle in this era against the new Christian–Jewish crusade led by the big crusader Bush under the flag of the Cross; this battle is considered one of Islam's battles,' declared Bin Laden.[47] In this context Islam is repeatedly employed to justify Bin Laden's motives. The motive is an explicit call to jihad against the United States of America (and smaller 'Satans') which, as I have already noted, is generally dismissed as legitimate by the majority of Muslim jurists. Orthodox *Sunni* jurisprudence did not condone such acts. According to orthodox jurisprudence jihad reflected the debate about inner struggle or as a defensive mechanism against the foreign invasion and occupation of Muslim territory. The call to defence engages the *mujahid* in defence of a territory under occupation in which Islam is prevented from flourishing. From this perspective it was argued that those who undertook the attacks on 11 September 2001, and earlier incidents against American targets could not from a *Sunni* juridic point of view be regarded as *mujahideen*, nor their deaths in such attacks as martyrdom. Indeed, according to some Muslim leaders, the virtues of jihad are undermined by the 11 September 2001 bombers and those who motivated them. One Hamas leader declared, 'what they did [the 9/11 bombers] is not jihad in our name. They are free and enjoy liberty yet they took it from innocents. Our struggle is not their [al-Qaeda's] struggle'.[48] The sanctity of jihad is perceived as undermined by crass fundamentalism as expressed by the terrorists. Crass fundamentalism and its dangerous and violent terrorist tendencies are not unique to Islam. As I have remarked elsewhere in this book fundamentalism represented in its Hindu, Christian and Jewish manifestations also go a long way in accounting for major terrorist atrocities and violence across the globe. The notion of crass fundamentalism held at the heart of this project by the majority of the bombers is also related to the nature and ideas associated with the export of neo-fundamentalist tendencies. This system of Muslim belief is a marginal *Sunni* phenomenon that cannot be considered representative of mainstream orthodox *Sunni* Islam. Many of the adherents of this neo-fundamentalism, however, consider it their divine duty to wage a war on the West and those in their own societies that they consider to be far from their strict and literal interpretations of Islam.

The scourge of terrorism and instability that has been underscored by al-Qaeda, the Taliban and other fanatic Islamist elements, it is alleged, has been supported, funded or established through a linkage to powerful individuals in *wahabbi* dominated Saudi Arabia. While it appeared to come as a shock to ordinary Americans and Europeans that young Saudi men had played a part in such terror and devastation, it was no surprise in many quarters of the Muslim domain that have experienced the influence of what they viewed as Saudi Arabia's *wahabbi* propagation agenda as a malign force in their own societies. Establishment and anti-establishment forces within Saudi Arabia are now charged with playing a major part in accounting for the arrogance of power and wealth that has been employed in the name of Islam across the contemporary globe to promote an antipathy founded on neo-fundamentalist practices.[49] Increasingly the more altruistic and peaceful motives of Saudi Muslim philanthropy are obscured by growing allegations that within Saudi Arabia there are those that have encouraged fundamentalism of the most extreme kinds, including al-Qaeda, and the Taliban; have oppressed other Muslim minorities – in particular the *Shi'a*; and nurtured a generation of citizens many of whom subscribe to the same fantastical and arrogant beliefs of *Wahabbi* hegemony built on a chimera of money and not orthodox mainstream Islamic belief.

Does the neo-fundamentalist religious nature of such societies go some way in explaining the motives and methods of madness so shatteringly demonstrated by al-Qaeda's operations? Is there anything sacred in the wanton destruction of the lives of ordinary people even if it is claimed in the name of Islam? Martyrdom and sacrifice as a religious phenomenon was effectively emptied of its meaning in the post-modern discourses of secularism. And in many respects such processes also allowed the fanatic fringe in Islam to get away with re-inventing and re-branding it to fit their own marginal interpretations. *Sunni* and *Shi'a* orthodoxy on the subject has emerged to provide a very modern interpretation of the phenomenon. In the *Shi'a* context there is a depth to the discourse that was promoted by necessity rather than timely reflection. This discourse, as Reuter's contends, was of its time. Today, he claims that Iran is a society deeply opposed to cultures of martyrdom that were perpetuated by the state in the early revolutionary phase.[50] The sacred dimension of violence in Iran has been altered. The wider debate about the sacred dimension of violence in the modern era should steer us to a wider discourse about faith and politics in a global context that is seen as increasingly consolidated by secularism. The myths surrounding conceptualisations of what it means to be modern have been challenged by the violence of Islam's self-declared jihad warriors. This is part of a wider tension between that which is secular and that which is religious in the modern era. The challenge has been manifest in a violent form through acts of terrorism but this in turn has diminished their sacred dimension. Will this change? Gray contends that, once al-Qaeda has disappeared, 'other types of terror – very likely not animated by radical Islam, possibly not overtly religious – will surely follow.'[51] Violence is often the helpmate of change and in this respect Islam is not unique in employing it for such purposes. The challenge is to offer alternatives to violence and disconnection through diversity and sociability.

5

Holy Terror: Representations of Violence in a Modern Age

Introduction

> From pacifist to terrorist, each person condemns violence – and then adds one cherished case in which it may be justified.
>
> Gloria Steinem

There are very few images, if any, in the post-modern era that have gripped the popular imagination more than the one of Muslim suicide-bombers. The image of Muslim fanaticism and the fear it perpetuates has, as other chapters in this book have highlighted, a historical predecessor and is exploited by a number of actors in political and other conflicts which engage combatants from Muslim domains. Nevertheless, the image of Holy Terror was irrevocably reinforced by the hijackers who steered their planes to such devastating consequences on 11 September 2001 and by the direction of Usama Bin Laden. From this image others have spawned and contributed to an environment where others who took stability and security for granted have been compelled to stop and re-assess everything that hitherto they had taken for granted in their lives. There is a growing perception, disseminated in modern media, that there is a worldwide Muslim terror phenomenon – global, part of a new wave of terrorism that animates and characterises Muslim domains and their interactions with others.

In this chapter then, I intended to pull out the strands of an argument that contests that dimensions of Huntington's thesis of a clash of civilisations (and between Islam and the West in particular) is an inevitable outcome of a changed global order in the wake of the ending of the Cold War. I contend that collision and its forgone violent consequence is not inevitable. Additionally, I believe there is evidence of a new construction of Islam within certain Western scholarly circles that deliberately contributes to the increasing distance, dissonance and misunderstanding that results in the lumping of a rich and diversified religious tradition into one homogenous and violent mass. From this perspective of contemporary terrorism, most

Muslims have become a subject of fear and suspicion. As Pipes remarks, 'whom are we fighting? Two main culprits have emerged since Sept. 11: terrorism and Islam. The truth more subtle, lies between the two – a terroristic version of Islam.'[1] Such an assertion can be countered with examples of the attempts at nuance in this debate by western political leaders such as President Bush of America or British Prime Minister Tony Blair to reach out to the Muslim community in their own countries and assert that the war on terrorism is not a war on Islam.

This reductive or simplistic approach far from alerting Western policy-makers, strategists and others to the real threats posed by Muslims who engage in acts of terrorism was partly responsible for the blinding confusion that contributed to the failure of the western intelligence community to recognise the true nature of the threat and meet it before the devastation wrought by events such as the al-Qaeda Embassy bombings in 1998 and the attacks on America in September 2001. As such, I am arguing that it is disingenuous to assert that because al-Qaeda carries out terrorism this can be equated with Islam represented as a faith system that is innately violent. Indeed, such assertions seem only likely to stoke the fires of conflict and promote a sense of persecution among mainstream Muslim elements. Additionally, I would contend that the way in which the label of Muslim Holy terror is currently employed is problematic in relation to the justifiable and legitimate reaction of Muslim communities against authoritarian governments and elements.

The Muslim mainstream, however, also has a task of getting its own house in order and through the promotion of internal discourse must begin to address the dilemmas presented through the manifestation of terrorism in the name of Islam. Ambiguity in this context is the enemy of Islam and fails to breach the chasm or eradicate the notion of threat and fear that currently resonates around the faith. In a sense then what I am saying is that the notion of accountability must be introduced to both sides of this debate, this conflict and this relationship; Muslims are not regarded of the West, even if physically located in the West; and its values creates a demand that makes scholars, thinkers and leaders of the global Muslim community accountable to the accusation.

Perception is everything

In a popular broadcast programme shown on mainstream TV, US psychologist Dr. Phil (and friend of Oprah Winfrey) offers advice to his mass audience. In outlining his life laws, Dr. Phil declares, 'Life Law #6: There is no reality; only perception.'[2] 'Perception', he tells overweight women, couples experiencing marital breakdown or teenagers with confidence problem, 'is what matters'. That most Muslims have become a subject of fear and suspicion is also about perception. It may appear to be exaggerated to speak of such a perception but when it exists it gives rise to an increasing suspicion that Muslims – increasingly transformed in the popular consciousness into potential terrorists – are bent on a holy war of destruction and annihilation not just of enemy states but also a prevailing international order in which western-based capitalism stands at its apex. Akhbar Ahmed described this in the following way, 'Muslims – whether living as a majority or a minority – felt especially vulnerable after 11 September. Any expression of Muslim identity risked the fear of being suspected as "terrorist" activity. Muslims felt that their religion Islam was under siege.'[3] Dimensions of Muslim holy and even 'transcendental unholy'[4] terror become a popular preoccupation of policy-makers, the intelligence community, economists, military strategists, diplomats, newspaper editors, news chiefs and academics. A consideration of the new phenomena of Muslim terror became a focus for re-thinking foreign policies, military spending, the development of the arms industry, the development of national economies and fresh reflection on the post-modern age where the secular order appears to be challenged and found wanting. The populations of Muslim communities from Kuala Lumpar to Harlem, Tajikistan to Birmingham, be they Black, Asian, Arab or Turk were increasingly portrayed or perceived as a conflated whole – their similarities of faith far greater than their differences. Put another way, I am contending, the boundary line between those within the Muslim domain who are extremist terrorists and those who are not becomes increasingly difficult to fix when discourse in the West increasingly focuses on the portrayal of Muslims as violent. Muslims have become homogenised through a series of symbols that are interpreted or reflected in the popular consciousness as denoting their identity in a reductive spiral that links to the symbols of violence and terror. From this vantage point, attempts made by Muslims and non-Muslim elements to wrestle with this stereotype and avoid such conflations become increasingly difficult and centred on rebuke.

Such images are easy to exploit, and the process by which a community of over a billion 'believers' of the Islamic faith became viewed as a 'threat' where all are potential terrorists began well before Bin Laden struck at American targets at home and abroad. The contention that most Muslims – whatever way being Muslim is defined – do not support the extremist doctrine of an individual Muslim such as Usama Bin Laden and are not terrorists are veiled in the assertion that it is as much the potential for violence among Muslims that is a threat within and to the modern Western order. Opinion polls conducted in the United States of America in 2003 demonstrated the growing perception that Muslims are more strongly associated with violence than those identified with other faith systems. The survey respondents demonstrated what was described as, 'an important shift in public perceptions of Islam. Of this, 44 per cent now believe that Islam is more likely than other religions 'to encourage violence among its believers'.[5] This was an increase rather than a decrease of perception with regard to the matrix between Islam and violence.

Does Islam encourage violence?

Islam encourages violence? (%)	March 2002 (%)	July 2003
Yes	25	44
No	51	41
Neither/DK	25	15
	100	100

Source: Pew Research Centre, July 2003.

The survey revealed that opinions of this nature were more likely expressed by those self-ascribed as conservatives than liberals and is some indication therefore of the impact of conservative governance in America and its impact on such issues.

Furthermore, the dissidence and dissatisfaction with the neo-liberal homogenising agenda expressed by, among others, people in Muslim communities in Bradford or Karachi or Nigeria are employed as evidence of the potential for a Muslim fifth column or transnational revolutionary force that will bring down the liberal democratic polities of the modern age. Muslim dissidence is measured against the yardstick of Bin Laden, no matter how fervently Bin Laden himself is rejected by such elements in the Muslim domain. As Hizb Allah MP Mohammed Fnaysh has argued, 'What Usama Bin Laden did was harmful to Islam ... and in relation to Afghanistan and the Taliban this is also not about using Islamic principles to address legitimate concerns, but now Islam is tainted with their violence'.[6] Such views may be interpreted as nothing more than a *Shi'a* rebuke to the internal contest between such elements and the *Sunni* fundamentalist forces of Bin Laden and the Taliban, but they also represent a real dilemma in terms of reading Islamism in the modern age. In the wake of suicide bombing attacks in the United States of America, Spain and the United Kingdom many ordinary citizens confronted this dilemma in terms of their day to day interactions with the Muslim members of their own society.

For now dissidence, a trait that in liberal-democratic terms might be acknowledged as important is interpreted as the potential for terror. So, it is no wonder when such 'dissidence' has been exploited by some Islamists to preach messages of hate against *kufrs* (non-Muslims), homosexuals and Jews. New myths are constructed and old ones resurrected to legitimate this new process of interpretation. The new myths underscore the notion that Muslims now represent or have the potential to represent a threat. Yet, myths are created for a reason. In the contemporary era such myths have a political purpose. This further confuses and clouds the way in which the political agendas associated with the major religious phenomenon of Islam are portrayed and around which individuals and communities are organised and others are opposed. Not only are political communities imagined as a process of creating themselves, as Benedict Anderson has convincingly asserted in his explanation of nationalism in the modern age, but imagined communities devise and employ myths of the 'other' and Islam in particular to assert the competitive strength of their ideologies. This is a two-way process for, as many in the West imagine 'myth' to be employed by more primitive nationalisms and religions, there is a case to be made for the gainful employment of such myth in modern developed political systems as well.

In association with Islam then terror takes on a mythic and more potent and urgent potential for instability in the post-communist order than hitherto more recently imagined. The contemporary evidence of a bearded Muslim fanatic holed up in Afghanistan as he masterminded his plan to take America underscored historic stories about an eternally linked leitmotif between Islam and violence. Such myths are then taken for granted and their presence qualifies and sanctions the need to take a position in a post-modern environment in which such appeals should really be irrelevant. The reason for this is clear, but only if we stop and think for a moment. In the post-enlightenment age of reason, democracy and global capitalism where plurality and the individual stand to prosper, it has been apparent, on more than one occasion, that the state which is most commonly identified with this age of reason, the individual and liberty is the United States of America. Yet, a counter-veiling force, built on a real and perceived experience of that which represents and is America has emerged. This 'anti-American' force has been given a particularly Muslim hue and has been significantly associated with an opposition that takes form in violence and more specifically terrorism.

Cradle of Holy Terror

> Terrorism is dangerous ground for *simplficateurs* and *generalisateurs*. To approach it, a cool head is probably more essential than any other intellectual quality.
>
> Walter Laqueur

It is important to reveal the process in which Islam becomes signified as terrifyingly potent in relation to violence and its lethal potential to alter environment and change patters of politics, economy and culture. Much contemporary theory on terrorism and political violence was nurtured and evolved in the context of the ideological battles of the Cold War era. Marxist and neo-Marxist explanations of violence in the modern age were as much a response to the right-wing and realist explanations of terrorism as a threat to legitimate state force, than the demand to support the legitimate right to raise arms in the course of self-determination and national liberation. The genre of terrorism studies revealed evidence of attempts at constructing a paradigm or typology to explain the terrorism of the left and the revolutionary and anarchic potential therein. Throughout the 1960s and 1970s when the spotlight fell on the Middle East, terrorism was almost singularly defined in terms of the threat posed by the PLO. Yet, it was the advent of mass revolution in Iran in 1979 and the establishment of a theocratic republic in its wake that led many to re-formulate their arguments and reflect a new dimension of terrorism. As Rapoport argued, 'a most arresting and unexpected development in recent years has been the revival of terrorist activities to support religious purposes or terror justified in theological terms.'[7] For the most part, Islam was identified as significant to the explanation of violence in Egypt, Lebanon and Iran, and other Muslim locales were consistently cited as evidence of the new terrorism.

One location where the new force was deemed manifest and significant was Lebanon. In the United States of America and Europe, the evocation of the word Lebanon is synonymous with violent, zealous, fanatical, atavistic, brutal and conflict. In many respects conflict in Lebanon was understood primarily by images of the 'bearded' 'stern-faced' murderous clerics and kidnappers of Islam; for it is through the interpretation of the Muslim dimension of Lebanon and the conflict that engulfed the country that many Western audiences know the country. As such war, violence and terrorism in Lebanon is not recognised in the context of the iniquities of deeply divided societies where the democratic model is abused to subordinate a demographic majority and where democratic rights are denied by a dominant community on the grounds of ethnic, national and religious animosities.[8] In Lebanon the West's image of Islam was forged on the ground of conflict, not cooperation. In Lebanon, it can be argued that many western states may have met their match and emerged from this particular engagement with dimensions of Islam battered and bruised. In one episode of what was to be multi-national UN-mandated support for the country involving thousands of American service personnel, Muslims only perceived America to be offering one-sided support for the Christian-led government. The *Shi'a* organisation, Hizb Allah that had formed as a result of Israeli occupation and invasion of Lebanon in 1982 and was subsequently supported by the post-revolutionary government of Ayatollah Khomeini in Iran had definitely constructed an ideological line of opposition to Western states such as the United States of America. Indeed, it can be argued that a significant dimension of Hizb Allah's anti-American agenda was forged, not only as a result as its opposition to liberal-democratic models and modernisation 'particularly as manifested by Westernisation', but due to a perception that since the 1920s successive Western governments had not only supported but directly intervened in the perpetuation of ethnic and religious inequality in Lebanon.[9] In addition, for the radical Islamist leadership (spiritual, as well as political and military) they contended that there was overwhelming evidence that US-support for neighbouring Israel had directly resulted in the suffering of Lebanese civilians. Radical Islamists and others, therefore, treated with suspicion the coalescence of Israeli and American interests in Lebanon that included US involvement in the multi-national peacekeeping mission that was eventually despatched to Lebanon by the international community in 1982.

Under such circumstances, was it antipathy to the 'West' or antipathy to a Western-state perceived as supporting hostile acts against Lebanese civilians that propelled radical Islamic elements into action? Hizb Allah's leaders contended the former; whatever the reasons, the consequences were significant. Terrorism was the strategy that was adopted. It started on 18 April 1983 when a pick-up truck packed with over 100 kgs of explosives was driven and detonated by its martyrdom-seeking driver outside the American embassy in Beirut. Of the 63 killed, including nearly 20 Americans, the CIA Bureau stationed in the Embassy had been significantly depleted. It was believed that the bureau-chief, his deputy and several others were among the dead. Six months later in another attack on US Marines stationed in the country, 241 were killed. In March 1984, Bill Buckley, the then-CIA chief in Beirut was subject to an audacious kidnapping and on 20 September that year another suicide-seeking operation executed by Islamist radicals on the US Embassy annex in Beirut left another 13 dead. America responded by taking its troops away and effectively shutting up shop in Lebanon. While it was true that they couldn't entirely abandon the country (US citizens were held as hostages throughout much of the 1980s largely because of its ties with Israel and its desire to contain both the Syrians and the Iranian threat that was all-too-apparent in their involvement in the conflict), it was clear that Islamist-inspired attacks on the United States of America and its military personnel had created the impression that the world's most powerful nation (even then) had met its match. As Smith notes, 'As American forces departed from Lebanon's shores in early 1984, the U.S. policy lay in ruins, the victim of the perceptions of its policy-makers as well as the entangled web of regional and communal hatreds.'[10] Radical Islamism was but one dimension of that entanglement.

In a play entitled the 'Militiaman',[11] Beirut's bloody and evil associations are inherently linked to a religious overtone in a multi-faceted political, sectarian, intra-state conflict in which an entire country was engulfed. This fatalistic account gives credence to a belief that religion motivates violence that is different in expression from other forms of violence. For, even though the central character in the play is a man brutalised by civil war, by the creation of landscapes dominated by landmines and snipers, it is the presence of a 'vengeful God' and the appreciation that 'sometimes fanaticism is all that you need to keep afloat' that distinguishes and marks this human experience out from others. It is the fact that religion appears to inspire a form of inhumanity that sets it apart from other traditions that seems to imbue acts of resistance, violence and terror with the same terrifying characteristics. In the context of Lebanon then, holy terror is reflected as a lived experience in the minds of many and has entered the cultural accounts of how the conflict was lived. Holy terror, however, is not about the destructive force of all religions but rather one; for in Lebanon, many accounts charge Islam as guilty.

Power matrix

The power-matrix from which many debates about terror in the modern age have emerged have been hinged on the dialectic debates about power and order rooted in western traditions of political thought. Such theorising held good for many decades with the battle lines firmly drawn around larger conflicts involving state and non-state actors. Nevertheless, one outcome of this debate was the growing consensus that terrorism had become a significant feature of the modern political landscape. In the post-Cold War era, where new frontiers of power and politics emerged with uneven and fractured frailty, so too have new responses to political violence been coined. Wars and conflict, the failure to prevent them and the failure to end them, have according to Kaldor demanded a new approach. The same, it should be argued, is demanded of explanations for contemporary terrorism. Kaldor contends that issues such as identity, global economy and the state remain important to explanations of new conflicts.[12] One other such response which has played on the strategic threats of the past is the so-called Holy Terror. One might presume that the Holy Terror thesis may shed light on the reasons why in the modern context young men and women feel compelled to engage in a form of politics – to make a political point to an opposing force – in which they turn themselves into human bombs. To know an individual who willingly undertakes a series of actions in which he or she ends their life in the hope that it might contribute to the resolution of a wider political struggle and more importantly victory for the cause has always demanded explanation, but all the more so when the battlefield is on a street or in a restaurant and the foes are unevenly matched. If the character of war had been traditionally defined by rules and norms, which attempted to keep civilians out of conflict, then the suicide phenomenon has challenged the old assumptions. Yet, it is not merely the suicide phenomenon that matters but also the religious mandate that appears attached to it.

Does the religious mandate or the context matter in terms of an explanation that means that somewhere down the line policy-makers and strategists have tools to counter the threat without compromising the democratic mandate and the rule of law? What is the context that compels people to such a form of direct action? The shanty refugee camp of Aida near the West Bank town of Bethlehem and the young refugee residents whose hopes and aspirations were constrained by the precarious nature of life under Israeli military occupation might give up some evidence; for to stand in such a refugee camp and survey its population and know that among them exists the willingness to end life in the name of the cause is surely an indication that all is not right in the world. In 1987 when hundreds and thousands of Palestinians took to the streets against Israel's defence forces, the image of those who tore open their shirts and demanded that the enemy make a martyr of them was all-too-willingly relayed as evidence of Palestinian conviction that they had a right to resist Israel as a consequence of its occupation of them. The notion of a martyr-syndrome grew and throughout the West Bank and Gaza Strip photographers were besieged to record the image of those who were willing to engage in annihilation of the self. Hasty marriages were made in order to lead to the birth of a human legacy of those who willingly opted for martyrdom. There are, however, hundreds of refugee camps across the globe where millions live in poverty but where suicide operations are not the means of communication. In the refugee camps of Western Sahara where the Sahrawi people reside in expectation that one day their internationally recognised right to self-determination will be fulfilled, its residents have not resorted to suicide bombs to further its cause.

Yet within the Palestinian Aida camp in the West Bank, and others like it, the resurgence of Islam in its political guise contributed to a new kind of consciousness raising and activism among its young residents; for one dimension of empowerment was an openness to new political appeal that was outside the monopoly of nationalism. And indeed among those refugees without a state and denied their rights, there was one among that number who was subsequently stepped on an Israeli bus in West Jerusalem with the intent of bringing terror to its passengers. This knife-wielding Palestinian succeeded in his task. The ways in which the knowledge of such sacrifices are made and felt; the ripples in the pool of humanity caused by such an act are unknowable. Yet, all are altered by it. All are affected and somehow made smaller and touched in ways that were previously unimaginable. Such acts diminish humanity; diminish power for good; and in the desire to succeed in the protection, the vulnerable is weakened. Indeed, defining the vulnerable or the victims in societies torn asunder by intrastate ethnic and nationalist conflicts becomes part of how the conflict is perpetuated and is self-defining. In such context, the legitimate claim to victimhood, the categorisation of the 'vulnerable' and the consequent moral obligation or demand to protect become subject to competing claims.

Yet, it was the international community that applauded such sacrifice or martyrdom-seeking behaviour by hundreds and thousands of young Palestinian men and women from 1988–93 and which went some way in rewarding it with diplomatic progress in attempted resolution of the Arab–Israeli conflict. The western media created a new image of Palestinians as victims not terrorists, and because they were no longer perceived as those wreaking havoc or chaos, their political acts of self-sacrifice were viewed from an entirely new perspective. Indeed, it was this volte-face in international opinion that appeared insensible to Israelis who were used to being portrayed as the victims of Palestinian terror rather than the perpetrators of terror against Palestinian victims. Western ambiguity, however, became increasingly apparent, when reflected on other acts of self-annihilation also labelled as Holy Terror. Surely, if the reasons for self-annihilation in the name of a political cause which has a particular Islamist association are explored, then a means to end such a destructive form of politics can be devised?

Most terrorologist conceptions of Islam contend that it is fixed, mono-lithic and static. Such accounts rarely acknowledge that Islam is multi-faceted – culturally, religiously, politically, economically and so on. Islam tends to be represented in a distorted one-dimensional caricature, lacking the animation of even the most crudely drawn cartoon.

Islam is understood and portrayed as uniform, but the plural vision or the particularistic manifestation that is appreciated in other faith systems, other ideologies or cultures is absent. The logic of such interpretations is that in embracing Islam (or even by virtue of being born a Muslim – for believers are not subject to a rite or ceremony of admission to the faith) the identity of the Muslim becomes one and the same as each and every other subscriber to Islam. This, in principle makes bedfellows of the Muslim Bin Laden who issued a declaration of war against Americans and legendry American boxing hero Mohammed Ali who condemned the attacks on Washington and New York on 11 September 2001.

Discerning the point, the element or factor by which all Muslims are divorced from the particular, the product of acculturation and interpreta-tion, a marriage of tradition and the modern, and represented as universal in character as it relates to the impulse for violence or terrorism is problematic to say the least. Yet, the terrorologist scholarship on Islam does just that. Yet, it should be noted that those who engage in such an endeavour are not nec-essarily malign but rather seek to make sense of what appears to be an 'us and other' situation where the 'other' appears to be hell-bent on the destruc-tion of 'us.' In this respect there is a unity between both 'the others' and 'us' that transcends the religio-cultural divides of 'Islam and the West'; for the majority of 'them' abhor the attempt at destruction of 'us'. If self-preservation is the order of the day then the aspiration is universal whether you are in Toronto or Tora Bora. The challenge here, I believe, is to undermine and defeat the root of the grievances that have made the theo-ideological assertions behind such acts relevant to people across the globe.

Warriors of the Prophet

Much contemporary research on Islamism has concentrated on aspects of political terror that have, in turn, been represented as dominating the lexicon of religion as a whole. While scholarship on Islam broadens the per-spective much, political science on Islamism continues to portray Muslims as 'Warriors of the Prophet' and an alien and hostile phenomenon that reflects a real threat to a common system of civilisation mostly represented as the West. Muslim terror became a phenomenon of such significant and frightening proportions that in the wake of the attacks of 11 September 2001 entire industries, such as those of travel, were shaken to its root; routine patterns of public behaviour were disrupted; thousands if not millions of people cancelled out on air-travel; a war in Afghanistan in which, even according to conservative estimates, as many civilian casualties were created as in the 11 September attacks was waged; and the boundaries of Operation Enduring Freedom expanded to other locations.

Indeed, there is evidence that since 11 September 2001, Muslim terror has clawed at the public imagination and this fear has been used by politicians and policy-makers on a scale which was previously unimaginable. North Americans were told that they were now living in a different world. In the United Kingdom, in the wake of the July 2005 suicide bombing, Prime Minster Tony Blair affirmed that 'There is no justification for suicide bombing whether in Palestine, Iraq, in London, in Egypt, in Turkey, anywhere. In the United States of America, there is no justification for it.'

Even the most benign forms of American television, such as Oprah with her hitherto soft focus on personal issues such as weight-problems and parenting, produced show after show in which the life altering effects of 11 September were programmed as a central motif. In the wake of 11 September a feature on homemaker extraordinaire, Martha Stewart, about 'Apple-Pie' and 'Marshmallows' was presented in the context of a 'new appreciation of the home' in the wake of a fear of public space. The American viewer, whether in Nebraska or New Mexico was made to feel touched, altered and fearful of the events that took place thousands of miles away. In addition for many months the US administration and a mostly unquestioning US media established the events of 11 September 2001 as globally relevant. The mantra of terrorism in its Muslim guise became an ever-present focus of media forms, particularly the news media. It is in the news media, for example, that the words of one Muslim individual – stripped of his citizenship, hiding out in a terrain that is virtually inaccessible and surrounded by a small cohort of supporters – are then attributed as evidence that 'Muslims [are] against the rest of the world.'[13] In a terrorist plot which millions are then supposedly signed up for it was clear that such perceptions underscored a fear: 'we have reason to be suspicious of Islam and treat it differently from other major religions, declared one controversial columnist.'[14] If western audiences started to believe such assertions then the events of 11 September and other terrorist attacks do put all Islam's adherents under the spotlight. The point here is that while there may be little empirical evidence of a mass-based hostility to Muslims and Islam in Western domains and vice versa, certain political elements do shamelessly exploit fears about episodes of Muslim perpetrated violence. Thus, while, for example, Americans may be genuinely reluctant to commit to fighting Islam they do want to destroy the terrorists, who in this case are as perceived happening to be Muslims. Empirical evidence of the domestic terror threat, before 11 September 2001, however, demonstrates that such fears were unfounded.[15]

Militant or fundamentalist Muslims were under suspicion, not just Muslims who were members of the Taliban, or Muslims who were members of the Philippine-based Abu Sayyaf group or the disparate cells of Yemen, nor even the hundreds of members of the Chechen Islamist forces, but Muslims the world over were increasingly regarded with suspicion and fear because their potentiality for terror was higher than any other faith or political group. Such assumptions generated a new perception.

While the US administration in the immediate wake of the 11 September attacks deplored attacks against Muslims in the United States of America, the reality was that the attacks in North America were an opportunity to legitimate the right-wing position hitherto promoted in many mainstream political circles that all Muslims had a dangerous potential to take up arms – to act as warriors of the Prophet. This had also been extensively demonstrated through the exploitation of such debates by the anti-immigration right wing in European states such as Holland and Denmark. Indeed such sentiments were publicly apparent in the wake of the attacks in America. As Daniel Pipes has argued while Islam was not the problem Islamism was; resembling 'fascism and Marxism/Leninism'. Islamists, according to Pipes, on the one hand are 15 per cent of the Muslim population across the globe and yet 'all must be considered potential killers.' Muslims in the West, he contended, were particularly susceptible to 'the lure of Islamist extremism' and he urged that 'steps should be taken to diminish their unique susceptibility to this totalitarian ideology'.[16] The sense of alarm in such sentiments couldn't be greater as there is an immediate impression that Muslims today are uniquely attracted to totalitarian forms of ideology, an obvious 'oriental trait' which has been the subject of past allegation and explanation of a political culture which is frequently described as despotic and embracing the authoritarian.[17] Only Muslims, western audiences have been encouraged to believe, are unique in exhibiting some innate desire for a human order in which no rival parties or loyalties are permitted and where the individual submits their will to God. Muslims are the new fascists and desire totalitarian political outcomes. Muslims become the subjected 'other' of Western nightmares. Additionally, the plural character of Islam is unaccounted for, alongside its liberal, reformist and community-spirited mainstream. Finally, such perspectives fail to explain the susceptibility of other faith systems – particularly Hindu and Christian fundamentalist dimensions – to totalitarian behaviours. It was after all the Hindu not Muslim political community in India that was elected in mass democratic elections in the late 1990s on platforms of Hindu ethnic exclusivity. Such platforms have been identified as responsible for promoting some of the most serious episodes of Hindu-inspired communal violence in modern history.

New dimensions of terrorism studies?

Terrorism studies are a relatively recent sub-discipline of academia; terrorism itself of course is not a recent or new phenomenon, and history (both ancient and modern) illustrates this. Samson as the first suicide bomber, the Muslim assassins and Tamil suicide bombers, all also highlight that religion and/or self-sacrifice (or self-annihilation) are part and parcel of what constitutes the dynamic manifestation of conflict and struggle for power in our societies. As I have already noted, terrorism studies emerged in an era of left-wing nationalist-inspired terrorism. The attention paid to the issue of terrorism in the Muslim domain, for example, became subject to new assessments, explanations and a discourse that attempted to re-draw the boundaries of contemporary understandings of political violence. The character of the terrorists, according to this new discourse, appeared to have transformed almost overnight, with one troupe of actors leaving the stage while a new troupe, sporting the mask of bloodlust and Islam took the limelight. Is this approach, however, helpful? Does it adequately explain a phenomenon and aid in the combat of terrorism in the context of what might be referred to as the Muslim arena? The evidence available to support the answer to this question allows a variety of contrasting explanations to be offered. Laqueur's insight, however, is helpful in this regard, when he recognises that terrorism 'was never in the mainstream' of the faith system and that a more varied, complicated and interrelated explanation of politics and conflict in the modern age explains the current radical Islamist phenomenon.[18] Additionally, the manifestation of terrorism by non-state actors in states which are nasty, brutish, authoritarian and have perpetrated terror against their opposition (at home and abroad) is left unexplained in this discourse. This may well be because in terrorism studies there has been a traditional disdain for characterising state violence as terrorism rather than extension of legitimate force.

Throughout the mid-to-late 1990s as the political violence or terrorism of secular groups like the IRA and PLO was perceived as entering decline, it was increasingly portrayed as a primary signifier in the way that Islam influenced policy-makers, media and the cultural norms of the Judeo-Christian West. The view that terrorism was not simply just a nuisance but a real threat in the closing epoch of this century was increasingly emphasised by those writers and researchers who embraced the thesis that there is such a phenomenon of religious terrorism, otherwise known as 'holy terror', 'sacred terror' and 'Islamic terror' and that it constituted a phenomena that threatened to upset the global balance of power. Although this construction of Islam was diametrically at odds with the real relationship between faith and struggle (jihad), the important point here was that acts of violence or terrorism associated with the news headlines were represented as 'divinely inspired' and were represented as an example of something about the inability of Islam to adapt to the demands of the modern age.[19] In this way the new terrorism studies in this area echoed standard orientalist positions about the inability of Islam and Muslims to modernise, liberalise and capitalise in ways that were deemed universally desirable and democratic. The epoch of 'Holy Terror' and 'Muslim Rage' that seemed to follow so hot on the heels of the declining menace of communism was evidence of the assertions by orientalists that Islam was violent and Muslims the purveyors of barbarity, inhumane practices and hatred. In this context any counter-assertion that Islam was a religion of peace was derided and ignored. Commentators asked, where was the Muslim Martin Luther King or Muslim Ghandi if Islam were truly such a peaceable religion? Muslims, it was argued, were determined to bring the battle between them and the 'West' to America's front door. Muslims in the East, Muslims in the West, Muslims in the North, Muslims in the South – experts on terrorism marked them out as the enemy in a new ideological battle.[20]

What becomes clear, however, is that certain theories of political violence, terrorism studies and international relations were then subjected to new thinking and responses. The compulsion of certain Egyptian Muslims to defy the state was explained by examining the nature of Islam as a faith founded and established through the sword as well as the Koran. The mass-based uprising of Palestinians against foreign domination condemned by the international community, were explained in terms of the desire by Muslims across the globe to 'liberate Jerusalem' by the wholesale destruction of the Jewish people in Israel. The resistance of Chechens to the hegemonic ambitions of the Russians was represented as evidence of the murderous intent of Muslims in the former Soviet republics and so on. The point here is that the boundaries between protest and terrorism became so blurred that in the majority of cases the violent event was subject to isolation in terms of context, circumstances and cause and effect. The roots of this Muslim terror were not explained to western audiences in terms of the direct pattern of relationships between and amongst actors and parties to certain political dynamics. The changed nature of the international order, the steadily increasing impoverishment of the developing world, the debt, the denial at international forums of rights that are considered legitimate to other parties, the deliberate interference with and assistance to regimes and states that make little secret of their poor human rights record, their authoritarian and anti-democratic tendencies all but ignored in the explanation or examination of the roots of Muslim violence. Did it, for example, matter that it was the CIA that played its part in making Bin Laden the menace that he is? As Moran is quoted as commenting, 'arming a multi-national coalition of Islamic extremists in Afghanistan during the 1980s – well after the destruction of the marine barracks in Beirut or the hijacking of the TWA Flight 847 – was [a] time when the United States should have resisted the temptation to ... hold its nose and shake hands with the devil for the long-term good of the planet.'[21]

For, the foundation stone on which any present study of Muslim protest and violence rests, according to the expert literature of terrorism studies, is the belief that among Muslims, more so than any other religious, ethnic or national group, violence and the predilection for terror are endemic. Indeed,

Muslims, it is argued in some right-wing quarters of the British press, are sometimes represented as no more than 'predatory destructive Orientals' who choose the 'crudest weapons available and use them with appalling violence'.[22] The weapons which this particular author referred to were in fact some three million AK-47 assault rifles which the American government, through the CIA, had armed Afghan's rebels with in the war against Soviet occupation in the 1980s. Such analysis of 'Muslim warfare' may account for the strategic failure in meeting the challenge posed by extremists who engage in violence to communicate their political message. Military history like any other history is open to interpretation and such assertions do stereotype Muslims as 'devious and underhand,' in a most unhelpful fashion. As Driver contends,

> reading Keegan is uncannily like reading British imperial accounts of military adventures across the globe ... during the long nineteenth century. The same assured confidence, the same rhetoric about 'Western' civilization and 'Oriental' treachery, all the more astonishing when one considers the technology of modern military conflict, which precisely enables unimaginable slaughter to take place without the inconvenience of 'face to face' confrontation. It is easy to unpick the racial stereotyping and cultural essentialism in such supposedly informed accounts, which crudely replicate the discursive structures of Orientalism. But in some ways this is all too easy. We are in danger here of missing a larger point, less about the power of sophisticated expertise than about the effects of thoroughgoing ignorance. This is not knowledge in the service of power, but hackneyed rhetoric betraying its own impotence.[23]

Clearly, Driver believes that such a body of knowledge is used to betray a dimension of modern power in a wilfully ignorant fashion.

Thus aspects of the universal and global appeal of the religion are obscured by the biases of many in the West who hold the key to popular understanding of a major faith whose adherents form significant communities in Europe and America. When Mohammed Ali, America's most famous of seven million Muslims stood up and preached tolerance in the wake of 11 September he did as both a Muslim and an American citizen with no evidence of a contradiction between the two positions. Does such a stand make Mohammed Ali, the great sporting legend of the twentieth century, an apologist for terrorists? Additionally, Christian and secular voices have called for a better understanding and tolerance of Islam in the wake of such attacks. For sure, a call for balance and comprehension rather than hatred and xenophobia against the Muslim 'other' will do more to meet the challenge and eradicate the threat of those who truly are embarked on a murderous task. Yet as the Chinese strategist Sun Tzu reminds us, 'If you know the enemy and know yourself, you need not fear a thousand battles. If you know yourself and not the enemy, for every victory you will suffer a defeat. But if you neither know yourself nor the enemy, then you are a fool and will meet defeat in every battle.'[24]

The works of the architects of the sacred or holy terror approach emerged in a political and cultural context in which they sought reactive explanation and theorised about a phenomenon that instilled fear and undermined security. The development of a discourse on this particular subject emerged from a specifically American context responding to the first terrorist offences in the country in the early to mid 1990s, including the World Trade Centre in 1999, the Oklahoma bombing in 1995 and the continued targeting of American military personnel in international locales such as Kuwait and Saudi Arabia. The American media, policy-makers and public were alarmed at this phenomenon of terror, more specifically they struggled to make sense of violence in the post-Cold war era where peace and security were supposed to be guaranteed. An obvious vulnerability had been exposed by these acts of terrorism and there was a growing fear that the perils of such could not be contained. Fortress America had been exposed, both at home and abroad by militarily weaker parties, to conflict because they engaged with previously unimaginable strategies.

Indeed, the extent to which there was recognition within the American mindset that there were elements existing in their own communities – the McVeigh-type patriots and abroad who had engaged in a conflict with the American state – is not easy to discern until after the events of 11 September 2001. The authors of the Muslim terror approach appeared to offer an explanation that also encouraged a real fear and hostility to all Muslims. They emerged from right-wing think tanks and had been employed to provide congressional committees, lobby groups and the media with a suitably stereotypical reductive explanation to increase arms and intelligence budgets. But did their profiles of the new terror threat assist in detecting the real menace of terrorism as perpetrated by al-Qaeda in 1998, 2000 and 2001?

The new explanation rested on the perception that a new threat to global security and the United States of America in particular lay at the heart of Muslim discourse. They constructed a virtual reality that actually differed quite radically from the reality of terrorism in the United States of America that was, until 11 September 2001, an almost exclusively 'home-grown' phenomenon. The discourse on Muslim terror, however, represented the entire faith system as a potential threat of gigantic proportions. In the light of the events of 11 September 2001, were the authors' fears and trepidations founded? Certainly, the record of domestic terror in a country like the United States of America until 11 September 2001 demonstrated that it was an almost exclusively home-grown phenomenon. Additionally the evidence suggests that when religion was a marker of terrorism in the American context it was manifest in Christianity not Islam. The 1999 FBI report highlights that animal liberation elements, or right-wing Nazi or Christian fundamentalist elements perpetrated most incidents. Yet it should also be noted that on 7 June 1999 the FBI added Usama Bin Laden on its top ten most wanted list.[25]

Nevertheless the arguments inherent to the discourse make sense on an internal level. From this perspective Islam is 'signified' in opposite relation to the cultural milieu from which these writers are located. Indeed, as such the Muslim terror discourse has as much to say about current understanding of Islam in the West as it does about contemporary manifestation of radical Islam. Its authors opted for an approach raising the threat of the religious spectre that had characterised past approaches to Islam. This understanding of Islam remains the province of traditional orientalist approaches to scholarship and discourse, and it is largely unaffected by the debates which have been conducted within the discipline of Middle East studies for more than 15 years. Some, such as Kramer, might applaud this approach for the very fact that it does indeed appear to be untainted. In relation to the study of Islam, Kramer argues that the dominant discourse in Middle Eastern Studies in North America has been shaped by a misty-eyed cling to the thesis on Orientalism published by Edward Said in 1978.[26] As such, this approach unconsciously embraces the perspective of Islam of orientalists and those such as Huntington who adopts an orientalising approach to Islam. The motifs that are related to this approach are drawn from a distinct perspective of Islam, its relation to violence and therefore terrorism. As such it has, as we shall see, not so much to do with the diversity of Islam, in particular political Islam in the current era. What it does represent is the manifestation of terrorism in its extreme form within the Muslim body politic and highlight the particular dimensions to debates about justification and legitimisation of this form of political violence in a modern age where religious norms and values are presumed marginal to the universal norms deemed applicable in secular societies. Consciously or otherwise, the contribution to the debate, the construction of a critique within terrorism studies that reflects on these dimensions of terrorism carried out by Muslims is not always apparent. Instead, what appears to emerge is a 'balancer' effect predicated on the assumption that if, for example, left-wing terrorism has gone in decline then there has been a concurrent rise in Muslim terrorism cradled in the Middle East. Often the emergence of dimensions of terrorism carried out by Muslims are not examined; rather it is taken as given that there is a symbiotic relationship between Islam and terror. Yet is all Muslim terror carried out in the name of Islam?

Who's Islam, which Islam?

It can be argued, therefore, that the holy terror approach sometimes assumes an unabashed proclivity to demonise Islamists, or rather 'fundamentalists' as they are referred to and to de-legitimise the rationality of all political violence. The violence of Islamists is perceived as unfathomable without the sole focus of the religion, for it is the religion that encourages the terror that threatens the entire world order.[27] The assumption here is that norms and values within Islam legitimate terrorism and reward the perpetrators. Time and time again the former government of Saddam Hussein and the government of Saudi Arabia are cited for 'rewarding' the families of Palestinian suicide bombers.[28] The Muslim clerical establishment and Muslim jurisprudence is frequently cited as contributing to the collusion within Islam to perpetrate terrorism. Through the discourse such figures are conveyed to Western audiences as 'representative' of something that lies deep in the Muslim soul.

As such, one is compelled to question whether the approach ignores the context in which this manifestation of political violence occurs and the realities of conflict and resistance which beset all modern-day societies. Indeed, it may be argued that because of the obvious attachment to the motif that Islam equals terror, the new approach failed to recognise a pattern that embraced the utility of violence in conflict-ridden arenas. Indeed the demonstration effect of the successful employment of terror and violence in such a context perpetrated by others needed to be taken into account when examining dimensions of violence and terrorism in which Muslims and Muslim groups participated in. Indeed the complex political emergencies which actually characterised many contexts of conflict which engaged Islamists the world over appear to have been eschewed in favour of traditional international-relations-based thinking on war and conflict. Yet, the world had changed, the era of old wars had passed and the modern phenomenon of intrastate conflicts whether in Rwanda, Afghanistan, East Timor or Kosovo dominated the international landscape. In these contexts of ethno-national tension, there is no single party or grouping that enjoys a monopoly of terror. For when societies and political orders and states collapse violence and unregulated violence in the guise of terrorism is an inevitable outcome. One interesting dimension of this context that has been under examined in relation to prevailing discourses on the topic relates to the motif of democracy. Such contexts were ignored because context didn't matter, faith did. Yet if intelligence experts, defence analysts, students of terrorism and policy-makers had kept such domains under the limelight, to what extent might the threat of Muslim terrorism have been met? Certainly there is a private view expressed by senior elements of the Western intelligence community that had Western governments not ordered their agents to abandon inputs into such domains the threat potential posed by Usama Bin Laden could have been detected earlier.[29]

The over-generalised version of Islam inherent in the discourse on Muslim terror also ignores another dimension of the political environment. The discourse encourages the assumption that Islam is conducting an assault against open, plural, fully democratic societies that respect the rule of law and encourage full representation of rights. This reflects the dominant thesis promoted by Huntington in the early 1990s on the 'Clash of Civilizations'.[30] Huntington contended that global conflict at the turn of the twentieth century was no longer ideological or economic but based on cultural dimensions. This was very much a thesis shaped by the end of the Cold War and the perception of a concurrent rise in the Green menace in place of the old Red threat. Huntington established divisions in the modern world into conflicts premised on monarchs, nations, ideologies and civilizations. Terrorism features as a manifestation of such conflicts and emerges with a degree of primacy in the conflict between civilisations that Huntington characterises the closing decade of the twentieth century by. Contending that Western culture was experiencing pressures and decline in the contest with rival civilizations, Huntington identified Islam as the primary point of friction. He seeks to redefine societies anew with culture the signifier of identity. Islam is singled out by Huntington from other civilizations – Western, Slavic, Sino-Confucian and so on – as the most confrontational and he also emphasizes the feature of inherent conflict that is both historical and contemporary between it (Islam) and other civilizations. Huntington embraces the Crusaders myth as relevant to his modern hypothesis. It would appear that empirically a glance at the post-Cold War order substantiated his argument, for in the bitter eruption of localised conflicts Islam appeared to be the chief culprit in 'fault-line' wars. Indeed, Huntington believed that his approach explained war in Afghanistan, the 1990 Gulf crisis, conflict in the former Yugoslavia, conflict in southern Europe and the rise of Muslim ethnic conflict states in the former Soviet Union. Indeed, those that embraced the thesis used the presence of militant Muslims as the reasons for conflicts in Sudan, Kosovo, Kashmir, Gujarat, between Ethiopia and Eritrea, Chechnya, the Philippines, and the Arab–Israeli and Palestinian–Israeli conflict. From this proposition a Muslim presence is almost a predictor of conflict under the rubric of civilizational impulse. In turn, this argument is extended with respect to democratisations; Muslim majority countries are inhibitors to democracy. For surely Huntington employs his thesis of civilisation as an identifier, as having a more primordial than invented character. He implies that Islam is innately conflictual and confrontational; that in fact, Islam is defined by the impulse to conquer other civilizations. Indeed, Huntington has been criticised for his monolithic approach to Islam and his failure to acknowledge that Islam and Muslim states are diverse, dynamic and not historically fixed to an event that took place in seventh century Arabia. For example, not all Muslim states are on the same trajectory of confrontation with the West though of course Huntington implies this and would, I suppose, be suspicious of those Muslims states that are pro-Western such as Pakistan under the rule of General Musharaff. Additionally, where do Muslim states such as Indonesia, Tunisia, Egypt, Turkey, Morocco or Mali fit on this trajectory of conflict against the West?

Nor, perhaps more importantly, I would argue, is Muslim identity so rigid as he presupposes. Indeed, there is no place on this trajectory of conflict for

Muslims that embrace western values, are pro-Western or indeed are Western Muslims. Once again the extreme fringe is conflated as a representative of the whole. Even the diverse nature and motives behind the radical fringe are lost. Indeed the differences between manifestations of radicalism in Gujarat and the secessionist nature of radicalism epitomised by Abu Sayyaf in the Philippines is lost. Huntington does not generally reflect the explanation of political factors that currently characterise the changed nature of war in modern societies in this approach. The authoritarian and repressive nature of states in which Muslims live, the ideologies of mono-culturalism that create hostility against them, anti-westernisation as an element of the anti-global counter-globalisation movement, the promotion of religion in public and political life, and legitimate demands for self-determination and independence, all appear to figure vaguely in the calculation that Islam is on a trajectory of terror against the West. The radical fringe Islamist appropriation of the *Dar al-Islam/Dar al-Harb* (Abode of Islam/Abode of War) dichotomy as justification for their theology of jihad is also cited as evidence of the internal embrace of Huntington's thesis. This may go some way in explaining the manifestation of terrorism perpetrated by al-Qaeda, but how much further does it go? Huntington's premise is not Islam but the development of a response to a changed international order that was shaped by the collapse of the ideological battle between the West and the Soviet Union. Huntington wants his Western audience to believe that Islam, not certain Muslim elements, emerged into some kind of ideological vacuum to replace one threat to the West with another and thus, give justification for the Western military complex. The Arab Afghans but not the Muslim populations of Hamburg, Trieste or Chicago typify such elements. Many Arab Afghans were subsequently engaged in acts of terrorism in their home states and against western targets.

Terrorism and trials in Egypt

> At the onset of the twentieth century, many Egyptians ... believed that the government was tyrannical and arbitrary. They reasoned it ruled without a constitution [and] ignored popular aspirations.
>
> M. Badrawi, *Political Violence in Egypt 1910–1925*, p. 230[31]

The manifestation of radical terror elements in Egypt in the early to mid-1990s, for example, does have demonstrable links to this particular phenomenon but should not be seen merely as a manifestation or evidence of the significance of Huntington's thesis but as a reflection of other factors too. The manifestation of terrorism as violence in Egypt cannot be explained by Huntington's thesis. Badrawi's historical account gives greater perspective to this phenomenon in the modern era.[32] Throughout the twentieth century

Egypt's relationship with the West was shaped by legacies of exploitation, imperialism and colonialism, as well as an earlier collapse from nonalignment to pro-Western client in the latter stages of the Cold War. Sadat had sealed Egypt's pro-Western fate with the conclusion of a peace treaty with Israel in 1978 and the promise from the United States of America of admittance into the Western-donor supported orbit. Once in the pro-Western orbit and despite the rise of radical elements at home, Egypt was more than happy to send Egyptian 'mujahideen' volunteers to Afghanistan to support the Western effort to get the Russians out of Kabul. It also conveniently removed the object of radical opposition from the domestic arena. Yet that element of opposition would return to haunt the governing authorities, further fuelled and fired by the experiences on the battlefields of Afghanistan. For victory brought belief that the road to liberation of repressed Muslim masses could be achieved by resorting to arms, even if that meant against fellow Muslim leaders. The reign of terror that descended on Egypt in the early 1990s was brought to an abrupt halt as a result of the government-inspired campaign against the Arab Afghans. Yet before that point the Arab Afghans were implicated in the wave of terror that gripped Egypt. They were connected with attacks against the regime and its political elite, on the local Christian Coptic community and with a wave of terror against tourists visiting the country's famous sites.

Extremist elements, forged in the maelstrom of Afghanistan, like '*Tala'i' al-Fath*' or *Gamma Islamiyyah* and smaller jihadist elements, were found responsible for the new wave of terror aimed at undermining the ruling pro-Western regime led by Hosni Mubarak. Terror attacks on Western tourists, including the Luxor massacre of November 1993 in which members of *Gamma Islamiyyah* murdered 58 tourists, additionally hit revenues to the state earned from lucrative tourist dollars. An Afghan trained operative named Mohammed Abdel Rahman led the attack. The jihadist terror attacks, however, were also waged against local citizens and many local innocent lives were lost to their campaigns. Public support for the principles behind opposing the Mubarak regime waned as more victims emerged. Additionally, Egyptian jihadist figures like Ayman Zahrawi, Mustafa Hamza and Ahmad Rifa'i Taha were discovered back in Afghanistan and other locales emerging as senior elements of the al-Qaeda network. The Egyptian authorities also took the initiative in their campaign against the radicals by deporting undesirable elements from the country.[33] The counter-campaign became increasingly successful and by the mid to late 1990s the Egyptian authorities had succeeded in the arrest and trial of many jihadist elements. By 1998 a fissure within the radical fringe was reported over future directions following the announcement of a cease-fire by the imprisoned leadership of *Gamma Islamiyyah*.[34] The cleft also revealed tensions between external and internal elements common to movements of this kind. Clearly Huntington's thesis is problematic.

It is true, however, that the assault on 11 September 2001 in America was indeed an attack on an open, plural, fully democratic society that respects the rule of law and encourages full representation of rights. This is a view that is held within and by other self-recognising democracies, yet the view as experienced by those outside of America is not filtered by any rose tinted glasses. Barlas illustrates this by exposing the conundrum surrounding the issue of the 'real America.' She asks whether the 'real US' is 'the one that advocates freedom, civil liberties, and democracy at home or the one that carries out wars and violence and repression abroad?'[35]

Identikit monsters

The experts on terror who address the issue of Islam have a tendency to view the religion as a solid monolith allowing them to link diverse elements under one umbrella. Islam and politics are also perceived as one and the same thing, the expression of which is always fundamentalist and rarely, if ever, anything else. In this discourse, Hizb Allah in Lebanon, the *Wahabbi salafi* of Saudi Arabia, Palestinian Hamas, Louis Farrakhan and the Nation of Islam, Bosnian rebels resisting Serb-enacted genocide, the Muslim Brotherhood in Jordan, and South Africa's Muslim-led anti-drug programmes are often conflated together.

In addition, because the discourse identifies the establishment of Islam by the Prophet Mohammad with 'terrorism', the entire religion is represented as violent. Even when textual evidence of the continuation of that legacy of violence is absent, authors like Rapoport believe that there is 'Still evidence of a connection (that) exists', part of a 'projective narrative' that allows contemporary fundamentalists to engage in acts of terrorism sanctioned by Islam. Robin Wright's remarks serve as ample retort to this argument:

> mining the Koran for incendiary quotes is essentially pointless. Religions evolve, and there is usually enough ambiguity in their founding scriptures to let them evolve in any direction. If Usama Bin Laden were a Christian, and he still wanted to destroy the World Trade Centre (WTC), he would cite Jesus' rampage against the moneychangers. If he didn't want to destroy the WTC, he could stress the Sermon on the Mount.[36]

Traditions of terrorism, as explained in earlier chapters of this book, or theological embrace of the efficacy of violence for theological means can be found and determined as common to most faith systems and certain interpretations of their holy texts and treatises.

Muslims' terrorism is believed to be associated with the doctrine of jihad, which the holy terror approach interprets as holy war. On both counts, however, the monolith is weakened by the existence of debates within the religion on the meaning of jihad and the erroneous assumption that jihad is holy war rather than a broad and diverse concept of striving. By perceiving and constructing Islam as monolith, the discourse on Muslim terror re-interprets important aspects of Islam and represents them as the entire religion. In this version of Islam – as Muslim Terror – the political space is limited and also populated by an extremely small group of exclusively male actors who are driven by a 'transcendental' and 'cosmic' force to lead Islam into the twenty-first century. They are interpreted as employing the force of the sword in the same way that the Prophet Mohammad is perceived as having first established the religion in the seventh century. Conquest and defeat of the 'other', and in this case more specifically the prevailing status quo whether within the Muslim world or outside is represented as the driving force of Islam. In this respect Islam has an anarchical character to its drive to destroy prevailing orders through whatever means, possible especially violent ones.

A further important dimension in the holy terror approach is the suggestion that there has been a long history between religion and terrorism and more specifically that the Middle East is a location where these forces are traditionally manifest. Evidence of this inextricable relationship between terror and location is drawn in particular historical overviews of religion and in which the historical precedents established by elements such as the Assassins are presented as evidence.[37] While helpful in terms of an interesting etymology of terms such as assassin and zealot, this is also a distinction drawn between what may be termed as religious and secular manifestation of terrorism. Thus distinct and separate characteristics are ascribed to the so-called religious terrorists. One argument made is that the historical religious antecedents of terror support the argument for a 'cyclical' character to modern terror. This has less to do with developments in modern technology and more to do with 'significant political watersheds that excited the hopes of potential terrorists and increased the vulnerability of society to their claims'.[38] Such an approach fails, however, to also address the philosophical relationship between religions and violence. In addition, it does not focus on state forms and their embrace of political violence in the name of faith that, for example, characterised Medieval Europe during the Inquisition. Similarly the manifestation of Christian fundamentalist violence in the modern era weakens the argument that somehow while Christianity has evolved from a bloody past, Islam remains wedded and defined by it. So to suggest that Christianity has evolved but Islam has lost its dynamism and remains attached to violence and terror betrays a lack of understanding in relation to the nature of evolutionary forces as they relate to these motifs. As Lewis contends, 'Compared with Christendom, its rival for more than a millennium, the world of Islam had become poor, weak, and ignorant.'[39] This understanding of Islam in evolution is not a linear process and nor is it advisable to employ the evolution of one phenomenon as a yardstick against which others may be measured. Additionally, as I have already highlighted, nor is Christianity or are Christian believers freed from a bloody past or present.

One needs only reflect on the liberation theology of Latin American clerics, the function of Christianity as a legitimator of ethnic violence in the former Yugoslavia, or the link between the Christian faith and terrorist violence in Northern Ireland or Lebanon to assess the relevancy of this argument.

Nevertheless, from this foundation of scholarship there emerged a small but influential group who perceived the modern manifestation of political violence as Muslim holy terror. This discourse was premised on an argument that manifestations of secular terror were in decline in the 1990s. As Hoffman remarks, 'What is particularly striking about holy terror compared to purely secular terror, however, is the radically different value systems, mechanisms of legitimisation and justification, concepts of morality, and Manichean world view that the holy terror embraces.'[40] A problem with this approach lies in the present difficulty in drawing firm boundaries and distinctions between manifestations of terror that are secular and those that are religious, particularly when one addresses the realm of ethno-national conflict. Was, for example, the sectarian murder of the Catholic postal worker Daniel McColgan in January 2002 in Northern Ireland by Protestant members of an outlawed loyalist paramilitary organisation religious or secular in motive? McColgan was identified for murder because of his faith by paramilitaries who embrace a mixture of both secular-socialist working-class emancipatory and protestant-inspired faith-based ideology and sectarianism.[41] This small example illustrates the fact that so-called secular terrorists can rely as much on religious motifs as their so-called holy counterparts and conversely that the so-called holy men of terror consciously and sub-consciously embrace and address the secular and secular-nationalist agendas of liberation and conflict. For example, Hamas leaders talk about the liberation of Palestine in terms of a nationalist duty as well as a religious one; for Hamas have had to operate and compete in an environment where the dominant political discourse and language of politics was predicated on 'secularised' notions of emancipation, liberation, democracy and self-determination. Hamas also represents itself to its constituency as a nationalist movement – 'Nationalism in the eyes of the IRM is part of religious faith ... nationalism is a religious precept.'[42] For the fundamentalist Protestant wing of Ulster unionism the theocratic dominance of society and the political system remains the same goal. While Hamas seeks to establish a future Palestinian state of Muslims – which have mechanisms of tolerance for minority groups – Protestant fundamentalist elements in Northern Ireland seek to eliminate perceived threats to their identity. As Bruce notes, 'the Northern Ireland situation gives even nonreligious Protestants good reason to support fundamentalists,' and such fundamentalism has led to terrorism in the name of faith.[43]

The holy terror thesis, however, also rests on the assumption that the religious terrorists are 'more lethal than their (secular) counterparts, regarding violence as a divine duty.' Indeed, the act of political violence particularly among Muslims is, argue proponents of the discourse, even 'mandated by God' as part of a wider rise in fundamentalism. This phenomenon of Muslim fundamentalism is in turn perceived as the explanation for the explosion of terrorism in the last decade of the twentieth century. An initial problem with this approach is the absence of any explanation of how such perpetrators of religio-political violence are any more lethal than their secular counterparts. While there are deep philosophical and political disputes over the semantics of terrorism, force and violence, without exception lethal force is accepted for what it is. Indeed, lethal force can only result in one thing, death or the intention to kill; it cannot be any more or less lethal, more dead than dead. The import of this ascription is largely left unexplained other than through an assumption that lethal violence is more deadly if it has connotations of some higher spiritual form. Do the authors mean to assert that somehow those Muslims who engage in acts of terror push at perverse 'boundaries' of acceptable and unacceptable, thinkable and unthinkable terror that other practitioners of terror, whether they be Spanish Basques, Tamil Tigers, the leftist Baader-Meinhof, ZAPU (Zimbabwe National People's Union) in Zimbabwe in 1979, do not?

The discourse also rests on a view of all Islamists as fundamentalists. In other words, all Muslims who engage in politics – for this is how Islamism is defined – whether that form of politics is high or low, local, national, regional or international, the politics of states, the politics of race, the politics of sport, the politics of the street, are all classified as fundamentalist expressions of Muslim identity. This understanding of Islam as purely an expression of fundamentalism raises some problems that are both implicit and explicit to the approach. It ignores the corpus of evidence and scholarship that demonstrates that Muslim politics is a broad and multi-faceted phenomenon.[44] Aside from the basic problems associated with defining fundamentalism certain theorists because of its orientalist foundations have rejected the term. In the discourse of holy terror, however, the notion of fundamentalist Islam is associated with a reductive strategy that also reflects the manifestation in a negative signifier, particularly in relation to the West. Indeed, not only is Islamism fundamentalist, it is also anti-Western in a way that marks it out as unique and alien to common political discourses of the twentieth and twenty-first century. Indeed the counter-global elements of Islamist discourse are ignored, their parallels to other anti-global and counter-global commentaries whether from the Greens in Germany or Seed Farmers in India are not drawn or recognised. The debate about the possible legitimacy of their arguments, ideologies or even parts of their approaches just does not take place.

It is easy in this context, therefore, to assert, as some of the writers on holy terror in its Muslim form have, that the 'Islamic' revolution in Iran in 1979 'is held up as an example to Muslims throughout the world to reassert the fundamental teachings of the Koran and to resist intrusion of

Western – particularly United States – influence.'[45] The easy transposition of fundamentalism to Islamism and even Islamic phenomena should, however, be questioned. This view of Islam has also been re-stated and re-worked in the post-Cold war era by Huntington who argues that 'Islam and the West are on a collision course. Islam is a triple threat: political, civilizational and demographic'.[46] The essence of Islam in this context is perceived as funda-mentalist, linking Islam and politics in a particular monolithic antagonistic expression of a conflict with the West that began in the twelfth century dur-ing the Crusades. Indeed, one writer, Taheri states that, 'Islamic politics inevitably lead[s] to violence and terror'.[47] Terrorism is then perceived as an expression of fundamentalist Islam. Indeed for the discourse of holy terror to remain significant Islam has to be signified and connected to the politics of fundamentalism. This is turn is based on a eurocentric presentation of Islam where, for example the fundamental doctrinal differences between *Sunni* and *Shi'a* forms or debates about modernist, reformist, militant, institutional and traditional forms of Islamic politics are subsumed under the fundamen-talist foundation stone of conflict, violence and eternal, indiscriminate war.

Additionally, elements of the discourse reflect that in the Muslim form vio-lence is a 'divine duty'. There is an assumption that the activist or perpetrator of such a deed is compelled into violent action as a profession of faith; that to accept the faith one must engage in acts of violence which are divinely inspired. Thus the religion is once again subject to the reductive categorisa-tion by a corpus of researchers and writers who engage with the faith from the perspective of terror, and terror only, not politics, sociology, law, economy or anthropology. They are engaged with a phenomenon only through a particu-lar and inevitable avenue in which terror and violence are always the domi-nant motif. Violence is placed atop the high minaret of Islam as the defining element of the faith system. The murderous acts of those who call themselves Muslims are utilised to demonstrate the strength of their arguments and as evidence that in dealing with this new manifestation of terror (for both the motives and the techniques are perceived as somehow innovatory) the fatal-istic realisation that Western culture and governments face a new menace which remains implacably tied to terror as politics. This reduction places vio-lence and more specifically acts of terrorism high on the Muslim agenda, par-ticularly in the contemporary era where they struggle with the forces of modernisation and development. This construction is sold as real, empirical and acceptable evidence that at least one of the three monotheistic faiths is fixed on a bloodthirsty, 'transcendental dimension' which is unfettered from the usual 'political, moral or practical constraints' that govern other faiths or other terrorists.[48] The subjective nature of this body of work is not widely acknowledged. The point here is not only that there is more than enough evi-dence to conclude that these are bad arguments for concluding that Islam is somehow inherently violent but also that this assumption in the first place is false. In addition the idea that religious terrorists act for no constituency but themselves leads to the assumption that their violence is 'limitless' and conducted against a 'virtually open-ended category of targets'.[49] As such it is clear that the approach does not regard the political context or environment in which these so-called terrorists are located as important in terms of explanation or in terms of informing future policy directions; for according to the logic of holy terror, this does not matter; all that matters is the imperative of holy terror to convert the globe to Islam through the force of violence. Indeed, there is no other way to understand Islam.

The construction of Islam established by the discourse of holy terror plays an important role in the way in which western-based governments manufacture their own policies towards Islam and encourage non-Western governments, particularly those in Muslim domains, to 'tackle' the threat that is perceived as inherent in the dominant milieu of society. Of course in the wake of 11 September 2001 many western governments and their policy-makers have argued that the approach is reinforced by the menace that Islamists present across the globe. Bin Laden's bombers have reinforced the view that the 'problem' is that a politics of signifiers has emerged in which Islam is understood in dominant discourse in Western societies as irredeemably hostile and negative. The wider range of opinions which characterise the Muslim world are ignored, the problems with underdeveloped and failed or weak states underestimated, the failure to play a part in resolving major conflicts in which western states originally had a hand in generating deemed as a 'sideshow' issue or simply not relevant, dialogue absent and instead the empty signifier is filled with a garbage-version of Islam. While Islam remains signified as negative by so many then the alternatives, no matter how lacking in real intrinsic value in terms of the principles which are outlined as defining modern nations (rule of law, respect for human rights, democracy etc.), are embraced without really ever admitting the consequences as dangerous. Islam becomes negative only through its signification with the West, and the West stands for everything that Islam lacks.

It ain't what you do it's the way that you do it ...

> I don't watch the news any more because I think Muslims are portrayed so badly. A huge part of the problem is ignorance – people can't be bothered to find out what our religion's all about. They think 'You're all the same – Muslims, fundamentalists, you just blow people up.' That's sad.
>
> Zaki Chentouf, quoted in Marie Clarie,
> December 2002, p. 71[50]

This issue of representation is also about how Islam is signified in the popular consciousness of Western audiences, particularly in the wake of 11 September 2001 and other attacks on western targets. Through this method of signification, the conception of good and evil becomes one-dimensional. It reflects President George Bush's totemic statement in the wake of the attacks, *'Whoever is not with us is against us. Peoples of the world, I bring you "Operation Enduring Freedom." '* This statement and statements like that embrace evil and good as finite oppositions and reflect theories of discourse that demonstrate that antagonism lies at the heart of such encounters. The boundaries of politics become contested and central to expressions of power and contestation. The foundation of the approach to holy terror recognises these constructions in the way it represents Islam. It doesn't matter whether construction is objectively correct or not because in and of itself it becomes an obstacle to mutual understanding based on a progressive dynamic. Specific representations or signifiers such as 'liberty', 'equality', 'the state', 'violence', 'Islam' and 'democracy', remain, therefore, essential in reflecting and examining the way in which political subjects are constituted. In the case of holy terror the signifiers of 'Islam', 'the nation', 'emancipation' and 'terrorism', for example, are constructed with pre-given assumptions that establishes a negativity.

This representation of 'Muslim' contributes to a furthering of the construction of an orientalist perspective to Islam in both the classical and modern sense. Muslims are depicted as a blight that seek not only to constrain but also overthrow the established capital-based liberal democratic hegemony epitomised by the United States of America in the wake of the Cold War. Islam is represented as a political force first and foremost and the myriad dimensions of Muslim identity are lost. The ethical and moral impulse within Islam and Muslim discourse is given scant attention. Ultimately Muslim terror only begins to obtain its meaning because it is different from secular terror, political violence and warfare. It is construed as different, both in terms of inspiration (where there might be a point here), and strategies and outcomes. Islam's terrorists, rather than Muslims who engage in acts of terrorism, represent an Islam that is perceived as fundamentalist, radical, anti-Jewish, authoritarian, totalitarian, monolithic and theocratic. Islamic terrorism appears to have challenged the old paradigms giving meaning to war, philosophy of war and the moral justification for wars. The character of war appears to be challenged and changed by the fact that Muslims have armed themselves and taken on their enemies. The stereotype of the opiate smoking supine oriental has been replaced by that of the zealous, fanatical oriental who will use any and every means possible to achieve the goal of establishing the abode of Islam across the modern globe. This version of Islam works on the premise of no compromise and a maximalist position that cannot be accommodated by its foes. Iraq in the wake of the fall of Saddam Hussein and the emerging Islamic insurgency has proved to be a case in point.

So while empirically the so-called Islamic terrorists remain an exceedingly small cohort of disparate groupings that have emerged out of a variety of political contexts, they are perceived by western audiences as powerful enough to wreck global havoc. If a plane falls unexpectedly from the sky, if an explosion sounds on the street of an American city, if someone is kidnapped in a remote and mountainous region, if rumours of chemical warfare and anthrax emerge, if a suspect package is found in an airport terminal, the finger of blame is initially pointed at Islam. Islam is now guilty until proven innocent of major global domestic and international acts of terrorism. Thus, although within the broad spectrum of political Islam groups like Islamic Jihad and *Gamma' Islamiyyah* may well be marginal players, not only on the world stage but within their own societies they are nevertheless interpreted and represented as epitomising 'the gospel for the youth' inaugurating a 'new era in Islamic thought'.[51]

The purpose of this aspect of the debate is not to deny that acts of political violence or terror have been perpetrated that employ the symbols of religion; nor is it to make an apology for terrorism perpetrated by people who claim to act in the name of Islam and legitimate their violence and terror in this way. Rather it is to question whether it is the nature of specific religions themselves and particularly Islam, which is violent and encourages the deathly embrace of terror or a cohort of certain Muslims who deliberately misconstrue the meaning of Islam to represent it as a form of terror? Perhaps this is all just a question of degrees of violence and terrorism or semantics but where the border between and within Islam and terrorism is drawn matters deeply and has implications for the nature of the modern international order and the relationships that take place within that orbit. Taheri asks, 'is Islam a religion of terror?' He seems to believe so. And while the authors who have constructed the 'holy terror, religious terror' thesis claim this is a worldwide phenomenon carried out by Japanese religious cults, and skin-heads in Arizona alike, their predominant focus in the contemporary era has been Islam. Islam regularly features as a religion in which the inextricable link between faith, politics, violence and its justification are asserted. This is an area of discourse in which another sharp divide has opened with strictly opposing views and positions on either side. The grey areas of politics abandoned for the maximalist positions and statements of opposing camps. In the 1980s, the academy engaging in the study of the Middle East and Islam had undergone a period of critical reflection and re-assessment of the contribution of Western scholarship to such topics in response to the debate about representing the 'other'. Supporters and critics alike acknowledge that this debate was ignited by Said's tome on *Orientalism* that was published in 1978. Martin Kramer believes that Said and his legion of 'progressive' and 'critical' scholars ignored the violent excesses and nature of Islam and the threat it posed in favour of blaming the West for its negative representation in the first place. 'Instead', he argues, 'each Islamist action became another opportunity for the repetitive and ritual denunciation of Western prejudice against Islam.'[52] By turns he blames this academy; 'It is no exaggeration,' he argues, 'to say that America's academics have failed to predict or explain the major evolution of Middle Eastern politics and society over the past two decades.'[53] In relation to Islam, Martin Kramer contends that the real threat and violent impulse at the heart of Islam and Islamists has been 'obscured' by the scholarship of the American academy. Self-reflection and critique within terrorism studies on the obscured vision of Islam that they have promoted is also in short supply. The example of authors like Rapoport who declares he has 'agonised' over his interpretation of sacred terror represented by figures like Abd-al Salam al-Faraj are few and far between and even Rapoport succumbs to traditional orientalist ascription's of Islam as 'puzzling', deviant and different from other religions. Instead, we are left with bald statements about Islam and terrorism that do nothing to enlighten and much to obscure. Conflict becomes the inevitable outcome of such encounters. Islam rarely enters the discourse of peace making, conflict resolution or the conceptual polar opposites to terror, violence and global chaos. Islam is rarely acknowledged as possessing a peaceful character in the contemporary era.

Events in Iraq since the fall of Saddam Hussein and the inauguration of the American-led western occupation of the country have also given rise to great instability and protest, including violent insurgency, from among Iraq's Muslim population. Both *Sunnis* and *Shi'as* have taken part in protesting the American-led occupation. Some religious leaders have tried to steer a nonviolent transition to self-rule. Their vision is for the re-insertion of faith back into the political life of modern-day Iraq. For others, however, the reality of foreign occupation has been enough to galvanise armed constituencies of support for violence against foreign armed forces as well as westerners living and working in Iraq. In the *Shi'a* community, the young cleric Muqtada al-Sadr has not found it difficult to win support among the impoverished of Iraq's largest cities. Among the *Sunni*, locally orchestrated insurgence against Allied targets and other Westerners has also garnered support from foreign *mujahideen* elements that now see Iraq as the new frontier in the battle between Islam and the West. The rapid collapse and the disestablishment of Iraq's state forces in the wake of the American-led occupation left the country vulnerable to radical neo-fundamentalist elements who had infiltrated and continue to infiltrate across the country's borders.

Islamic insurgents – whether in Iraq, Chechnya, Kashmir or Palestine – are now considered to be a transnational criminal phenomena that hold their own as well as other populations to ransom with their extreme aims and demands. They are perceived as enjoying little by way of popular support. Muslim insurgents, however, have been able to exploit a wellspring of injustice that many in Muslim communities across the globe believe they have experienced as a result of their encounters with the West. Following the US campaigns and showdowns with Muqtada al-Sadr in the Summer of 2004 and against Fallujah in November 2004 it appeared that the Islamic insurgency in Iraq had been put down. Yet such impressions were only fleeting. Violence and insecurity still stalked the landscape of Iraq.

Badshah Guffar Khan: a Muslim Gandhi or Martin Luther King

Many commentators opine that Islam lacks an attachment to pacifism that is apparent in other monotheistic faiths. Christianity is cited as embracing a pacifist tradition that holds violence and its manifestation as both unethical and unprincipled in terms of a set of beliefs sustained by the faith system. Islam, it is contended, sanctions violence if the faith system is in need of defence, and the just war tradition enshrines this approach. The just war tradition in this context must be linked to the explicit rules set out within the Islamic framework regarding conditions for self-defence and defence of the faith.[54] Indeed it could be argued that such 'rules' demonstrate an apostate element in al-Qaeda's relish for targeting non-combatants in pursuit of any form of jihad as such actions are not, according to the Koran and mainstream traditions of jurisprudence permissible. Returning to the main point here there are some who suggest that there is no Muslim Martin Luther King or Gandhi. Such a perspective ignores that rich tradition of reconciliation, pacifism, quietism and address of social injustice through peaceful means acknowledged within Islam in its modern manifestations. The issue of social injustice is, for example, an issue deeply relevant to those Muslims that seek a variety of avenues to connect with the modern era. They are motivated by blatant acts of injustice not just against or within their own communities but outside them as well. It is an inadequate explanation of the manifestation of violence in the modern era to argue that the only language of change that Muslims understand is violence. Muslims have embraced peaceful routes to address social injustice and found themselves stymied and ignored by state elites and other powers.

Indeed, as with manifestations in other contexts, violence, as perpetrated by Muslims, does become the route of last not first resort. Additionally there are manifestations of Muslim perpetrated violence that are a route of first resort and a product of environments where Muslims have been habituated to violence as a dimension of politics that has suited the strategic needs of others, including superpower actors. None of these scenarios can be conflated to represent Islam per se. There are plenty of Muslim Martin Luther King's – men and women adherents of the faith of Islam who have engaged in acts of non-violent resistance to achieve social change and who don't advocate violence to achieve change. Yet so little is known among Western audiences about such individuals. There are also thousands of communities of Muslim Sufis who have sustained Muslim order according to principles of quietism and pacifism. Such orders are responsible for influencing and supporting thousands of projects aimed at bringing a sense of tranquillity to Islam. Such movements have inspired many leaders and thinkers of the contemporary resurgence phenomenon, yet are condemned by fundamentalists and largely ignored by Western audiences.

It is with some irony that the same territory that is thought to provide a haven to Bin Laden in the twenty-first century had also cradled Badshah Guffar Khan, known as the 'peaceful-mujahideen' and a contemporary of Ghandi. Khan was a devout Muslim and advocate of non-violence. During his lifetime the British and Pakistan authorities jailed him. Born in 1890, Badshah Khan grew up in a territory subject to constant contest and battles for control. A well-known social reformer, he embraced the same orbit of non-violence as his colleague Ghandi. He argued that there was no tension between Islam and non-violence, asserting that 'There is nothing surprising in a Muslim or a Pathan like me subscribing to the creed of non-violence. It is not a new creed. It was followed 1400 years ago by the Prophet all the time he was in Mecca.'[55] Badshah Khan was a genuinely representative voice of a Muslim community engaged, like their Hindu brethren, in resisting social injustice and the rule of the British.

His followers became known as 'Non-violent soldiers'. But another way of representing them is to recognise that they were mujahideen striving to stand against injustice without resort to violence. As Johansen asserts the oath of these mujahideen is symbolic of everything that they, as Muslims in their attachment to non-violence, stood for:

> I am a Servant of God, and as God needs no service,
>   but serving his creation is serving him,
> I promise to serve humanity in the name of God.
> I promise to refrain from violence and from taking revenge.
> I promise to forgive those who oppress me or treat me with cruelty.
> I promise to refrain from taking part in feuds and quarrels
>   and from creating enmity.
>
> ...
>
> I will live in accordance with the principles of non-violence.
> I will serve all God's creatures alike; and my object shall be
>   the attainment of the freedom of my country and my religion.
> I will always see to it that I do what is right and good.
> I will never desire any reward whatever for my service.
> All my efforts shall be to please God, and not for any
>   show or gain.[56]

The resolve of Badshah Khan's recruits was tested in April 1930 when his peaceful mujahideen stood against British forces who opened fire against their unarmed numbers. Over 200 of these unarmed protesters against injustice and exploitation were massacred; 'the carnage stopped only because a regiment of Indian soldiers', writes Pal, 'finally refused to continue firing on the unarmed protesters, an impertinence for which they were severely punished' by their British overlords.[57] Badshah Khan put his principles into action. He wasn't an armchair mujahid for peace but asserted that the fundamental principles of Islam were governed and ruled by peaceful and non-violent frameworks.

His organisation, Khidmatgar, grew in size throughout the 1930s and 1940s to an estimated 120,000 members. Close to Ghandi and other members of the Indian congress, Badshah Khan promoted an Islamic vision underpinned by his theocratic understandings of Islam as a polar opposite of violence and injustice. As such he opposed ethnic division of territory, making him an enemy of the newly emerging political elite of Pakistan. Perhaps it was while reflecting on the nature of his 'threat' that the elite of the new state imprisoned Badshah Khan and prohibited membership of his movement. This act demonstrated more about the violent and authoritarian tendencies of newly created states than the impulse for violence within Islam. For Khan the symbiotic nature of Islam and peace was more than a reflection of a 'moment in time' but a timeless characteristic of the faith system. Khan, in relating this immutable peaceful core to a fellow Muslim, is said to have declared, 'I cited chapter and verse from the Koran to show the great emphasis that Islam laid on peace, which is its coping stone ... I also showed to him how the greatest figures in Islamic history were known more for their forbearance and self-restraint than their fierceness'.[58]

Is Bashah Khan an exception to the rule? The Muslim peacemakers are there but they mostly remain hidden from Western audiences. Western audiences forget that it is Muslims with a stake in peace rather than war which, for example, signed up to the Dayton Accords, signalling an end to the ethnic bloodbath of the former Yugoslavia. Muslim peacemakers wrought an end to the civil conflict that tore Lebanon apart for 15 years. Muslim peacemakers in India have sought to bring an end to the hate-filled campaigns of Hindu fundamentalists – without resorting to violence. Muslim social activists have organised sustained campaigns of social support, welfare and development. Muslim activists have promoted social reform without violence in thousands of locations across the globe. Such activists work to achieve positive change, and social and political justice, yet without confrontation.

The majority of social activism projects undertaken by Muslim are non-violent and account for the greater impact on local social orders than manifestations of violence. In failed and weak states such activism has resulted in vital support offered to the most vulnerable elements of society. As Bayat argues, 'social Islam is a significant means through which some disadvantaged groups survive hardship or better their lives.'[59] In Lebanon, Hizb Allah has played a major part in sustaining a local, socially deprived and marginalised population – not only through war but in peace also. In south Lebanon, the Hizb Allah's presence was manifest not only in the military sphere but also in terms of offering a wide range of social services to the population. In Jordan the Muslim Brotherhood has remained out of formal politics and generated support through a range of socio-religious activities.[60]

Leaders of the Muslim Brotherhood there have not been drawn into violent opposition with the state and have demonstrated a longevity sustained by a commitment to social activism. Such social non-violent activism demonstrates one part of a spectrum of change where, to paraphrase Lapidus, 'Islamic beliefs ... represent an effort to generate and legitimate new forms of political and social action in radically changing societies.'[61] In Malaysia such activism has met with illiberal resistance from the state. Liberal voices for democratic change, such as those of Anwar Ibrahim, are stifled and gagged. Liberal Muslims are under attack from Muslim state elites who understand the potential for change that they embody. Ibrahim, who was a government member and former deputy prime minister advocated a modernised interpretation of Islam that demonstrated its plural, democratic and social justice agenda. He and others like him represented a genuine attempt to generate an internal challenge to the fundamentalist agenda's of so many others. As Esposito points out, Anwar Ibrahim's Islam is a dynamic, developing tradition that responds to diverse times and places. He rejected the conservative imitation (*taqlid*) of the past in favour of independent analysis and re-interpretation (*ijtihad*), believing that Islam is 'a pragmatic religion whose real strength and dynamism was in its ongoing revitalization'.[62] Ibrahim's dissent led him to jail on the orders of a ruling elite subsequently condemned by the international community. His imprisonment symbolises the limited space for such voices in contemporary Muslim domains.

Muslim peacemakers achieve conflict resolution and reconciliation on a daily basis in communities where dispute leads to a call for their intervention. Muslim peacemakers draw on a rich tradition and framework in Islam that facilitates such processes. Discourse, historical and contemporary focus on reconciliation, settlement of disputes and cease-fire are not as absent from the Muslim arena as one might believe. Yet such approaches remain largely absent from modern debates about peace, settlement, conflict resolution and reconciliation in the modern era. The absence of such recognition explains why so many in Western locales continue to believe that violence is the only path for Islam.

Conclusion

Peace is not only better than war, but infinitely more arduous.

George Bernard Shaw

The al-Qaeda attacks on America on 11 September 2001 created a sense of disbelief as millions across the globe watched or listened to the terrifying accounts of death and destruction in New York, Washington and beyond. In the immediate aftermath of the attacks the ether of a million media imploded with the same questions; Was everything changed? Why did it happen to us? Who were the perpetrators? What had compelled them to commit such evil? Moreover many of the new questions cast a spotlight on Islam and its adherents. At a time when popular knowledge of Islam in western consciousness had been negligible a new thirst for information was apparent. The British Prime Minster was reported to be reading the Holy book of Islam – the Koran and the shelves of countless bookshops filled rapidly with accounts of the 'new phenomenon'. The majority of these books and other media, however, had little to say about Islam per se and a lot to say about al-Qaeda, Usama Bin Laden and the 11 September terrorists. The Islam that was represented in such accounts was Bin Laden's Islam and a kind of sole property faith founded on a fundamental hatred for the United States of America.

Muslim terrorism is now presented to western and other audiences as the most significant threat of the modern era. Muslim terrorism is understood as presenting a monumental challenge to the defenders of the free world. Muslim terror plots and the attempts to gain weapons of mass destruction, including chemical, nuclear and biological capability, explain in part the unfolding instability besetting global relations in the twenty-first century. The response to such a threat has been to announce a war on terrorism and the tools of terrorism that the Muslim terrorists might seek to acquire. The spectre of international terrorism in the twenty-first century is undeniably Muslim in character. Any war on terror, counter-terrorism effort and international campaign to end terrorism, thus, necessitates a penetrating gaze upon Muslim communities and domains. In this respect Islam is found wanting. For Muslim regimes, Islamic leaders, Muslim states, Islamist movements, Islamic congregations and Muslim communities are presented as failing 'the rest' in the secularised environment of the new global order. In this sense, Muslims residing in the 'Islamic world' are partly identified as the new enemy. These enemies are presented as fundamentally at odds with the political and economic forces that currently dominate the international order. They are rarely understood as the victims of such orders.

The war on terror has established some notable successes, and it did at first appear that a military-type response might be enough to get rid of Usama Bin Laden and the Taliban regime that hosted him in Afghanistan. As such the war on terror has led to the collapse of the Taliban regime, a war on Iraq and the capture of hundreds of 'militants' imprisoned in Guantanemo in Cuba. Yet, by 2005 like a hydra, the menace of al-Qaeda and its affiliates still remained undiminished. Bomb attacks and missiles in Spain, Iraq, London, Kenya, Turkey, Bali, Saudi Arabia, Tunisia, Morocco and elsewhere seem to confirm the fear that al-Qaeda has not diminished in its menace. The appeal of its message seemed almost enhanced by the ability of Bin Laden to elude and endure along with his other closest allies. In this respect the perpetrators ignore the adage that terrorism doesn't work. Religious clerics sanction violence and especially suicide acts and undermine the security of countless millions across the globe. The fear grows that the day when the terrorists have WMD capacity is getting nearer.

Finishing off al-Qaeda?

On the eve of Operation Iraqi Freedom, US Defence Secretary Donald Rumsfeld outlined the objectives of the Coalition Forces:

> First, end the regime of Saddam Hussein. Second, to identify, isolate and eliminate Iraq's weapons of mass destruction. Third, to search for, to capture and to drive out terrorists from that country. Fourth, to collect such intelligence as we can related to terrorist networks. Fifth, to collect such intelligence as we can related to the global network of illicit weapons of mass destruction Sixth, to end sanctions and to immediately deliver humanitarian support to the displaced and to many needy Iraqi citizens. Seventh, to secure Iraq's oil fields and resources, which belong to the Iraqi people. And last, to help the Iraqi people create conditions for a transition to a representative self-government.[1]

Cruise missiles, amphibious assaults, B-52 bombers, Tomahawk missiles, Expeditionary Forces, Royal Marines, Mechanised divisions, bombing missions, ground forces numbering over 150,000, and thousands of air strikes ensued in the military campaign to achieve Rumsfeld's objectives. By 9 April

2003 Iraqi forces and Saddam Hussein had fled Baghdad as the city fell to US control. With this a major victory over terrorism had been achieved. Rumsfeld's number one objective had been obtained. The Coalition Forces had flexed their muscles and the regime of Saddam Hussein had toppled. There was cause for early optimism that if the war had been so easy to win then a drop in terrorism was bound to occur. Neighbouring states, such as Syria and Iran, were warned moreover to take stock of their own positions regarding terrorism and be cognisant of an unwillingness to join the international campaign against the terrorist networks and their attempts to acquire 'illicit' weapons of mass destruction.

The short-term consequences of this successfully prosecuted war seemed to demonstrate that a military response to the threat of terrorism was working. The Coalition Force occupation of Iraq, however, has not in the short term actually succeeded in diminishing the terror threat in Iraq or beyond its borders. In Iraq incidents of terrorism, including the bombing of the Jordanian Embassy and the United Nations Headquarters, insurgency, kidnappings of Westerners, and locals alike have increased and thus diminished security throughout the country for both its citizens and internationals present there. The rise of insurgency in Iraq – much of it with an Islamist colour – has effectively de-stabilised the country and made the task of democracy promotion and post-war reconstruction increasingly difficult. While the occupation of Iraq may have officially ended in the Summer of 2004 when American administrator Paul Bremner handed it over to local Iraqi administrators, even the highest ranking American military officials admit that their forces will remain for at least a decade. Insurgency in Iraq is characterised by a dangerous mix of local as well as foreign *Sunni* and *Shi'a* elements, all of who seek to wield power in post-Saddam Iraq.[2] As Rumsfeld himself admitted in August 2003, the global war on terror was 'far from over'. Yet a rise in the acts of global terrorism seemed to confound. In some respects it would appear that the military solution in Iraq or Afghanistan and other locations has had limited effect in terms of achieving a drop in terrorism. Revenge and retribution would not be enough. Al-Qaeda was still undertaking attacks belying the aspiration that this new network of transnational terrorism had been hopelessly undermined. There is a need to recognise that a more multi-faceted and multi-variant approach to the issue would have to be developed. Such an approach would be undermined if primacy were given to military solutions for countering terrorism of such mythic proportions. There is no simple answer, but historical record demonstrates that following a hearts and mind campaign after a military campaign has often failed to win over the very populations that are targeted. In January 2005, US officials also admitted that occupied Iraq had replaced Afghanistan as the major location for the training of 'terrorists'.

More than four years after the 11 September attacks Usama Bin Laden and many of his most important colleagues remained at large, and his political message continued to resonate and spread in Muslim domains characterised by authoritarian and non-democratic rule. Western coalition handling of Taliban suspects and lack of concern for their due rights only served to confirm Muslim suspicions against the United States of America. Western democracies undermine their own futures as well as give grist to the mill of Muslim propagandists when the suspended human rights and the rule of law as a strategy for countering terrorism. Many judicial and other authorities in the West have commented on the compromise of western values and principles that such action has established. International human rights organisations have alleged that Western and particularly US moral authority in the war on terrorism has been damaged by the cruelty to prisoners in Iraq and the secretive detention and coercive techniques used against detainees in American custody elsewhere. In 2005 the Human Rights Watch (HRW) organisation reported that 'human rights suffered a serious setback worldwide in 2004 as a result of the Abu Ghraib scandal and the failure of the global community to protect victims of ethnic massacres in the Darfur region of Sudan'. In setting itself up as a defender of human rights around the world the United States of America and European states such as the United Kingdom have failed themselves to stick to legal standards and furthermore lended dubious credibility to brutal customs undertaken by other states for 'security reasons'. HRW further stated that, 'in the midst of a seeming epidemic of suicide bombings, beheadings and other attacks on civilians and non-combatants – all affronts to the most basic human-rights values – Washington's weakened moral authority is felt acutely.'[3]

By remaining un-captured Bin Laden remains a threat. Yet even if Bin Laden were captured Muslim terrorism would be unlikely to evaporate overnight. The grievances that have been exploited by Bin Laden and other Islamist extremists, including significant complaints against the West and the outcome of their policies or interactions with Muslim domain, would remain and continue to fester in the absence of new policies. Thus the terrorists may be battered and bruised but their beliefs and the contexts that established them remain potent. The Taliban and al-Qaeda may have been ousted from Kabul but they and the causes they represent have not been eradicated. Post-war Afghanistan has suffered as a result of a lack of commitment to forward the economic and military assistance necessary to transform this failed state from a community of warlords to peace-loving and democratic citizens. In this respect locally held elections are not sufficient guarantors that the transition from Islamic authoritarianism to peace and freedom has been successfully secured. The Taliban and al-Qaeda, in sustained alliance with local warlords, remain in the wings. Outside of Kabul, Afghanistan remains lawless and the majority of its citizens lack basic rights and a sense of security. Moreover under the guise of the global war on terrorism states benighted by pre-existing ethno-national conflicts tend to further rely on military and other coercive measures to beat down restive populations and opponents further fuelling the cycle of violence.

The age of terror

Looking for more than military measures as a solution to global terrorism and its Muslim manifestation demands that political, diplomatic, economic and legal dimensions and issues are addressed. As I have demonstrated elsewhere in this book there is evidence that such an approach has played a part, albeit in a somewhat piecemeal fashion, in fashioning a multi-faceted approach to the issue. In many western democracies a raft of legal measures have been taken to counter the threat of terrorism but in many cases these are undermined by fear of the extent to which such measures undermine the principles of rights that make states democratic in the first place. Moreover unprecedented improvements in public security and preparedness and awareness have taken place right across the globe. Improved security measures are in evidence on public transport, around diplomatic missions, at borders and in government institutions. Improved security measures, however, have not deterred the terrorists; merely resulting in 'soft targets' such as hotels, holidaymakers, apartment complexes, clubs and bars becoming targets. Military reprisal has largely failed due to the indiscriminate manner of its execution in domains such as Afghanistan, Egypt and Iraq. Such attacks may 'take out' the bomb-maker or terrorist 'mastermind' but they 'fail' to counter the problem in other ways. First, the indiscriminate nature of such attacks give rise to civilian casualties that consolidate rather than eradicate grievance. Second, although the instruments of terror or its operatives may be eliminated in such attacks the political environment that gives rise to such violence remains marginal or un-addressed.

What appears to be missing from the current equation, however, is full international subscription to the principles of the war on terrorism as they are currently identified. Furthermore, the absence of the United Nations as a significant actor in formulation of a response is telling and could be read as underscoring the rift that has opened in the international community over this issue. International solidarity grew in the wake of the attacks on 11 September 2001 but such support failed to translate into a more sustainable, significant or better-resourced role for the international community through the forum of the United Nations. It is clear that diplomacy has not been the weapon of choice in the global war on terrorism although it is obvious that there have been some limited diplomatic trade-offs that have impacted positively in terms of the Palestinian–Israeli peace process. The difficulty in the diplomatic approach is that the main target – in the global war on terrorism, the al-Qaeda – represents the ideas of fringe fantasists with nihilistic tendencies.

Dialogue is thus rendered meaningless unless some distinctions are drawn about who's who in the Islamist fold. If all Muslims are considered beyond the pale then only annihilation will work, but if those Islamist elements with legitimate and representative objectives and grievances are recognised then dialogue and negotiation could work. Such dialogue, however, demands concession from both sides and would better succeed if confidence building and trust building measures have been achieved beforehand. Such a move would signal an acknowledgement that terrorism must be countered through a diverse and graded series of responses to dimensions of violence that include terrorism but not exclusively so. In undertaking this task Muslims and Muslim communities must join in the rejection rather than in the celebration of those tactics that target civilians. Muslim clerics who justify violence against Jewish worshippers in Jerusalem and office workers in Manhattan must be held to account by their own communities for supporting acts of wanton violence and terror that belittle the demand for equitable treatment in hearing the grievances and complaints that beset embattled Muslim communities across the globe.

The response to terrorism must, however, be proportionate and those who lead the response must be careful to be seen to wage war fairly; responses that appear to target communities rather than the terrorists only serve the interests of the terrorist. Otherwise, cyclical violence and terror will be generated. Countering terrorism should also demand a reflection on the part of policy-makers across the globe on power and its uses. Blind rage, revenge and righteousness can only succeed in establishing a world of polar opposites between good and evil that betray the true complexities of dealing with such issues. In this way the tie between terrorism and Islam in the modern era may be broken.

Notes

Introduction

1. Rashid, A., http://www.worldpress.org/Mideast/1941. cfm
2. Raban, J., 'The Greatest Gulf', *The Guardian*, 13 April 2003.
3. For a discussion of instrumentalism within identity formation, see: Maalouf, A., *On Identity*, London, Harvill Press, 2000.
4. Ayatollah Mohammed Hussein Fadlallah, interview with author, Beirut, April 2000.
5. Such a perspective is explored in Western scholarship on Islam, including Kedourie, E., *Politics in the Middle East*, Oxford, Oxford University Press, 1992.
6. Ibid., p. 1.
7. Akenson, D. H., *God's People, Covenant and Land in South Africa, Israel and Ulster*, Ithaca, Cornell University Press, 1993.
8. Allen, D. (ed.), *Religion and Political Conflict in South Asia, India, Pakistan, and Sri Lanka* (Contributions to the Study of Religion), Westport (CT) and London, Greenwood Press, 1992.
9. For example see: Elliott, M., 'Hate Club: al-Qaeda's web of terror' *Time*, 4 November 2001 or Kaplan, D. E., 'Playing offense: the inside story of how US terrorist hunters are going after al-Qaeda', *New Republic*, 6 February 2003. Alternatively read the account of journalist Jason Burke, *Al-Qaeda: Casting a Shadow of Terror*, London, IB Tauris, 2004.
10. For example: Jenkins, B. M., *Countering al-Qaeda: an appreciation of the situation and suggestions for strategy*, Rand, 2002 or Corbin, J., *The Base: al-Qaeda and the changing face of global terror*, London, Pocket Books, 2003.
11. Recent works that devote attention to this axis include: Kepel, G., *The War for Muslim Minds*, Cambridge (MA), Harvard University Press, 2004; Lewis, B., *What Went Wrong? Western Impact and Middle Eastern Responses*, London, Phoenix, January 2004; or Hiro, D., *War without End, the Rise of Islamist Terrorism and Global Response*, London, Routledge, 2002.
12. Burke, J., op. cit., p. 23.
13. Goldstein, J. and Keohane, R. O., 'Ideas and foreign policy: an analytical framework', in Goldstein, J. and Keohane, R. O. (eds), *Ideas and Foreign Policy: Beliefs, Institutions and Political Change*, Ithaca, Cornell University Press, 1993, pp. 3–30.
14. Roy, O., *Globalised Islam, the Search for a new Ummah*, London, Hurst, 2002, pp. 124–37.
15. Ahmed, A. S., *Islam under Siege*, Cambridge, Polity Press, 2003 and Sardar, Z. and Wyn Davies, M., *Why Do People Hate America*, London, Icon Books, 2002 explores these themes.
16. Esposito, J. L., *Unholy war, terror in the name of Islam*, New York, Oxford University Press, 2002, pp. 118–25.
17. See: Lawrence, B. B., *Shattering the Myth, Islam Beyond Violence*, Princeton, Princeton University Press, 1998; Huband, M., *Warriors of the Prophet, the Struggle for Islam*, Boulder (CO), Westview Press, 1999 and Hafez, M., *Why Muslims Rebel, Repression and Resistance in the Islamic World*, Boulder (CO), Lynne Rienner, 2004.

18. Such locales include countries in the Middle East such as Lebanon or Israel and the Palestinian territories of the West Bank and Gaza Strip, in western Europe Northern Ireland and in Africa Somalia, Sierra Leone and Sudan.

19. On the absence of democracy in Muslim majority states see: Diamond, L., and Plattner, M. (eds), *The Global Resurgence of Democracy*, Second Edition, Baltimore, Johns Hopkins University Press, 1996; Huntingdon, S., 'Will more countries become democratic?', *Political Science Quarterly*, 99:2, 1984 and Diamond, L., Linz, J. and Lipset, S. M., *Politics in Developing Countries: Comparing Experiences with Democracy*, Boulder (CO), Lynne Rienner, 1995.

20. There is a growing body of literature on gender and conflict which reveals evidence of the extent to which environments of conflict and violence are dominated by men and the extent to which women become targets, victims and symbols of conflict. See: Enloe, C., *The Morning After: Sexual Politics at the End of the Cold War*, Berkeley, University of California Press, 1993; or Jacobs, S., Jacobson, R. and Marchbank, J. (eds), *States of Conflicts, Gender, Violence and Resistance*, London, Zed Books, 2000.

21. Cockburn. C., 'The gendered dynamics of armed conflict and political violence' in Moser, C. and Clark, F. (eds) *Victims, Perpetrators or Actors?: Gender, Armed conflicts and Political Violence*, London, Zed Books, 2001, p. 21.

22. See: Downer, J. W., 'Don't expect democracy this time: Japan and Iraq', *History and Policy*, http://www.historyandpolicy.org, March 2003.

23. Said, E., *Covering Islam: How the Media and Experts Determine How We See the Rest of the World*, London, Vintage, 1997, p. 163.

24. Hamas Covenant, http://www.yale.edu/lawweb/avalon/mideast/hamas.htm, 1988.

25. See: Mansur, S., 'The father of assassins', *Toronto Globe and Mail*, 11 October 2001 and E. Margolis, 'Is the gun smoking? Experts disagree on bin Laden's home video', *Toronto Sun*, 17 December 2001.

26. Kaldor, M., *New Wars and Old Wars, Organized Violence in a Global Era*, Cambridge: Polity, 2001, p. 76.

27. Remarks of President Hosni Mubarak to International Press, March 2003.

28. Eickelman, D. F. and Piscatori, J., *Muslim Politics*, Princeton, PUP, 1996, p. 138.

1 Religion and Violence: A History of Entanglement

1. In December 2004, minor controversy broke out over the death of Iraqi civilians since the American led war and occupation of the country in April 2003. Counting the cost of civilian death in modern conflicts has become a political issue but remains overlooked when compared to military casualties such as those of American soldiers killed in the Iraq conflict.

2. Walker, C. *Ethnonationalism: The Quest for Understanding*, Princeton: Princeton University Press, 1993 and Horowitz, D. L., *Ethnic Groups in Conflict*, Berkeley, California University Press, 2001.

3. Mary Kaldor's explores this phenomenon in op. cit.

4. Eickelman D. F. and Piscatori, J., op. cit., p. 28.

5. See: http://www.ppu.org.uk/learn/infodocs/st_war_peace.html

6. In both the NATO bombing of Kosovo and the Allied Campaign against Afghanistan civilian casualties were higher than military losses. See: Milne, S. 'The innocent dead in a coward's war', *The Guardian*, 20 December 2001 and Kaplan, F. 'Bombs killing more civilians than expected', *The Boston Globe*, 30 May 1999.

7. The apparent policy of 'assassination' of Palestinian leaders and others, carried out by Israeli state forces demonstrates the tensions and sensitivities associated with this issue. In August 2001 then Israeli Deputy Defence Minister Ephraim Sneh declared, 'I can tell you unequivocally what the policy is … If anyone has committed or is planning to carry out terrorist attacks, he has to be hit … It is effective, precise and just.' See: http://news.bbc.co.uk/1/hi/world/middle_east/ 1258187.stm
8. Von-Clausewitz, C., *On War*, London, Pelican Books, 1968, p. 203.
9. Juergensmeyer notes that Timothy McVeigh, the Oklahoma bomber was influenced by 'Christian identity ideas'. Juergensmeyer, M., *Terror in the Mind of God*, Berkeley, California University Press, 2000, p. 31.
10. Armstrong, K. 'Cries of rage and frustration', http://www.cs.hofstra.edu/~vbarr/ Politics/armstrong .html
11. A Human Rights Report outlined state involvement in violence against Muslims. See: *Human Rights Watch*, 'We Have No Orders To Save You, State Participation and Complicity in Communal Violence in Gujarat', April 2002, New York: HRW.
12. Rushdie, S. 'Religion, as ever, is the poison in India's blood', *The Guardian*, 9 March 2002.
13. The role of religious leaders in such conflicts is open to debate with regard to their negative and positive powers. In Northern Ireland, figures such as Pastor Kenny McClinton liaised actively with the Loyalist LVF and in Israeli Rabbi Meir Kahane gained notoriety for his views on the Arabs and the right of Jews to settle the land of Eretz Israel.
14. *CBS, 60 Minutes* – Gerry Falwell. 6 October 2002. A week later, during which a call by a leading Iranian Aytollah for his death was made, Falwell issued an apology for his remarks, 'I sincerely apologize that certain statements of mine made during an interview for CBS's *60 Minutes* were hurtful to the feelings of many Muslims. I intended no disrespect to any sincere, law-abiding Muslim.'
15. Ansell, A. E. (ed.), *Unraveling the Right: The New Conservatism in American Thought and Politics*, Boulder (CO), Westview Press, 1998, and Berlet, C. and Lyons M. N., *Right-Wing Populism in America: Too Close for Comfort*, New York, Guildford Publications, 2000.
16. Franklin Graham quoted by NBC, November 2001.
17. See: http://www.guardian.co.uk/uselections2004/comment/story/0,14259,1348262, 00.html
18. This is often through aggressive exploitation of modern media and technologies. Many Muslim populist leaders and protest movements have exploited such technologies.
19. Rushdie, S., 'Yes, this is about Islam', *New York Times*, 2 November 2001.
20. See: Address to Congress by President G. W. Bush, 20 September 2001 where he makes his 'For or Against us' speech.
21. Images that represent Islam – as conveyed through much mass media in the West tend to portray Islam in pictorial/image form alongside symbols and images of violence as faith associated.
22. Lewis, B., 'The roots of Muslim rage', *Atlantic Monthly*, 266:3, September 1990, pp. 47–60.
23. Lubotsky, A. 'Shabbat Shalom', *The Jerusalem Post*, 26 February 1991.
24. The event was widely reported in the media. See: Human Rights Watch, 'Saudi Arabia: Religious Police role in School Fire criticised', *Human Rights Watch Press Release*, New York, 15 March 2002.

25. Simon, B. 'Falwell brands Mohammed a "Terrorist" ', 60 Minutes, CBS News, 6 October 2002, www.cbsnews.com/stories/2002/10/03/60minutes/main524268. shtml
26. Yet such automatic identification with Israel angered other elements within Loyalism and its right-wing support base in British groups such as Combat 18 with its overtly anti-Semitic and racist philosophy.
27. Tucker, R. C. (ed.), *The Marx-engels Reader*, New York, WW Norton and Co, 1978, pp. 53–4.
28. Hourani, A., *A History of the Arab Peoples*, London, Faber, 1991, p. 144.
29. Van Ess, J., 'Political ideas in early Islamic religious thought', *British Journal of Middle Eastern Studies*, 28:2, 2001, p. 151.
30. Lewis, B., op. cit., 1990, pp. 47–60.
31. See: Hourani, A., op. cit., or Lapidus, I. M., *A History of Islamic Societies*, Cambridge, Cambridge University Press, 1990.
32. Engineer, A. A., *Theory and Practise of the Islamic State*, Lahore: Vanguard Books, 1985.
33. Ayubi, N., *Political Islam, religion and politics in the Arab world*, London, Routledge, 1993, p. 6.
34. Lapidus, I. M., op. cit., p. 63.
35. Saunders, J. J., *A History of Medieval Islam*, London: Kegan Paul International, 1965, p. 147.
36. Mawdudi, A., as quoted by Rudolph Peters, *Jihad in Classical and Modern Islam*, Princeton (NJ), Marcus Wiener Publishers, 1996, p. 128.
37. Khan, Q., *The Political Thought of Ibn Taymiyyah*, Delhi, Ansar Press, 1992, p. 57.
38. Keegan is quoted as pointing out that the tradition of ancient leadership was always linked to military prowess, 'The legitimacy of all their roles was established and sustained by readiness to go to the battlefield and fight with courage once there.' Keegan, J., *The Mask of Command*, London: Jonathan Cape, 1987, p. 312.
39. See: al-Mawardi, Adu'l Hassan, *al-Ahkam as-Sultaniyyah*, London, TaHa Publishers, 1996.
40. Saunders, J. J., op. cit., p. 33.
41. Taji-Farouki, S., 'Islamic state theories and contemporary realities', in Sid-Ahmed, A. S. and Ehteshami, A. (eds), *Islamic Fundamentalism*, Boulder, (CO), Westview Press, 1996, p. 37.
42. Saunders, J. J., op. cit., p. 71.
43. Hourani, A., op. cit., p. 143.
44. Mawardi, Abu'l Hassan, op. cit., p. 64.
45. Sheikh Abduallah Shammi, interview with author, Gaza, September 2002.
46. Khan, Q., *The Political Thought of Ibn Taymiyyah*, Delhi, Ansar Press, 1992, p. 168.
47. Ibid., p. 169.
48. Keddourie, E., op. cit., 1992, p. 13.
49. The point here is that somehow Usama Bin Laden is emblematic for both Muslims and non-Muslims.
50. Frankenthal, Y. 'I would have done the same', *The Guardian*, 7 August 2002, p. 16.
51. Huntington, S. 'The Clash of Civilizations?', *Foreign Affairs*, Summer 1993, p. 31.
52. Kelsay, J., *Islam and War – the Gulf War and Beyond*, Kentucky, Westminster John Knox Press, 1993, p. 47.
53. Ibid., p. 65.
54. Fnaysh, M., MP Bint Jubayl, interview with author, Beirut 15 August 2002.
55. New York Times, 'Iranian President denounces terrorism', *New York Times*, 11 November 2001. It should be noted that a degree of hostility and mistrust lays in

the relationship between *Sunni*-based al-Qaeda and *Shi'a* Iranianism under clerical rule. Yet, to this statement should be added the many others from the *Sunni* religious leadership's condemnation of Bin Laden's method and message as unrepresentative.

56. Jihad is quite often cited as the sixth fundamental obligation of Islam. For example, many websites refers to Jihad as the sixth pillar of Islam. See: http://churchofassumption.com/9232001.shtml for an example of a homily on Islam that includes Jihad.
57. Guelke, A., *The Age of Terrorism and the International Political System*, London, IB Tauris, 1995, p. 8.
58. Taheri, A., *Holy Terror: The Inside Story of Islamic Terrorism*, London, Sphere, 1987.
59. Kelsay, J., op. cit., p. 46.
60. Fnaysh, M., MP Bint Jubayl, interview with author, Beirut 15 August 2002.
61. Ismail Haniyeh, Hamas leader, interview with author, Gaza city September 2002.
62. Hoffman, B., *Inside Terrorism*, New York, Columbia University Press, 1998, p. 87.
63. Lewis, B., *The Assassins: A Radical Sect in Islam*, London, Weidenfeld and Nicolson, 1980, pp. 129–30.
64. Dafarty, F., *The Assassin Legends: Myths of the Isma'ilis*, London, IB Tauris, 1994, p. 121.
65. Ibid., p. 34.
66. Jones, T. and Ereira, A., *Crusades*, London, Penguin, 1994, p. 52.
67. Dr. Atef Adhwan, interview with author, Islamic University of Gaza, Gaza, 9 August 2002.
68. Armstrong, K., *Holy War: The Crusades and their Impact on Today's World*, Houndmills, Palgrave, 1988, p. 89.
69. Rees, S. 'Extremist: "Mad Mahdi"', *Military History Magazine*, June 2002 or Furnish, T. R., 'Bin Laden: the man who would be Mahdi', *Middle East Quarterly*, 9:2, Spring 2002, http://www.meforum.org/article/159
70. See: Holt, P. M., The Mahdist state in Sudan 1881–1898: *A Study of Its Origins, Development and Overthrow*, London, Clarendon, 1958 and Lapidus, I. M., op. cit., 1988, p. 854.
71. Rashid Rida in Egypt or Sheikh Izz-a-din al-Qassam in mandate Palestine. See: Milton-Edwards, B. *Islamic Politics in Palestine*, London, IB Tauris, 1996.
72. Schleifer, A., 'The Life and Thought of Izz ad-din al-Qassam', *Islamic Quarterly*, pp. 63–4.
73. See: quote from http://www.yuni.com/quotes/hegel.html
74. Kaldor, M., op. cit., 2001, p. 111.

2 The West's Terror of Islam

1. For example see: Keane, J. 'Cosmocracy', *New Statesman*, 23 May 2002 with references to apocalyptic terrorism, or Benjamin, D. and Simon, S. *The Age of Sacred Terror*, New York, Random House, 2002.
2. Lieven, A., 'Strategy for Terror', *Prospect*, vol. 67, October 2001, p. 19.
3. Ibid., p. 19.
4. Dershowitz, A., *Why Terrorism works*, Yale, Yale University Press, 2002, p. 1.
5. Ariel Sharon, Address to the Israeli people, September 2001.
6. A World of Difference, *The Guardian* – G2, 11 October 2001, pp. 2–5.
7. Huntington, S., op. cit., pp. 22–49.
8. Barber, B., *Jihad vs. McWorld*, New York, Ballantine Books, 1996, p. 215.
9. Ibid., p. 205.

10. The author is grateful to Jorgen Nielsen for raising this issue.
11. See: Lewis, B., op. cit., p. 48.
12. Ibid.
13. Ibid.
14. Islamophobic tendencies in non-western societies have characterised domestic Indian politics in the latter twentieth century manifest in the rise and electoral successes of fundamentalist Hindu political parties and ongoing conflicts over secessionist claims in Kashmir and ethnic violence in Gujarat. See: Misra, A., *Identity and Religion, foundations of anti-Islamism in India*, New Delhi, Sage, 2004.
15. See: Sadar, Z. and Wyn Davies, M., op. cit.
16. Kaplan, R., Address on National Public Radio, 23 September 2001, extracts from http://www.siliconvalley.com/mld/siliconvalley/business/columnists/gmsv/2844 387.htm
17. Lewis, B., 'The revolt of Islam, when did the conflict with the West begin and how could it end?', *New Yorker*, 19 November 2001, p. 17.
18. Ibid., p. 17.
19. See: Conley, C.A., *Melancholy Accidents: The Meaning of Violence in Post-Famine Ireland*, Lanham (MD), Lexington Books, 1999, and Ignatiev, N., *How the Irish Became White*, London, Routledge, 1996.
20. Wright, F., *Northern Ireland: A Comparative Analysis*, Dublin, Gill and Macmillan, 1988, p. 11.
21. Sadar, Z. and Wyn Davies, M., op. cit. In chapter 1 they draw on the example of the US programme 'The West Wing' to demonstrate how identity and values in the modern age (including those against Muslims) are created and consolidated through mass mediums such as the television.
22. Al-Hawali, S., 'An Open Letter to President Bush', 16 October 2001.
23. Al-Hawali, S., 'Infidels without and within', *New Perspectives Quarterly*, 8:2, 1990, www.npq.org, p. 2; trans. Bayan, 1990.
24. Al-Hawali, S., Ibid., p. 2; trans. Bayan, 1990.
25. See: Milton-Edwards, B., 'Political Islam and the Palestinian-Israeli conflict', in Karsh, E. and Kumaraswamy, K. (eds) *Israel and the Islamic World*, London, Frank Cass, 2006.
26. See: Milton-Edwards, B., op. cit., pp. 27–35 and Mattar, P., 'The Mufti of Jerusalem and the politics of Palestine', *Middle East Journal*, vol. 42, 1989, pp. 227–40.
27. See: http://www.moqawama.tv/page2/f_oreali.htm
28. Sheikh Nabil Qa'ouk, Commander of Hizb Allah southern forces, interview with author, Sidon 11 May 2000.
29. The text of the letter is quoted in Augustus Norton, R., *Amal and the Shi'a: Struggle for the Soul of Lebanon*, Austin, Texas (TX), University of Texas Press, 1987, pp. 167–87.
30. Saad-Ghorayeb, A., *Hizbu'llah, Politics and Religion*, London, Pluto Press, 2002, pp. 106–7.
31. Haj Naim Kassem, Deputy Secretary-General Hizb Allah, interview with author, Beirut, April 23, 2000.
32. Kramer, M., 'Hezbollah's vision of the West', *Washington Institute for Near East Policy, Hezbollah's Vision of the West*, Policy Paper no. 16, Washington, 1989, p. 75.
33. According to US State Department assessments, 'Although Hizb Allah has not attacked US targets in Lebanon since 1991, animosity has not abated', US State Department, *Patterns of Global Terrorism*, 2000, p. 6; Middle East Section, Lebanon.
34. Haj Naim Kassem, Deputy Secretary-General Hizb Allah, interview with author, 9 May 2000.

35. Haj Mohammed Raad, Head of Hizb Allah's 'Loyalty to the Resistance' Parliamentary Bloc, interview with author, 9 November 2001.
36. In October 2002 Israeli Shin Bet acknowledged that they were holding a Canadian passport holder named Fawi Ayoub who they alleged was a Hizb Allah leader operating and supporting Palestinian militants in the West Bank town of Hebron.
37. The oft-quoted role of the CIA in Afghanistan in supporting Mujahideen efforts to end the Soviet occupation illustrated the attempt to use Islam for strategic advantage.
38. Runnymede Trust, *Islamophobia: A Challenge for Us All*, London, Runnymede Trust, 1997.
39. Halliday argued that anti-Muslimism is 'not so much hostility to Islam ... but hostility to *Muslims*, to communities of peoples whose sole or main religion is Islam and whose Islamic character, real or invented, forms one of the objects of prejudice.' Halliday, F., *Islam and the Myth of Confrontation*, London, IB Tauris, 1996, p. 160.
40. Lacayo, R., 'Rushing to bash outsiders', *Time*, May 1, 1995, p. 70. Also, ACCLU press releases, December 1995.
41. http://www.aclu.org/ImmigrantsRights/ImmigrantsRights.cfm?ID=10774&c=98
42. Guelke, A., op.cit., pp. 113 and 115.
43. *Human Rights Watch*, Press Release, 'Ensure protection for foreign detainees', 1 December 2001.
44. John Ashcroft, as reported on CNN, http://www.cnn.com/2001/US/12/06/inv.ashcroft.hearing/, December 2001.
45. Jaggi, M., 'Civil wrongs', *Guardian Weekend*, 22 June 2002, p. 57.
46. Cole, D., 'National Security State', *The Nation*, 17 December 2001.
47. See: Ford, P., 'Crusade: A Freudian Slip? Europe Cringes at President Bush's 'Crusade' Against Terrorists,' *Christian Science Monitor*, 19 September 2001.
48. Sheikh Abdullah Shammi, interview with author, Gaza, 9 September 2002.
49. Fukuyama, F., 'Fighting the 21st century Fascists', *The Age–Australia*, 5 January 2002, http://www.theage.com.au/news/state/2002/01/05/FFXE5PLU0WC.html
50. The phenomenon of many faiths in revival is examined by Juergensmeyer, M., op. cit., p. 18.
51. Juergensmeyer, M., op. cit., p. 19.
52. Statement issued by Hizb ur Tahrir, United Kingdom, 8 November 2003.
53. *Human Rights Watch*, press release, 'UK: New anti-terror law rolls back rights', 14 December 2001.
54. Only two non-nationals arrested have opted to quit the United Kingdom on a voluntary basis.
55. *Amnesty International*, 'News release issued by the International Secretariat of Amnesty International', Press release, 17 July 2002, EUR 45/012/2002.
56. Anti-terrorism, Crime and Security Act, November 2001, Section 27. http://www.hmso.gov.uk/acts/en/2001en27.htm
57. Anti-terrorism, Crime and Security Act, November 2001, Section 21–3, http://www.hmso.gov.uk/acts/en/2001en21.htm
58. *The Guardian*, December 16, 2004. http://politics.guardian.co.uk/homeaffairs/story/0,11026,1374970,00.html
59. Bright, M., 'Blunkett attacked dying "terrorist" ', *The Observer*, 21 July 2002.
60. Amnesty International expressed concerns about the Act. See: AI Index: EUR 45/007/2001, 20 February 2001.
61. BBC, 'Hamas suspect supported bin Laden' 9 May 2002.
62. In Australia the same issues face the Muslim migrant community. Despite its relatively small size of 300,000 it is reported as experiencing undue and negative

attention in the media and its representation of them. See: Saeed, A. and Akbarzadeh, S. (eds), *Muslim Communities in Australia*, New South Wales, University of New South Wales Press, 2001.

63. *The Guardian*, 'A Map of Muslim Britain', 17 June 2002, p. 5.
64. Barber, B., op. cit., p. 164.
65. See: Bunce, S., 'The Forgotten Prince', *The Observer*, 11 November 2001.
66. The campaign to establish the first Sikh school, which was opened in November 1999, took two years of organisation by Sikh parents.
67. See: *Daily Telegraph* 26 May, 1996, 28 November 1998, *Jewish Chronicle*, 'Investigation rejects Muslim charity "link to Hamas terrorism" ', June 7 1996.
68. See: CAIR Letter, 11 June 1997.
69. Comments from New York Police Commissioner, Raymond Kelly, 26 February 2003, CBS News.
70. Sardar, Z. and Wyn Davies, M., op. cit., p. 12.
71. Huntington, S., op. cit., pp. 22–49.
72. Visit: http://www.math.nyu.edu/phd_students/amirishs/Html/shariati.html# quotations – quotations from Shariati on the role of intellectuals.
73. The Algerian democracy debate demonstrates this point.
74. '61% [of Muslims in the Guardian/ICM poll] said relations with non-Muslims had deteriorated since September 11' compounding the sense of exclusion which as many as 69% said they felt in terms of being an integral part of British society. *The Guardian*, 'Muslims reject image of a separate society', 17 June 2002, p. 1.
75. Maalouf, A., op. cit., p. 28.
76. Pew Research Center, June 2003: http://people-press.org/reports/display. php3?ReportID=185
77. Robinson, F., 'Islam and the West: clash of civilisation?', *Journal of RSAA*, vol. XXXIII, Part III, October 2002, pp. 307–20.

3   Islam and Violence

1. Bailie, G., http://www.salsa.net/peace/quotes.html
2. Weber, M. 'Politics as vocation' in Gerth, H. H. and Mills, C. W. (eds), *From Max Weber*, New York, Oxford University Press, 1972, p. 78.
3. Turner, B., *Weber and Islam, a Critical Study*, London, Routledge and Kegan Paul, 1974, p. 3.
4. See: McKenna, T., *Muslim Rulers and Rebels: Everyday Politics and Armed Separatism in the Southern Philippines* (Comparative Studies on Muslim Societies, 26), Berkley, University of California Press, 1998.
5. Gunaratna, R., *Inside Al-Qaeda: Global Network of Terror*, Berkley, Berkley Publishing Group, 2003.
6. The indigenous and fluid Afghan culture of localised Islam was considered altered by the influences of Arab-based and initiated salafi and revivalist discourses, movements and preaching across the Muslim world.
7. As quoted in: http://www.chron.com/cs/CDA/story.hts/special/terror/response/ 1064293
8. At that time Abu Sayyaf were also were holding two US citizens for ransom.
9. Crenshaw, M. (ed.), *Terrorism, Legitimacy and Power: the Consequences of Political Violence*, Middletown (CT), Wesleyan University Press, 1983, pp. 5–6.
10. Guelke, A., op. cit., p. 23.

11. Weber, in Turner, B., *Weber and Islam, a Critical Study*, London, Routledge and Kegan Paul, 1974, p. 34.
12. Nasr, Seyyed Hossein, 'Islam and the question of violence', *Al-Serat*, 13:2, 2002, p. 1.
13. Koran, Sura 104, The Backbiter, p. 659.
14. Sardar, Z., 'Islam has become its own enemy', *The Observer*, 21 October 2001.
15. Vakili-Zad, Cyrus, 'The power of religious rituals and revolution – Iran and South Africa, a comparative perspective', *Iranian Journal of International Relations*, 2:4, Winter 1990–91, p. 628.
16. US Troops face suicide attacks: http://www.lebanonwire.com/0303/03031514DS.asp
17. Slim, H., 'Why protect civilians? Innocence, immunity and enmity in war', *International Affairs*, 79:3, 2003, pp. 481–501.
18. Dr Mahmoud Zahar, Hamas leader, interview with author, Gaza, September 2002.
19. See: Armstrong, K., *The Battle for God: Fundamentalism in Judaism, Christianity and Islam*, London, Harper Collins, 2001.
20. Jeurgensmeyer, M., op. cit., 2001, p. 5.
21. President Bill Clinton, 1995, Address to the United Nations.
22. Priestland, G., 'The Future of Violence', London, Hamish Hamilton Ltd, 1974, p. 14.
23. Koran, Sura 49:5.
24. Koran, Sura 2:30.
25. MacFarlane, L., 'The right of self-determination in Northern Ireland and the justification for IRA violence', *Terrorism and Political Violence*, 2, 1990, p. 46.
26. Nasr, Seyyed Hossein, 'Islam and the question of violence', *Al-Serat*, 13:2, 2002, p. 1.
27. Hajj Naim Qassem, Deputy Secretary general of Hizb Allah, interview with author, 9 May 2000, Beirut.
28. Hashmi, S. H., 'Islamic Ethics in International Society' in Said, A. A., Funk, N. C. and Kadayifci, A. S. (eds), *Peace and Conflict Resolution in Islam*, Lanham, University Press of America, 2001, p. 110.
29. As quoted in Hashmi, p. 111.
30. Koran, Sura 2:256.
31. Schmid, A. P., *Political Terrorism*, New York, Transaction Publishers, 1985, p. 36.
32. Qutb, S., *Milestones*, 1978, p. 111.
33. Azzam, A., *Join the Caravan*, n.p., Ahle Sunna wa Jamaah, n.d, p. 30.
34. Ibid., p. 29.
35. Azzam, A., *Defence of Muslim Lands*, n.p., Ahle Sunna wa Jamaah, n.d, p. 15.
36. See: Nass bayan al-jabah al-islamiyyah al-Alamiyah li-jihad al-Yahud wa al-Salibiyan, *al-Quds al-Arabi*, 23 February 1998, p. 3.
37. See: Ruthven, M., *A Satanic Affair, Salman Rushdie and the Rage of Islam*, London: Chatto, 1990.
38. See: http://www.meij.or.jp/new/Osama%20bin%20Laden/jihad1.htm
39. See Zogby International Polling – http://forums.macrumors.com/archive/topic/22248-1.html
40. Fanon, F., *The Wretched of the Earth*, New York, Grove Press, 1986, p. 37.
41. Ibid., 1986, pp. 94 and 42.
42. Ghannoushi, R., 'On the dilemma of the Islamic movement', in el-Affendi, A (ed.), *Rethinking Islam and Modernity, Essays in Honour of Fathi Osman*, London, The Islamic Foundation, 2001, p. 116.
43. Paul Bremer, http://www.pbs.org/newshour/bb/military/july-dec98/war_8–25.html, 25 August 1998.
44. Fandy, M., *Saudi Arabia and the Politics of Dissent*, Houndmills, Palgrave, 1999, p. 25.

45. Ibid., p. 25.
46. Bin-Laden, U., Declaration of War: http://www.islamic-news.co.uk/declaration.htm
47. Ibid.
48. 'Mohammed', Senior Academic in Saudi Arabia, interview with author, November 1999.
49. Khaldun Ibn, 'Foundations and Purposes of Political Authority' in Said, A. A., Funk, N. C. and Kadayifci, A. S. (eds), *Peace and Conflict Resolution in Islam*, Lanham, University Press of America, 2001, p. 41.
50. Sardar, Z., 'Islam has become its own enemy', *The Observer*, October 21, 2001.
51. Esposito, J. L., *Islam, the Straight Path*, New York, Oxford University Press, 1994, p. 193.
52. Bin Laden, U., 'Declaration of war Against Americans occupying the land of the two holy places', 1996.
53. Ibid.
54. Barber, B., op. cit., p. 215.
55. Hefner, R. W., 'Secularization and citizenship in Muslim Indonesia', 1998, pp. 148–9.
56. Khomeini, on 'Just Fiqh'.
57. Ehteshami, A., *After Khomeini, the Iranian Second Republic*, London, Routledge, 1995, p. xiv.
58. Zubaida, S., *Islam, People and the State*, London, Routledge, 1988, p. 16.
59. Saad-Gorayeb, A., *Hizbu'llah Politics and Religion*, London, Pluto Press, 2002, p. 67.
60. Hourani, A., op. cit., 1991, p. 223.
61. See: Milton-Edwards, B., 'Iraq, past, present and future: a thoroughly modern mandate', *History and Policy*, http://www.historyandpolicy.org/archive/policy-paper-13.html
62. Interview with Dr. Lamia Ghaiylani, London, December 2002.
63. Anwar, Z., 'To claim their rights, Muslim women cannot leave it to men to define Islam', 2002, http://www.time.com/time/asia/covers/501030310/viewpoint2.html
64. Mrs Wazir, Minister of Social Affairs, Palestinian Authority, interview with author, Gaza, July 2003. She related that a shelter for victims of violence established in the West Bank for women from Gaza had been empty for three years as Israeli closure and travel restrictions meant that women victims of violence were prevented from travelling out of the Gaza Strip via Israel to the West Bank.
65. Kandiyoti, D., 'Women, Islam and the state: a comparative approach', in Cole, J. R. (ed.), *Comparing Muslim Societies*, Ann Arbor, University of Michigan Press, 1992, p. 251.
66. Vickers, J., *Women and War*, London, Zed Books, 1993, p. 106.
67. Lorentzen, L. A. and Turpin, J. (eds), *The Women and War Reader*, New York, New York University Press, 1998, p. 4.
68. Ibid., p. 64.
69. Siddiqi, D., 'Taslima Nasreen and others: the contest over gender in Bangladesh', in Bodman, H. L. and Tohidi, N. (eds), *Women in Muslim Societies*, Boulder (CO), Lynne Reinner, 1998, p. 209.
70. See: *The Observer*, 12 May, 2002.
71. See: Mernissi, F., *Beyond the veil: Male-female dynamics in modern Muslim society*, London, Saqi Books, 1985 and Afshar, H., *Islam and Feminisms, An Iranian Case Study*, 1998.
72. Sunan of Abu Daoud, trans. Ahmad Hasan, http://www.usc.edu/dept/MSA/fundamentals/hadithsunnah/

73. Afshar, H., op. cit., 1998, p. 146.
74. Marcus, R. 'Violence Against Women in Bangladesh, Pakistan, Egypt, Sudan, Senegal and Yemen', *Institute of Development Studies*, Brighton, 1993, p. 8.
75. See for example: Hammami, R., 'From immodesty to collaboration: Hamas, the women's movement and national identity in the Intifada', in Beinin, J. and Stork, J. (eds), *Political Islam, Essays from Middle East Report*, London, IB Tauris, 1997.
76. Qutb, S., *Islam, the Religion of the Future*, Kuwait, International Islamic Federation of Student Organizations, 1971, p. 64.
77. Tibi, B., *Islam between Culture and Politics*, Houndmills, Palgrave, 2001, p. 113.
78. Islam, Y., 'Faith and the future', *The Guardian*, 18 September 2001, p. 7.
79. Ostling, R., 'Bin Laden's idea of "jihad" is out of bounds, scholars say', *Associated Press*, 22 September 2001.

4 Sacred Violence

1. Prior, M., 'The clash of civilisations', draft text, July 2002, p. 4.
2. Gellner, E., *Muslim Society*, Cambridge, Cambridge University Press, 1983.
3. Keddie, N. and Monian, F., 'Militancy and religion in contemporary Iran', in Marty, M. E. and Appleby, R. S. (eds), *Fundamentalisms and the State*, Chicago, University of Chicago Press, 1993, p. 512.
4. Joffe, G., http://www.megastories.com/islam/analysis/violent.htm
5. ABC News poll: http://abcnews.go.com/sections/us/DailyNews/Islam_poll021025.html
6. Most conventional historical accounts of the war underplay this dimension of the conflict: Milton-Edwards, B. and Hinchcliffe, P., *Conflicts in the Middle East since 1945*, London, Routledge, 2001.
7. Dafarti, M., (trans.), *The Texts of Letters Exchanges between the Presidents of the Islamic Republic of Iran and the Republic of Iraq 1990*, p. xii.
8. This included putting Islamic verses on the Iraqi national flag and calling on Muslim leaders in the Middle East to support his 'jihad'.
9. Former Iranian soldiers and citizens, interviews with author, March 1991 and October 2002.
10. Beeman, W. O., 'Ta'ziyeh performance conventions: a short sketch', *Asia Society*, http://www.asiasociety.org/arts/taziyeh/beeman.html
11. Interview with Iranian reform elements, October 2002.
12. Aburish, S., *Saddam Hussein: The Politics of Revenge*, London, Bloomsbury, 2001.
13. See: Black, J., 'Kashmir fundamentalism takes root', *Foreign Affairs*, 78:6, 1999, pp. 36–42, and Schofield, V., *Kashmir in the Crossfire*, London, IB Tauris, 1996.
14. Franchetti, M., 'Russia's "Black widow" revenge', *The Sunday Times*, 26 September 2004.
15. Selection of advertising slogans from copy of *Marie Claire* magazine, March 2002, UK edition.
16. Girard, R., *Violence and the Sacred* (trans. P. Gregory), Baltimore, John Hopkins University, 1972.
17. See: Williams, J. G., *The Bible, Violence and the Sacred*, San Francisco, Harper, 1995.
18. 'Hoon stands firm over UK troop decision', *Financial Times*, 21 March 2002.
19. See: Rashid, A., *Taliban: Story of the Afghan Warlords*, London, Pan, 2001.
20. Anspach, M. R., 'Violence against violence: Islam in comparative context' in Jurergensmeyer, M. (ed.) *Violence and the Sacred in the Modern World*, London, Frank Cass, 1992, p. 24.

21. Girard, R., op. cit., p. 14.
22. Ibid., pp. 14–15.
23. Scruton, R., *The West and the Rest – Globalization and the Terrorist Threat*, London, Continuum, 2003, p. 38.
24. Hall, J. R., Schuyler, P. D. and Trinh, S., *Apocalypse Observed: Religious Movements and Violence in North America, Europe and Japan*, London, Routledge, 2000.
25. Yeats, W. B., 'The Rose Tree', *The Poems*, London, Dent, 1990, p. 231.
26. Interesting illumination of this issue can be found by watching the Oscar winning film Fog of War: Eleven Lessons from the Life of Robert S. McNamara.
27. See opinion polls conducted by the Palestinian Center for Policy and Survey Research 1994–2004. http://www.pcpsr.org/
28. Hamas Covenant, http://www.yale.edu/lawweb/avalon/mideast/hamas.htm, 1988, articles 7 and 13.
29. Dr Abdel Aziz al-Rantisi, Hamas leader, interview with author, Gaza city, August, 2002.
30. Hamas leaflet, entitled 'Rabin's attempt to cover up his criminal policies with fictitious battles' 16 April 1994.
31. Ismail Haniyeh, Hamas Leader, interview with author, Shatti refugee camp, Gaza, September 2002.
32. Sheikh Shammi, Islamic Jihad leader, interview with author, Shujahiyeh, Gaza Strip, September 2002.
33. Hafez, M., *Why Muslims Rebel, Repression and Resistance in the Islamic World*, Boulder (CO), Lynne Rienner, 2004, p. 158.
34. Prusher, I. R., 'When bombs rip where is Islam?', *CSMI*, 11 August 1997.
35. Transcript of interview with Sheik Yusef al-Qaradawi, BBC, 8 July 2004.
36. Sarraj, E., 'Why we have all become suicide bombers', http://www.missionislam.com/conissues/palestine.htm
37. As quoted in Haaretz, May 2002.
38. Hammami, R. and Budeiri, M., on suicide bombings in *al-Quds* Arabic daily newspaper, 21 December 2001.
39. Hamas Covenant, http://www.yale.edu/lawweb/avalon/mideast/hamas.htm, 1988, article 12.
40. Cockburn, C., 'The gendered dynamics of armed conflict and political violence', in Mosner, C. and Clark, F. (eds), *Victims, Perpetrators or Actors? Gender, Armed Conflict and Political Violence*, London, Zed Books, 2001, p. 21.
41. Dworkin, A., 'The women suicide bombers', *Feminista*, 5:1, http://www.feminista.com/v5n1/dworkin.html, 2002.
42. Alison, M., 'Women as agents of political violence', *Security Dialogue*, 35:4, 2004, p. 460.
43. Hamas Covenant, http://www.yale.edu/lawweb/avalon/mideast/hamas. htm, 1988, articles 17 and 18.
44. Mohammed Fnaysh, MP Bint Jubayl, interview with author, Beirut 15 August 2002.
45. Alison, M., op. cit., p. 460.
46. *The Washington Post*, 11 October 2001, http://www.washingtonpost.com/wp-dyn/articles/A40545–2001Oct10.html
47. Text of Statement from Osama Bin Laden, Associated Press, Monday, 24 September 2001.
48. Usama Hamdan, Hamas leader, interview with author, Beirut, May 2004.
49. An example of these kinds of allegation are found in Schwartz, S., *The Two Faces of Islam, Saudi Fundamentalism and its Role in Terrorism*, New York, Anchor Books, 2003.

50. Reuter, C., *My Life is A Weapon, A Modern History of Suicide Bombing*, Princeton, Princeton University Press, 2004, pp. 170–1.
51. Gray, J., *Al-Qaeda and What It Means to Be Modern*, London, Faber and Faber, 2003, p. 2.

5 Holy Terror: Representations of Violence in a Modern Age

1. Pipes, D., 'Aim the war on terror at militant Islam', *Los Angeles Times*, 6 January 2002, http://www.danielpipes.org/article/106
2. See: http://www.drphil.com/advice/advice.jhtml?contentId=090302_lifestrategies_lifelaws.xml&section=Life%20Strategies
3. *The Globalist*, interview with Akhbar Ahmed, 20 July 2003.
4. Helmreich, J. 'Beyond political terrorism: the new challenge of transcendent terror', *Jerusalem Letter*, Jerusalem Centre for Public Affairs, 15 November 2001, no. 466.
5. See: Pew Research Centre, 'Religion and politics: contention and consensus growing number says Islam encourages violence among followers', 24 July 2003.
6. Mohammed Fnaysh, MP Bint Jubayl, interview with author, 15 August 2002.
7. Rapoport, D. C., 'Sacred terror: a contemporary example from Islam', in Reich, W. (ed.), *Origins of Terrorism, Psychologies, Ideologies, Theologies, States of Mind*, Cambridge, Cambridge University Press, 1990, p. 103.
8. See: Dekmejian, R., 'Consociational democracy in crisis: the case of Lebanon', *Comparative Politics*, 10:2, 1978, pp. 251–65.
9. See: Saad-Ghorayab, A., op. cit.
10. Smith, C. D., *Palestine and the Arab-Israeli Conflict*, New York, St Martin's Press, 1992, p. 272.
11. By Egyptian playwrighter, Abdel Hakin.
12. Kaldor, Mary, op. cit., pp. 1–12.
13. Gardner, D., 'An Eye for an Eye', *Financial Times*, 13 October, p. I, II. 2001.
14. Burchill, J., 'Some people will believe anything', *The Guardian Weekend*, 18 August 2001, p. 7.
15. See FBI Reports on domestic terrorism www.fbi.gov/publications/terror/terror98.pdf or www.fbi.gov/publications/terror/terror99.pdf for evidence that domestic terror during this period was a non-Muslim phenomenon and related to right-Christian collations, radical animal liberation elements etc.
16. Pipes, D., 'Protecting Muslims while rooting out Islamists', *The Daily Telegraph*, 14 September 2001, p. 22.
17. See: Keddourie, E., op. cit.
18. Laqueur, W., 'Left, right and beyond, the changing face of terror', in Hoge, J. F., and Rose, G. (eds), *How Did This Happen? Terrorism and the New War*, New York, Public Affairs Reports, 2001.
19. Studies by terrorism experts into the manifestation of political violence in Egypt in the 1980s was treated in this way. See: Sivan, E., *Radical Islam: Medieval Theology and Modern Politics*, New Haven and London, Yale University Press, 1990; or Jansen, J. G., *The Neglected Duty: The Creed of Sadat's Assassins and Islamic Resurgence in the Middle East*, New York, Macmillan, 1996.
20. See: Hadar, L., 'What Green Peril?', *Foreign Affairs*, 72:2, Spring 1993, p. 27.
21. Quoted in Robinson, A., *Bin Laden, Behind the Mask of the Terrorists*, Edinburgh, Arcade Publishing, 2001, p. 95.

22. Keegan, J., 'In this war of civilisations, the West will prevail', *Daily Telegraph*, 8 October 2001, p. 22.
23. Driver, F., 'The geopolitics of knowledge and ignorance', *Transactions of the Institute of British Geographers*, 28:2, 2003, p. 131.
24. See: http://www.kimsoft.com/polwar.htm
25. See: www.fbi.gov/publications/terror/terror99.pdf, p. 23.
26. Kramer, M., *Ivory Towers on Sand: The Failure of Middle Eastern Studies in America*, Washington (DC), Washington Institute for Near East Policy, 2001.
27. See: Hoffman, B., 'Holy Terror: the implications of terrorism motivated by a religious imperative', Santa Monica (CA), RAND paper, 1993.
28. See: Israel Insider on allegations against Saudi Arabia – http://www.israelinsider. com/channels/diplomacy/articles/dip_0202.htm
29. Interview with X, Senior MI6 and Y, Senior Israeli intelligence, May 2004.
30. See: Huntington, S., op. cit. and Huntington, S., *The Clash of Civilizations and the Remaking of World Order* New York, Simon & Schuster, 1996.
31. Badrawi, M., *Political Violence in Egypt 1910–1925*, London, Richmond, 2000, p. 230.
32. Ibid., p. 231.
33. Hence the controversy in states like the United Kingdom where such individuals were granted asylum from the persecution agenda of the Egyptian authorities and its poor record of respect for human rights.
34. See: Vincent Durac, 'Islamic modernism in contemporary Egypt: an evaluation', unpublished PhD, Queen's University, Belfast (Northern Ireland), 2000.
35. Barlas, A., 'Interpretation and exceptionalism', Palestine-forever@usa.com, 2001.
36. Wright, R., 'Muslims and Modernity', *Slate*, October 2001, http://slate.msn. com/id/2057529/
37. See: Rapoport, D., 'Religion and Terror: Thugs, Assassins and Zealots' in Kegley, C. W., Jr (ed.), *International Terrorism, Characteristics, Causes, Controls*, New York, St Martin's Press, 1990 and Lewis, B., *The Assassins*, London: Weidenfeld and Nicholson, 2003.
38. Rapoport, D. C., 'Fear and trembling: terrorism in three religious traditions', *The American Political Science Review*, 78:3, September 1984, p. 672.
39. Lewis, B. *What Went Wrong? Western Impact and Middle Eastern Responses*, London, Phoenix, January 2002.
40. Hoffman, B., ' "Holy Terror": The implications of terrorism motivated by a religious imperative', *Studies in Conflict and Terrorism*, vol. 18, 1995, pp. 271–84.
41. McDonald, H., 'Hannibal the Loyalist', *The Observer*, 20 January 2002.
42. Hamas Covenant, http://www.yale.edu/lawweb/avalon/mideast/hamas.htm, 1988, articles 9 and 13.
43. Bruce, S., 'Fundamentalism, Ethnicity and Enclave', in Marty, M. E. and Appleby, R. S. (eds), *Fundamentalisms and the State*, Chicago, University of Chicago Press, 1993, p. 51.
44. See: Eickelman, D. F. and Piscatori, J., op. cit., p. 7.
45. Hoffman, B., op. cit., p. 274.
46. Huntington, S., op. cit., p. 23.
47. Taheri, A., *Holy Terror: The Inside Story of Islamic Terrorism*, London, Sphere, 1987, p. 1.
48. Hoffman, B., op. cit., p. 272.
49. Ibid., p. 273.
50. Zaki Chentouf, a Muslim woman living in Britain quoted in *Marie Claire*, December 2002, p. 71.
51. See: Sivan, E., op. cit.

52. Kramer, M., *Ivory Towers on Sand: The Failure of Middle Eastern Studies in America*, Washington (DC), Washington Institute for Near East Policy, 2001, p. 44.
53. Ibid., p. 2.
54. See: Kelsay, J., op. cit.
55. Easwaran, E., *Non-violent Soldier of Islam, Badshah Khan a Man to Match his Mountains*, California, Nilgiri Press, 1999.
56. As quoted in Johansen, R. C., 'People power: Non-violent political action in Muslim, Buddhist and Hindu tradition', 1993, http://www.wcfia.harvard.edu/ponsacs/DOCS/s93johan.htm
57. Pal, A., 'A Pacifist uncovered', *The Progressive*, February 2002.
58. Ibid.
59. Bayat, A., 'Activism and social development in the Middle East', *International Journal of Middle Eastern Studies*, vol. 34, 2002, p. 11.
60. Milton-Edwards, B., 'A temporary alliance with the crown: the Islamic response in Jordan', in Piscatori, J. (ed.), *Islamic Fundamentalism and the Gulf Crisis*, Chicago, AAAS, 1991.
61. Lapidus, I. M., op. cit., 1988, p. xiii.
62. Esposito, J. L., op. cit., p. 135.

Conclusion

1. General Tommy R Franks, 'Briefing on military operation in Iraq', 22 March 2003, quoting Rumsfeld. See: http://www.centcom.mil/CENTCOMNews/Transcripts/20030322.htm
2. Human Rights Watch Annual Report 2004, January 2005. http://www.hrw.org/wr2k5/
3. Ibid.

Glossary

Glossary of Islamic terms

ashura	the commemoration by *Shi'a* Muslims of the martyrdom of Imam Hussein at Karbala
Ayatollah	*Shi'a* religious leader
Allah	God
Caliph(ate)	a successor to the Prophet Mohammed (the institution of Islamic government after Mohammed)
chadour	clothing worn by women to cover themselves according to Koranic instruction
dar Al-harb	'abode of war'
dar Al-salam	'abode of peace'
dawah	call to Islam
dawla	the state
Dhimmi	People of the Book accorded protected status
faqih	jurisconsult – a man with good comprehension of the technicalities of Islamic jurisprudence
fatwa	a religio-juridic verdict or counsel issued by a religious scholar
hadith	commentary and report of the Prophet Mohammed
hajj	pilgrimage to Mecca
halal	permitted; sanctified
haram	prohibited
hijab	headscarf worn by women
hijra	the emigration of Prophet Mohammed and his followers from Mecca to Medina
hodna	form of ceasefire during the holy war
ijma	consensus
ijtihad	independent reasoning with regard to religious issues
ikhwan	brethren
imam	the leader of prayers in the mosque
islah	reform
Islam	submission or surrender to Allah
jahiliyya	originally referred to the total pagan ignorance during the pre-Islamic era; used in the contemporary era to characterise all societies which are not genuinely Islamic
jihad	exertion, striving and struggle by all means, including military
jizya	poll tax on *Dhimmi*
kaba	shrine in Mecca
kadi (Qadi, Qadhi)	a Muslim judge of *Shari'a* law
kibla (Qibla)	the direction of Mecca
madrassa	a religious place of learning
majlis	Muslim council/legislative body
masjid	mosque
mihrab	a niche in a mosque pointing in the direction of Mecca, where the Imam leads the prayers

minaret	the tower of the mosque where the call to prayer is broadcast
minba	the pulpit in a mosque
muezzin	the man who calls the people to prayer
mufti	Muslim legislator
mujahid(een)	fighter for Allah
mullah	a local religious leader
Muslim	follower of Islam
Muslim Schools of Jurisprudence	every Muslim is governed by a particular school to which s/he belongs. The four main schools are: Hanifi, Hanbali, Maliki and Shafi. The smaller schools are Wahabbi (mainly of Saudi Arabia), Ibadhi and Zaidi.
purdah	exclusion of women from public space
riba	usury
salafi	relates to the example and inspiration of the Prophet Mohammed and the four rightly guided caliphs; fundamentalist in inspiration.
sawm	fasting
shahadah	profession of faith
Shari'a	Islamic law
sheikh	an honorary term with religious connotation
shi'a	Party of Ali; followers of Ali.
shura	consultation
sunnah	the sayings and actions of the Prophet Mohammed
tajdid	revival
taqlid	imitation
tawhid	unity
ulama	scholars or people trained in the religious sciences
umma	community
usulia	fundamentalist
vilayat Al-fiqh	governance by an Islamic expert
zakat	tax for the poor

Bibliography

Books and journals

Aburish, S., *Saddam Hussein: The Politics of Revenge*, London: Bloomsbury, 2001.

el-Affendi, A (ed.), *Rethinking Islam and Modernity, Essays in Honour of Fathi Osman*, London: The Islamic Foundation, 2001.

Ahmed, A. S., *Islam under Siege*, Cambridge: Polity Press, 2003.

Akenson, D. H., *God's People, Covenant and Land in South Africa, Israel and Ulster*, Ithaca: Cornell University Press, 1993.

Allen, B and Herman, T., 'Rape warfare: the hidden Genocide in Bosnia–Herzegovina and Croatia', *Peace and Change*, 22:2, 1997, pp. 228–9.

Allen, D. (ed.), *Religion and Political Conflict in South Asia, India, Pakistan, and Sri Lanka* (Contributions to the Study of Religion), Westport (CT) and London: Greenwood Press, 1992.

Alison, M., 'Women as agents of political violence', *Security Dialogue*, 35:4, December 2004, pp. 447–63.

Amnesty International, 'News release issued by the International Secretariat of Amnesty International', 17 July 2002, EUR 45/012/2002.

Ansell, A. E. (ed.), *Unravelling the Right: The New Conservatism in American Thought and Politics*, Boulder (CO): Westview Press, 1998.

Anspach, M. R., 'Violence against violence: Islam in comparative context', *Terrorism and Political Violence*, 3:3, 1991, pp. 9–29.

Arberry, Arthur (trans.), *The Koran*, Oxford: Oxford University Press, 1982.

Armstrong, K., *Holy War: The Crusades and their Impact on Today's World*, Houndmills: Palgrave, 1988.

Armstrong, K., *The Battle for God: Fundamentalism in Judaism, Christianity and Islam*, London: Harper Collins, 2001.

Augustus Norton, R., *Amal and the Shi'a: Struggle for the Soul of Lebanon*, Austin (TX): University of Texas Press, 1987.

Ayubi, Nazih, *Political Islam, Religion and Politics in the Arab World*, London: Routledge, 1991.

Azzam, A., *Defence of Muslim Lands*, n.p.: Ahle Sunna wa Jammah, n.d.

Azzam, A., *Join the Caravan*, n.p.: Ahle Sunna wa Jamaah, n.d.

Badrawi, M., *Political Violence in Egypt 1910–1925*, London: Richmond, 2000.

Barber, B., *Jihad vs. McWorld*, New York: Ballantine Books, 1996.

Barlas, A., 'Interpretation and exceptionalism', Palestine-forever@usa.com, 2001.

Beeman, W. O., 'Ta'ziyeh performance conventions: a short sketch', *Asia Society*, http://www.asiasociety.org/arts/taziyeh/beeman.html

Beinin, Joel and Stork, Joe (eds), *Political Islam, Essays from Middle East Report*, London: IB Tauris, 1997.

Benjamin, D., and Simon, S., *The Age of Sacred Terror*, New York: Random House, 2002.

Berlet, C. and Lyons, M. N., *Right-Wing Populism in America: Too Close for Comfort*, New York: Guildford Publications, 2000.

Bin Laden, Usama, 'Declaration of war against the Americans occupying the land of the two holy places', n.p., 1996.

Black, Jonah, 'Kashmir fundamentalism takes root', *Foreign Affairs*, 78:6, 1999, pp. 36–42.

Bodman, H. L. and Tohidi, N. (eds), *Women in Muslim Societies*, Boulder (CO): Lynne Reinner, 1998.

Boyce, D. G. and O' Day, A. (eds), *The Making of Modern Irish History – Revisionism and the Revisionist Controversy*, London: Routledge, 1996.

Bruce, S., 'Fundamentalism, ethnicity and enclave', in Marty, M. E. and Appleby, R. S. (eds), *Fundamentalisms and the State*, Chicago: University of Chicago Press, 1993.

Burke, J., *Al-Qaeda: Casting a Shadow of Terror*, London: IB Tauris, 2004.

Burke, E. and Lapidus, I. M., (eds), *Islam, Politics and Social Movements*, Berkley (CA): University of California Press, 1988.

Chomsky, N., *9–11*, New York: Seven Stories (An Open Media Book), 2001.

Cockburn, C., 'The gendered dynamics of armed conflict and political violence', in Mosner, C., and Clark, F. (eds), *Victims, Perpetrators or Actors? Gender, Armed Conflict and Political Violence*, London: Zed Books, 2001.

Cole, D., 'National Security State', *The Nation*, 17 December 2001.

Cole, J. R. (ed.), *Comparing Muslim Societies*, Ann Arbor: University of Michigan Press, 1992.

Conley, C. A., *Melancholy Accidents: The Meaning of Violence in Post-Famine Ireland*, Lanham (MD): Lexington Books, 1999.

Connor, Walker, *Ethnonationalism: The Quest for Understanding*, Princeton: Princeton University Press, 1993.

Corbin, J., *The Base – In Search of al-Qaeda, the Terror Network that Shook the World*, New York: Simon & Schuster, 2002.

Crenshaw, M. (ed.), *Terrorism, Legitimacy and Power: the Consequences of Political Violence*, Middletown (CT): Wesleyan University Press, 1983.

Dafarty, F., *The Assassin Legends: Myths of the Isma'ilis*, London: IB Tauris, 1994.

Daftari, M. (trans.), *The Text of the Letters Exchanged between the Presidents of the Islamic Republic of Iran and the Republic of Iraq 1990*, Tehran: IIIS, 1991.

Dekmejian, R., 'Consociational democracy in crisis: the case of Lebanon', *Comparative Politics*, 10, 2 (1978), pp. 251–65.

Dershowitz, A., *Why Terrorism Works*, Yale: Yale University Press, 2002.

Diamond, L., Linz, J. and Lipset, S. M., *Politics in Developing Countries: Comparing Experiences with Democracy*, Boulder (CO): Lynne Rienner, 1995.

Diamond, L. and Plattner, M. (eds), *The Global Resurgence of Democracy*, Second Edition, Baltimore: Johns Hopkins University Press, 1996.

Downer, J. W., 'Don't expect democracy this time: Japan and Iraq', *History and Policy*, http://www.historyandpolicy.org, March 2003.

Driver, F., 'The geopolitics of knowledge and ignorance', *Transactions of the Institute of British Geographers*, 28:2, 2003, pp. 131–2.

Durac, V., 'Islamic modernism in contemporary Egypt: an evaluation', unpublished PhD, Queen's University, Belfast (Northern Ireland), 2000.

Dworkin, A., 'The women suicide bombers', *Feminista*, 5:1, http://www.feminista.com/v5n1/dworkin.html, 2002.

Easwaran, E., *Non-violent Soldier of Islam, Badshah Khan a Man to Match his Mountains*, California: Nilgiri Press, 1999.

Ehteshami, A., *After Khomeini, the Iranian Second Republic*, London: Routledge, 1995.

Eickelman, D. F. and Piscatori, J., *Muslim Politics*, Princeton: Princeton University Press, 1996.

Engineer, A. A., *Theory and Practise of the Islamic State*, Lahore: Vanguard Books, 1985.

Enloe, C., *The Morning After: Sexual Politics at the End of the Cold War*, Berkeley: University of California Press, 1993.

Esposito, J. L., *Islam, the Straight Path*, New York: Oxford University Press, 1994.

Esposito, J. L., *Unholy War*, New York: Oxford University Press, 2002.

Fandy, M., *Saudi Arabia and the Politics of Dissent*, Houndmills: Palgrave, 1999.

Fanon, F., *The Wretched of the Earth*, New York: Grove Press, 1986.

Fukuyama, F., 'Fighting the 21st century Fascists', *The Age–Australia*, 5 January 2002, http://www.theage.com.au/news/state/2002/01/05/FFXE5PLU0WC.html

Furnish, T. R., 'Bin Laden: the man who would be Mahdi', *Middle East Quarterly*, 9, 2 (2002), http://www.meforum.org/article/159

Gamage, S. and Waton, I. B. (eds), *Conflict and Community in Contemporary Sri Lanka*, New Delhi: Sage, 1999.

Gellner, E., *Muslim Society*, Cambridge: Cambridge University Press, 1983.

Gerth, H. H. and Mills, C. W. (eds), *From Max Weber*, New York: Oxford University Press, 1972.

Girard, R., *Violence and the Sacred* (trans. P. Gregory), Baltimore: John Hopkins University, 1972.

Goldstein, J. and Keohane, R. O., 'Ideas and foreign policy: an analytical framework', in Goldstein, J. and Keohane, R. O. (eds), *Ideas and Foreign Policy: Beliefs, Institutions and Political Change*, Ithaca: Cornell University Press, 1993.

Gray, J., *Al-qaeda and What It Means to Be Modern*, London: Faber and Faber, 2003.

Guelke, A., *The Age of Terrorism and the International Political System*, London: IB Tauris, 1995.

Gunaratna, R., *Inside Al-Qaeda: Global Network of Terror*, Berkley: Berkley Publishing Group, 2003.

Hadar, L., 'What Green Peril?', *Foreign Affairs*, 72:2, Spring 1993, pp. 27–42.

Hafez, M., *Why Muslims Rebel, Repression and Resistance in the Islamic World*, Boulder (CO): Lynne Rienner, 2004.

Hall, J. R., Schuyler, P. D. and Trinh, S., *Apocalypse Observed: Religious Movements and Violence in North America, Europe and Japan*, London: Routledge, 2000.

Halliday, F., *Islam and the Myth of Confrontation*, London: IB Tauris, 1996.

Hamas Covenant, http://www.yale.edu/lawweb/avalon/mideast/hamas.htm, 1988.

Hammami, R., 'From immodesty to collaboration: Hamas, the women's movement and national identity in the Intifada', in Beinin, J. and Stork, J. (eds), *Political Islam, Essays from Middle East Report*, London: IB Tauris, 1997, pp. 194–240.

al-Hawali, Safar, 'An open letter to President Bush', n.p., 16 October 2001.

—— (trans. M. Fandy), 'Infidels without and within', *New Perspectives Quarterly*, 8, 2 (1990), www.npq.org, pp. 1–3.

Hefner, R. W., *Civil Islam: Muslims and Democratisation in Indonesia*, Princeton: Princeton University Press, 2000.

Helmreich, J., 'Beyond political terrorism: the new challenge of transcendent terror', *Jerusalem Letter*, Jerusalem Center for Public Affairs, 15 November 2001, no. 466.

Her Majesty's Stationery Office (HMSO), 'Anti-terrorism, Crime and Security Act' (ATCSA), November 2001.

Hiro, D., *War without End, the Rise of Islamist Terrorism and Global Response*, London: Routledge, 2002.

Hoffman, B., 'Holy Terror: the implications of terrorism motivated by a religious imperative', Santa Monica (CA): RAND paper, 1993.

Hoffman, B., ' "Holy Terror": The implications of terrorism motivated by a religious imperative', *Studies in Conflict and Terrorism*, vol. 18, 1995, pp. 271–84.

Hoffman, B., *Inside Terrorism*, New York: Columbia University Press, 1998.

Hoge, J. F. and Rose, G. (eds), *How Did This Happen? Terrorism and the New War*, New York: Public Affairs Report, 2001.

Holt, P. M., The Mahdist state in Sudan 1881–1898: *A Study of Its Origins, Development and Overthrow*, London: Clarendon, 1958.

Horowitz, D. L., *Ethnic Groups in Conflict*, Berkeley: California University Press, 2001.

Hourani, A., *A History of the Arab Peoples*, London: Faber, 1991.

Huband, M., *Warriors of the Prophet, the Struggle for Islam*, Boulder (CO): Westview Press, 1999.

Huntingdon, S., *The Clash of Civilizations and the Remaking of World Order*, New York: Simon & Schuster, 1996.

——, 'The Clash of Civilizations?', *Foreign Affairs*, 72:3, Summer 1993, pp. 22–5.

——, 'Will more countries become democratic?', *Political Science Quarterly*, 99:2, 1984.

Hutchinson, J., 'Irish nationalism' in Boyce, D. G. and O' Day, A. (eds), *The Making of Modern Irish History – Revisionism and the Revisionist Controversy*, London: Routledge, 1996.

Ignatiev, N., *How the Irish Became White*, London: Routledge, 1996.

Islam, Y., 'Faith and the future', *Guardian*, 18 September 2001, pp. 6–7.

Jaber, H., *Hezbollah – Born with a Vengeance*, New York: Columbia University Press, 1997.

Jacobs, S., Jacobson, R. and Marchbank, J. (eds), *States of Conflicts, Gender, Violence and Resistance*, London: Zed Books, 2000.

Jaggi, M., 'Civil wrongs', *Guardian Weekend*, 22 June 2002, pp. 54–60.

Jansen, J. G., *The Neglected Duty: The Creed of Sadat's Assassins and Islamic Resurgence in the Middle East*, New York: Macmillan, 1996.

Johansen, R. C., 'People power: Non-violent political action in Muslim, Buddhist and Hindu tradition', 1993, http://www.wcfia.harvard.edu/ponsacs/DOCS/s93johan. htm

Jones, T. and Ereira, A., *Crusades*, London: Penguin, 1994.

Juergensmeyer, M., *Terror in the Mind of God*, Berkeley: California University Press, 2000.

Kaldor, Mary, *New Wars and Old Wars, Organized Violence in a Global Era*, Cambridge: Polity, 2001.

Kandiyoti, D., 'Women, Islam and the state: a comparative approach', in Cole, J. R. (ed.), *Comparing Muslim Societies*, Ann Arbor: University of Michigan Press, 1992.

Keane, J., 'Cosmocracy', 2002, http://www.wmin.ac.uk/csd/ Staff/Keane/cosmocracy.htm

Keddie, N. and Monian, F., 'Militancy and religion in contemporary Iran', in Marty, M. E. and Appleby, R. S., *Fundamentalisms and the State*, Chicago: University of Chicago Press, 1993.

Kedourie, Elie, *Politics in the Middle East*, Oxford: Oxford University Press, 1992.

Keegan, J., *The Mask of Command*, London: Jonathan Cape, 1987.

Kegley, C. W., Jr (ed.), *International Terrorism, Characteristics, Causes, Controls*, New York: St Martin's Press, 1990.

Kelsay, J., *Islam and War – the Gulf War and Beyond*, Kentucky: Westminster John Knox Press, 1993.

Kepel, G., *The War for Muslim Minds*, Cambridge (MA): Harvard University Press, 2004.

Khaldun, Ibn (trans. F. Rosenthal), *Al-muqaddimah – An Introduction to History*, Princeton: Princeton University Press, 1969.

Khan, Q., *The Political Thought of Ibn Taymiyyah*, Delhi: Ansar Press, 1992.

Korac, M., 'Women, war violence and women organizing: the case of post-Yugoslav states', *ISA: International Sociological Association*, 1998.

Kramer, M., 'Hezbollah's vision of the West', *Washington Institute for Near East Policy, Hezbollah's Vision of the West.*, Policy Paper no. 16, Washington, 1989.

Kramer, M., *Ivory Towers on Sand: The Failure of Middle Eastern Studies in America*, Washington (DC): Washington Institute for Near East Policy, 2001.

Lapidus, I. M., 'Islamic political movements: patterns of historic change', in Burke, E. and Lapidus, I. M. (eds), *Islam, Politics and Social Movements*, Berkeley and London: University of California Press and IB Tauris, 1988.

Lapidus, I. M., *A History of Islamic Societies*, Cambridge: Cambridge University Press, 1990.

Laqueur, W., 'Left, right and beyond, the changing face of terror', in Hoge, J. F. and Rose, G. (eds), *How Did This Happen? Terrorism and the New War*, New York: Public Affairs Reports, 2001.

Lawrence, B. B., *Shattering the Myth, Islam Beyond Violence*, Princeton: Princeton University Press, 1998.

Lewis, B, *The Assassins: A Radical Sect in Islam*, London: Weidenfeld and Nicolson, 1980.

——, *What Went Wrong? Western Impact and Middle Eastern Responses*, London: Phoenix, January 2004.

——, 'The roots of Muslim rage', *Atlantic Monthly*, 266:3, September 1990, pp. 47–60.

——, 'The revolt of Islam, when did the conflict with the West begin and how could it end?', *New Yorker*, 19 November 2001, pp. 1–20.

Lieven, A., 'Strategy for terror', *Prospect*, vol. 67, October 2001.

Lorentzen, L. A. and Turpin, J. (eds), *The Women and War Reader*, New York: New York University Press, 1998.

Maalouf, Amin, *On Identity*, London: Harvill Press, 2000.

MacKenzie, W. J. M., *Power, Violence, Decision*, Harmondsworth: Penguin, 1975.

McKenna, T., *Muslim Rulers and Rebels: Everyday Politics and Armed Separatism in the Southern Philippines* (Comparative Studies on Muslim Societies, 26), Berkley: University of California Press, 1998.

Marcus, R., 'Violence against women in Bangladesh, Pakistan, Egypt, Sudan, Senegal and Yemen', *Institute of Development Studies*, Occasional Paper, 1993.

Marty, M. E. and Appleby, R. S. (eds), *Fundamentalisms and the State*, Chicago: University of Chicago Press, 1993.

Mattar, P., 'The Mufti of Jerusalem and the politics of Palestine', *Middle East Journal*, vol. 42, 1989, pp. 227–40.

al-Mawardi, Abu'l Hasan, *Al-ahkam As-sultaniyyah*, London: TaHa Publishers, 1996.

Milton-Edwards, B. and Hinchcliffe, P., *Conflicts in the Middle East since 1945*, London: Routledge, 2001.

——, *Islamic Politics in Palestine*, London: IB Tauris, 1996.

——, 'A temporary alliance with the crown: the Islamic response in Jordan', in Piscatori, J. (ed.), *Islamic Fundamentalism and the Gulf Crisis*, Chicago: AAAS, 1991.

—— 'Hizbollah after withdrawal', *Middle East Insight*, 15:4, 2000, pp. 47–9.

Mosner, C. O. N. and Clark, F. C. (eds), *Victims, Perpetrators or Actors? Gender, Armed Conflict and Political Violence*, London: Zed Books, 2001.

Nasr, Seyyed Hossein, 'Islam and the question of violence', *Al-Serat*, 13:2, 2002, pp. 1–3.

Pal, A., 'A pacifist uncovered', *The Progressive*, February 2002, pp. 1–5.

Peters, Rudolph, *Jihad in Classical and Modern Islam*, Princeton (NJ): Marcus Wiener Publishers, 1996.

Pipes, D., 'Aim the war on terror at militant Islam', *Los Angeles Times*, 6 January 2002, http://www.danielpipes.org/article/106

Prior, Father Michael, 'The clash of civilisations', draft text, July 2002.

Qutb, S., *Islam, the Religion of the Future*, Kuwait: International Islamic Federation of Student Organizations, 1971.

Rapoport, D. C., 'Fear and trembling: terrorism in three religious traditions', *The American Political Science Review*, 78:3, September 1984, pp. 658–77.

Rapoport, D. C., 'Religion and terror: thugs, assassins and zealots', in Kegley, C. W., Jr (ed.), *International Terrorism, Characteristics, Causes, Controls*, New York: St Martin's Press, 1990.

Rapoport, D. C., 'Sacred terror: a contemporary example from Islam', in Reich, W. (ed.), *Origins of Terrorism, Psychologies, Ideologies, Theologies, States of Mind*, Cambridge: Cambridge University Press, 1990, pp. 103–30.

Rashid, Ahmed, *Taliban: Story of the Afghan Warlords*, London: Pan, 2001.

Rees, S., 'Extremist: "Mad Mahdi"', *Military History Magazine*, June 2002, http://britishhistory.about.com/library/prm/blextremistmadmahdi2.htm

Reich, W. (ed.), *Origins of Terrorism, Psychologies, Ideologies, Theologies, States of Mind*, Cambridge: Cambridge University Press, 1990.

Reuter, C., *My Life is a Weapon, a Modern History of Suicide Bombing*, Princeton: Princeton University Press, 2004.

Robinson, A., *Bin Laden, Behind the Mask of the Terrorists*, Edinburgh: Arcade Publishing, 2001.

Robinson, F., 'Islam and the West: clash of civilisation?', *Journal of RSAA*, vol. XXXIII, Part III, October 2002, pp. 307–20.

Roy, O., *Globalised Islam, the Search for a new Ummah*, London: Hurst, 2002.

Runnymede Trust, *Islamophobia, a Challenge for Us All*, London: Runnymede Trust, 1997.

Ruthven, M., *A Satanic Affair, Salman Rushdie and the Rage of Islam*, London: Chatto, 1990.

Saad-Gorayeb, A., *Hizbu'llah: Politics and Religion*, London: Pluto Press, 2002.

Saeed, A. and Akbarzadeh, S. (eds), *Muslim Communities in Australia*, New South Wales: University of New South Wales Press, 2001.

Said, A. A., Funk, N.C. and Kadayifci, A. S. (eds), *Peace and Conflict Resolution in Islam*, Lanham: University Press of America, 2001.

Said, E., *Covering Islam: How the Media and Experts Determine How We See the Rest of the World*, London: Vintage, 1997, p. 163.

Sardar, Z. and Wyn Davies, M., *Why Do People Hate America*, London: Icon Books, 2002.

Saunders, J. J., *A History of Medieval Islam*, London: Kegan Paul International, 1965.

Schleifer, S. A., 'The life and thought of Izz Ad-din al-Qassam', *Islamic Quarterly*, 23:2, 1979, pp. 60–81.

Schmid, A. P., *Political Terrorism*, New York: Transaction Publishers, 1985.

Schofield, Victoria, *Kashmir in the Crossfire*, London: IB Tauris, 1996.

Schwartz, S., *The Two Faces of Islam, Saudi Fundamentalism and its Role in Terrorism*, New York: Anchor Books, 2003.

Scruton, R., *The West and the Rest – Globalization and the Terrorist Threat*, London: Continuum, 2003.

Sid-Ahmed, A. S. and Ehteshami, A. (eds), *Islamic Fundamentalism*, Boulder (CO): Westview Press, 1996.

Siddiqi, D., 'Taslima Nasreen and others: the contest over gender in Bangladesh', in Bodman, H. L. and N. Tohidi (eds), *Women in Muslim Societies*, Boulder (CO): Lynne Reinner, 1998, pp. 209–29.

Siddiqui, H., 'Exposing the theology of hate', www.thestar.com, 13 October 2002.

Simon, B., 'Falwell brands Mohammed a "Terrorist"', *60 Minutes*, CBS News, 6 October 2002, www.cbsnews.com/stories/2002/10/03/60minutes/main524268.shtml

Sivan, E., *Radical Islam: Medieval Theology and Modern Politics*, New Haven and London: Yale University Press, 1990.

Smith, C. D., *Palestine and the Arab-Israeli Conflict*, New York: St Martin's Press, 1992.

Taheri, A., *Holy Terror: The Inside Story of Islamic Terrorism*, London: Sphere, 1987.

Taji-Farouki, S., 'Islamic state theories and contemporary realities', in A. Sid-ahmed and A. Ehteshami (eds), *Islamic Fundamentalism*, Boulder (CO): Westview Press, 1996, pp. 37–52.

Taylor, S., *Durkheim and the Study of Suicide*, London: Macmillan, 1982.

Tibi, B., *Islam between Culture and Politics*, Houndmills: Palgrave, 2001.

Thompson, W. I., *The Imagination of an Insurrection, Dublin, Easter 1916: A Study of an Ideological Movement*, New York: Oxford University Press, 1967.

Trawick, M., 'Reasons for violence: a preliminary ethnographic account of the LTTE', in Gamage, S. and Watson, I. B. (eds), *Conflict and Community in Contemporary Sri Lanka: 'Pearl of the Indian Ocean' or 'the Island of Tears'* (Studies on Contemporary South Asia, no. 3.), Beverley Hills (CA): Sage Press, pp. 139–63.

Tucker, R.C.(ed.), *The Marx-engels Reader*, New York: WW Norton and Co, 1978.

Turner, B., *Weber and Islam, a Critical Study*, London: Routledge and Kegan Paul, 1974.

Vakili-zad, Cyrus, 'The power of religious rituals and revolution – Iran and South Africa, a comparative perspective', *Iranian Journal of International Relations*, 2:4, Winter 1990–91, pp. 628–50.

Van Ess, Josef, 'Political ideas in early Islamic religious thought', *British Journal of Middle Eastern Studies*, 28:2, 2001, pp. 151–64.

Vickers, J., *Women and War*, London: Zed Books, 1993.

Von-Clausewitz, C., *On War*, London: Pelican Books, 1968.

Williams, J. G., *The Bible, Violence and the Sacred*, San Francisco: Harper, 1995.

Wright, Frank, *Northern Ireland, a Comparative Analysis*, Dublin: Gill and Macmillan, 1988.

Wright, R., 'Muslims and Modernity', *Slate*, October 2001, http://slate.msn.com/id/2057529/

Yeats, W. B., *The Poems*, London: Dent, 1990.

Zubaida, S., *Islam, People and the State*, London: Routledge, 1988.

Newspapers and periodicals

The Age–Australia
The Atlantic Monthly
The Boston Globe
Christian Science Monitor
Christian Science Monitor International
Daily Express
The Daily Star
The Daily Telegraph
The Financial Times
The Globalist
The Guardian
The Jerusalem Post
The Jewish Chronicle
Los Angeles Times
Marie Claire
New York Times
The Nation
The New Yorker
The Observer
Prospect Magazine
Al-Quds
Slate
The Sunday Times
Time Magazine
Toronto Globe and Mail
Toronto Sun
The Washington Post

Index

Abbasid caliphate   37, 39
    decline of   39
Abdelah, A.   74, 75
Abubakar, Y.   117
Abu Ghraib   194
Abuja   117
Aburish, S.   129
Abu Sayyaf   88, 90, 168, 176
acts
    hostile   163
    see also   international terror
administration   31, 45, 66, 69,
        110, 167
    Bush   23, 69, 89
    Clinton   65, 66, 67, 96
    US   167
    see also   Bush, G.
    see also   Clinton, B.
adultery   114, 116
    accused of   117
    act of   117
Afghanistan   1, 8, 17, 20, 68, 74, 78, 81,
        89, 99, 114, 119, 133, 134
    Arab mujahideen forces of   17, 103
    British role in the war in   81–2,
        132–33
    jihad movement   99
    labelled as Islamist   8
Africa   2, 28, 29, 35, 40
Afshar, H.   115, 116, 207
Afula bombing   144
agenda   11, 13, 49, 66, 71, 81, 104, 118,
        119, 130, 160, 162
    anti-American   162
    asserting the Islamic   130
    fundamentalist   49
    human rights   118
    international security   71
    Islamist   81
    modern   119
    national policy   11
    policy   13
    political   81, 104, 160
    state security   66

aggression   125, 126
    act   125
    Iraqi   126
agreement
    cease-fire   65
    political   65
al-Ahkam as-Sultaniyyah   37
Ahmed, H.   49
Ahmed, A.   159
Akhras, A.   149
Algeria   8, 47, 92, 96, 104, 139
Ali, M.   49, 77
Allah   2, 38, 41, 77, 115, 120, 123, 124,
        130, 142, 143, 145
    state governed by   35
allegiance   40
    oath   138
Allied War   14
Amnesty International   72
Anderson, B.   161
Anspach, M.R.   134
anti-westernism
    locus of   63
Antonio, M.B.   77
Anwar, Z.   112
Arabia   29, 31, 35, 90, 101, 192
    tradition of tribal rule in   31
    warriors of   90
Arafat, Y.   28, 45, 147
armed force
    disciplined use of   34
Armstrong, K.   21, 48
Ashcroft, J.   67, 68
Asia   2, 28, 29, 35, 40, 57
Asian states
    minority Muslims   76
Assam   140
assassin   30, 45, 46
Atlanta   67
attacks
    human wave   126
Australia   2
authorities   36–40, 45, 49, 74, 89, 102
    Amirate   38

Printed in the United States
147132LV00003B/25/A

9 781403 986184